SPALDING®

COACHING FOOTBALL

TOM FLORES & BOB O'CONNOR

MASTERS PRESS

A Division of Howard W. Sams & Co.

Published by Masters Press
(A Division of Howard W. Sams & Co.)
2647 Waterfront Parkway E. Dr., Suite 300
Indianapolis, IN 46214

Printed in the United States of America

Library of Congress Cataloging-in-Publication Data

Flores, Tom
Coaching Football / Tom Flores and Bob O'Connor.
     p.   cm. — (Spalding sports library)
    At head of title: Spalding
    ISBN: 0-940279-71-1
    1. Football— Coaching. I. O'Connor, Robert, 1932-
    II. Title. III. Series
GV954.4.F56 1993   93-5185
796.332'07'7—dc20   CIP

Acknowledgments

We would like to acknowledge the following people:

Mark Montieth, editor at Masters Press.

Ben Agajanian, the most knowledgable man in the world on kicking the football, for his help in the kicking section of the book; and Jim Bush, track coach at USC, for his assistance in the running program.

The photographers: Christina Kranzler and Claudia Figueroa.

Our models: Bob Kyman, Barry Drucker, and Cesar Parra from Pierce College.

Our reviewers: Don Fuoss of The California State University at Sacramento, John Johnson of California State University at Dominguez Hills, and Bill Williams of the Football Coaches Professional Growth Association.

Also: typesetters Misty Lockman York and Leah Marckel, production associate Christy Pierce, and Julie Biddle for designing the cover and producing the diagrams.

Contents

About the Authors

Tom Flores is one of the most respected and experienced men in all of football. Now the head coach and general manager of the NFL's Seattle Seahawks, he is a veteran of 33 NFL seasons. Flores began his career in professional football as a quarterback with the Oakland Raiders in 1960. He also played with Buffalo and Kansas City, and was a backup quarterback on the Chiefs' Super Bowl championship team. He was an assistant coach with the Bills for one season before returning to Oakland in 1972. He was an assistant with the Raiders until 1978, and was their head coach from 1979-87. The Raiders won Super Bowls in 1977, 1981 and 1984 during his tenure. Flores is one of only two men in NFL history to have Super Bowl rings as a player, assistant coach and head coach, and has more Super Bowl rings — five — than anyone.

Bob O'Connor has coached football for more than 40 years, at nearly every level. He is an honorary member of the American Football Coaches Association, and has coached with two Super Bowl coaches. He is now the head coach at Hollywood High School and a professor at Pierce College in Los Angeles. He also is the author of 17 books on health and physical education.

Preface

Those of us who are lucky enough to have chosen to work with enthusiastic young people in the great game of football are among the most fortunate people in the world. We have the opportunity to work with people we love — both our fellow coaches and our players. And we have this opportunity in the context of the most fascinating game ever devised. Because of our blessings we must make every effort to know how we can make football, and the lessons it can teach, as vibrant in the lives of our charges as it is with us.

To be effective coaches, we must learn about the game, learn about our players, then utilize our knowledge and teach the game effectively so that our players can win on the playing fields as they learn how to win in life.

We have organized this book according to the principles of Gestalt psychology. This approach has been shown to be the most effective in learning. We will begin with the philosophy of why we play the game. Over the next eight chapters we will discuss the game in its broad generalities — attempting to illustrate numerous possibilities of how the game can be played. The reader can then make the choices of which aspects of the game he will emphasize in developing the theory he will use in his coaching.

Understanding history, whether of our civilization, our nation, or our chosen occupation, is important. We will therefore briefly mention some of the men and ideas that have aided in the evolution of our dynamic game.

We then will discuss fundamentals. Whichever fundamentals are used will be determined by the theory the coach has chosen, so not all teams will use the same fundamentals. For example, a running team that doesn't pull its linemen may opt for a four-point stance with a great deal of weight forward while a passing team would be more likely to use a balanced three-point stance.

The intelligent coach will choose the fundamentals that help his players more easily accomplish what he is attempting to do in his theoretical approach to the game. An example of this was when Hayden Fry at Iowa decided to have his tight end stand in a two-point stance rather than the traditional three-point stance. Hayden said that while the end was a little less effective as a blocker, he was far more effective as a pass receiver. Hayden had changed what had been a "universal" fundamental in order to make his attack more effective.

The final chapters will deal with the organization of the program — the practices, coaching staff, and the relations with people outside of the immediate team concern.

The book will give an overview of what is necessary for understanding the coaching process, but it is just the beginning. The concerned coach will continue to educate himself by reading books and periodicals, by attending clinics, and by watching practices of successful coaches at every level.

Key to Diagrams

○	Offensive player
⊗	Offensive center or snapper
V	Defensive lineman
B	Linebacker
C	Cornerback or defensive halfback
S	Safety
●	Ball carrier
◑	Player who handles the ball but does not complete the play as the ball carrier
——	Path of player
- - - - -	Path of the ball (pass or lateral)
~~	Path of the man in motion

1

Upholding a Legacy

"Football's been good to me. I've laughed and I've cried my heart out, just like, probably, many of you. But all in all, I wouldn't take anything for having the opportunity to do what I wanted to do most of my life, and that is to coach football."

— Charlie McClendon (recently retired as the Executive Director of the American Football Coaches Association and former head coach at Louisiana State University on accepting the AFCA's highest award, the Amos Alonzo Stagg Award in 1992)

As a coach you have a deep responsibility to your players. It is your job to know the young people you are teaching, to know the game itself and to help bring your players to their highest potentials as happy and contributing citizens.

Those of us who have chosen to coach this great game follow in the footsteps of thousands of beloved coaches who have gone before us: from the gods of the game, such as Amos Alonzo Stagg, Knute Rockne, and Glenn "Pop" Warner, to the educational leaders of today, such as Joe Paterno, Eddie Robinson, and Grant Teaff. We have a legacy to uphold. We must strive to defeat the widespread idea that we must win at all costs. Rather, we must always seek to win within the rules. Victory gained by any other means is a personal loss to the players and coaches.

In order to win fairly, we must understand as much of this complicated game as possible. We must know our players well and, more importantly, understand them. We must choose the possibilities of the game that best fit our players and organize effectively so that we can make the most out of the

limited time available. And finally, we must try to out-think our opposing coaches in the week before the game and during the game. This is the challenge of football — a challenge no other game can match.

Approaching Coaching

As with any other worthwhile occupation, coaching football requires a thorough understanding of a wide body of knowledge. Many coaches are knowledgeable only about the system of football that they played, and therefore limit themselves in what they can offer their players and how they prepare for opponents.

The venerable former coach of the Ohio State Buckeyes, Woody Hayes, once outlined the structure of how football should be analyzed. Coach Hayes believed football can be analyzed according to philosophy, theory, strategy, and tactics.

Philosophy is the reason you coach or play the game. What drives the participants? What outcomes result because of playing and coaching? Every player and every coach learns something every year from

1

the game. Sometimes the things learned are negative, but hopefully the great majority of a coach's experiences are positive. It is the coach's job to ensure that the experiences of his players are primarily positive as well. Later in this book, some of the greats of the game will share with us what they have gained from football.

The theory of the game is the overall approach a coach takes toward playing. On offense, do you try to get a first down on every series (as most teams do), or do you play a more conservative "field position" game while you attempt to eliminate your mistakes and capitalize on those of your opponents? On defense, do you attack and gamble on creating losses, or do you attempt to limit your opponent's gains for three downs and then force a fourth down punt? How important is the kicking game in your plans? Is it a necessary evil while you wait to play offense, or is it a key part of your approach to the game? These are important decisions concerning a team's play that many coaches do not think through.

Because the time available to teach players is limited, you cannot teach your players everything you want them to know. You must develop a system of priorities based on your theory of play, then use the time available to teach those parts of the game that you believe are most important.

Planning strategy is one of the most interesting parts of the game for most coaches. After scouting your opponent, you attempt to find how you can match your strengths against the opponent's weaknesses — in personnel, formations, and situations.

Handling the tactical situations is often the key to winning, particularly in close games. This is where knowledge and experience count most in coaching. How do you cope with your opponent's unexpected changes in attack and defense? How do you force your opponent to play your game? Remember that every technical strength of a team results in a technical weakness somewhere on the field. Can you find it and exploit it?

Along with knowing the game, you must know how to organize your program. How do you buy and fit equipment? How do you organize your practices and your off-season program. What is your role with the administration of your school, the parents of your players, the booster club, the community, and the media? What are your duties as an assistant? What are your duties toward your assistants if you are the head coach?

Coaching football takes a great deal of time. It requires constant study to keep up with the changes in the game, long hours with the players in weight training programs and working on fundamentals, and, of course, many meetings and functions with people outside of the team. Few coaches ever make a significant amount of money for their time and effort, but money is not the reason people become coaches. We coach because our lives are enriched by the people with whom we work and those whom we teach. We are rich because we are spending our time doing what we enjoy most. We are lucky!

2

Why We Play the Game

The great composer Franz Liszt once said, "Every theater is a lunatic asylum and opera is the ward for the incurables." The same might be said about football coaches and players — for whatever reason, *football is fun.*

Every type of game excites its participants. Whether it is Monopoly, hide-and-seek, or football, people play for the sheer enjoyment of it. Those of us who have made lifelong commitments to the game obviously have some deep attachments to it. People love the sport for many reasons.

Football tests the raw physical courage of a man more than any other sport. All cultures recognize the value of courage and applaud it, whether it is the killing of a lion by a young African or the lonely battle against the elements of a young Native American in his initiation to the circle of braves. In our society, the tackling of an opponent by a young football player provides the same outlet.

If psychologist Alfred Adler was right, we all have a drive for power — a drive to overcome our feelings of inferiority. This could certainly explain the joy felt in making an aggressive block or tackle, throwing or catching a pass, kicking a field goal, or blocking a punt. It might also explain the fascination of the coaches in designing an offense or defense and molding a group of young people into an effective team. Of course, there also is the unparalleled satisfaction of leaving the field victorious.

Comradeship also is an important element of the game. When 30 or 40 young people and coaches have gone through the preseason practices or "hell weeks" together, a feeling of mutual respect and trust develops. When you see the defensive team huddled and holding hands, you are witnessing a feeling of family. How many times has the coach become the psychological father to the boy whose biological father hasn't taken the time to care for him?

Motivations for Playing

People play football for different reasons, and obtain different benefits from it. A boy may begin to play because he perceives it as the prestige sport, or because his father wants him to play, or because it is the only thing to do after school. However, the benefits of participation in an organized sport are much more widespread: a feeling of accomplishment, the development of a concept of self-worth, a college scholarship, or, perhaps, a lifetime job in playing or coaching.

Hall of Fame linebacker Sam Huff, of the Giants and Redskins, said that he started playing just because it was expected of him. In the small coal mining town of West Virginia where he grew up, boys were expected to go out for all three sports — football, basketball, and baseball. "I was pretty good at football and baseball, but I never could dribble, shoot, or jump!" he said. "And I liked the contact inherent to football. I liked the contact in baseball, too. I was a catcher.

"I was always a competitor and always did everything I could to win. Football has never been a hobby with me. It has been a career. I played it in college because of my athletic scholarship and it was the only way I could go through school."

Huff received unexpected benefits from playing the game he felt obligated to play. "It taught me how to compete in life," he said. "It taught me patience. It taught me to give and take. But most of all, it taught me to survive in a tough world." Sam's drive for success has landed him the vice-presidency of Marriott Hotels.

Otto Graham, the Hall of Fame quarterback, started playing for the simple reason that it was fun. But Otto also had other motivation. His father had a great interest in music, and Otto learned to play several instruments. He enjoyed the violin and French horn, but they did not provide him with the excitement of sports that so many young men crave. Basketball and football soon took up more of his time than the strings and woodwinds. Otto's fascination with both playing and coaching has always been for the fun of the game, even at the professional level.

Otto went to Northwestern on a basketball scholarship. He didn't play football until he was a sophomore, but he had great success as a quarterback. Paul Brown, then coaching Ohio State, was impressed. So when Paul approached Otto about signing with a new pro league (the All-American Conference), he knew what he was getting.

During World War II, Otto signed his first pro contract. As a naval cadet, he was making $75 a month, but Paul Brown offered him $1,000 to sign, $7,500 a year for two years and $250 per month until the war ended. It lasted only six more months.

After his first pro year Coach Brown tore up the $7,500 contract and replaced it with a $12,000 agreement. When Otto finally resigned from playing he was making $25,000 a year—the highest salary in pro football. Even so, Otto was still playing for the fun of it.

Otto Graham

Mel Hein, the Hall of Fame center of the New York Giants, attended Washington State. In college, his coach got him a job that paid $25 a month — enough to pay half of his monthly tuition and expenses. Mel started his college career as the third-string center on the freshman team. During the last game of the year, against the University of Idaho, the varsity coach told the freshman coach to play him. So during the second half of the last freshman game, he finally got a chance.

"I felt a surge of elation and strength when I entered the game. I wanted to prove to the head coach and to myself that I could play football. After the game, Coach Hollingberry patted me on the shoulder and said 'nice game.' This bolstered my ego and I became determined to make good.

"During spring practice I set a goal of being second string on the varsity. (The first string center was a three-year starter.) During the summer, I got a job clearing trails for the forestry department. Each day I ran in the mountains. By the beginning of fall practice, I was as tough and as hard as a rock. As a sophomore, I beat out the returning starter.

"My confidence, morale, and self-esteem was now tops. My individual goal now was to become All-Coast and All-American. Our team also had high goals. We won all of our games my senior year except the Rose Bowl, where we lost to Alabama.

"I encountered the same problem in the pros as in college. The Giants had two veteran centers, and the squad limit of 25 allowed only two of us to make the team. I got 10 minutes of playing time, total, in the two preseason games, so I had to make it in the first league game or be cut. In that game, the starting center developed leg problems. The second string center made two bad passes to our tailback, so coach Steve Owens yelled at me, 'Hein, do you think you can throw that damn ball back straight?' I didn't answer, I just tore out on the field.

"All I could think of on offense was to snap the ball back straight, then make a block. On defense I just tried to make the tackle. We won the game. After that I played 60 minutes nearly every game.

"Pride, hard work, and believing I could be the best helped me considerably during my career. But

Mel Hein

it is important that this desire should be kept to yourself. Action speaks louder than words. The man who 'mouths off' on what he can or will do is not respected by his fellow athletes."

Former longtime Raider offensive line coach Sam Boghosian says that he played because he was always success-oriented. He was a hard-working farm boy in Fresno, but when he got the chance to play sports he excelled. His chance for excelling was dealt a severe blow when he contracted polio at the age of 11. Both he and his brother were taken to the hospital with polio on the same day his sister died in the same hospital from polio.

He was told that if he ever walked again it would be with a cane and that he would never be able to run. However, his drive to succeed helped Sam overcome the paralysis in his lower leg. He excelled in baseball and was offered a pro contract, but accepted a UCLA football scholarship and played guard on the 1954 national championship team, where he made All-Coast and Academic All-American. One of his fondest memories was playing in the East-West Shrine Game for the benefit of crippled children.

"Participating in athletics has given me so much — an education, the joy of competition, and lifelong work as a football coach," he said.

George Blanda

Jim Otto

George Blanda, another Raider legend, played for the excitement of competition and for the camaraderie of his friends on the team. As with most people who have achieved in any area, George had a fire in him that lit the way for his teammates. Even during the grueling twice-a-day practices when others were tired and listless, George was "up."

Jim Plunkett made so many "comebacks" it was amazing. Not many athletes were counted out so many times and then came back to prove the "experts" wrong.

Plunkett had a burning desire not only to be the best, but to do it without fanfare. His pride and strong commitment helped him earn the Heisman Trophy and then kept him in the pro game for many years. He could have retired in 1978, but instead he helped the Raiders win two Super Bowls. Jim played to meet and beat the challenges the game presented.

The Raider Hall of Fame center Jim Otto began to play for the recognition of being an athlete. As a young man from "the other side of the tracks," he saw that a person could gain recognition from either breaking the law or through athletics. "I chose football," he said. "I had a reputation, even in high school, of not backing down and of being able to play with pain. In my junior year in high school, I played the whole season with a broken ankle. As a senior I had head and neck injuries, but I wouldn't quit. During my second week in college, I blew out my first knee. The next year the other one went. But I never quit.

"The combination of loving the game of football and desiring recognition kept me in the game through college and into the pros. Money was never really a factor. I just wanted to be best. First to get a scholarship to college, then to get a pro contract, then to become All-Pro, and finally to get into the Pro Hall of Fame. I was lucky enough to achieve each goal."

As you can see, the rewards of competing in football are many.

The Fascination of Coaching

Perhaps John Robinson said it best when, after leaving the head coaching position at USC for a three-month stint as a university vice-president, he took the job as the head coach of the Rams. "The thing that shocked me the most was that outside of the sports world, there isn't the passion for what you do."

Otto Graham got into coaching because of his love of the sport and the desire to help young men develop as individuals and as officers in the U.S. Coast Guard. He gave up a lucrative insurance business and a television program in Cleveland to move to Connecticut and the Coast Guard Academy. George Steinbrenner, a mutual friend of the Academy commandant and of Otto's, asked the Hall of Famer to return to the game as coach of the Division III team. This meant no recruiting, no pressure to win, and working in a wholesome environment.

Otto never liked the "win at all costs" pressure that was so evident at the professional and major college levels, so the Coast Guard Academy seemed like fun. After seven highly successful years, a new commandant was appointed to the academy. His approach to athletics did not agree with Otto's, and Otto left the Academy and became head coach of the Redskins.

Otto's easy-going attitude was not what was needed to be successful at the pro level. One time at a Green Bay game Vince Lombardi told him that "in order to be successful at the pro level, you must be an S.O.B." While coaching Division III football was fun for Otto, coaching at the pro level wasn't. "I'm just not a win-at-all-costs kind of guy."

One of the things that excites coaches is the challenge of molding a team from a group of individuals. Former San Francisco 49er coach Bill Walsh, now the coach at Stanford, is an innovative "X's and O's" coach. Like many coaches, he has a penchant for drawing plays on tablecloths, napkins, and scraps of paper.

Looking back on his career with the 49ers, he admitted that "Our fans liked our technical football, but I was really more concerned with two other things — the chemistry of the team and the proper evaluation and selection of talent. Nothing on a pro football team is more important than the talent."

A second area of excitement, which is more evident at the high school and college levels, is the chance to make a positive change in the lives of the young men who play for the coach. John Pont, after 22 years as a college coach at Indiana, Northwestern, Miami of Ohio and Yale, and a few years of business, returned to coaching at a high school, and later took a job in Japan. He loves it because he says "I like making an impact on another person's life." Many other dedicated coaches would echo Pont's sentiments.

Ralph McKinzie, who coached former President Ronald Reagan at Eureka College, was still coaching at age 91. His 65 years of coaching had brought him a great deal of joy. "I always liked to work with boys and try to make them better men," he said. "I feel pretty good about most of them."

Coach McKinzie stated that President Reagan told him that he learned many things from football that helped him in his life — particularly to never give up and to keep on trying to do what's right.

For many high school, college, and Pop Warner coaches, there is that keen desire and ability to help the young men of America. As Otto Graham has said, "The high school coaches are the unsung heroes of America, because so many of our youths will listen only to their coaches." Certainly knowing that they can be an important instrument in directing the lives of our youth is enough to make many coaches feel they are living worthwhile lives.

There is certainly a feeling of power a coach derives when he develops a new concept of offense or defense or when a strategy aids in beating a favored opponent. There is a feeling of satisfaction when he makes personnel evaluations that turn out to help the team. There is the joy felt when he can help a player or his family. And there is the feeling of accomplishment when his team has won a game, especially a big game.

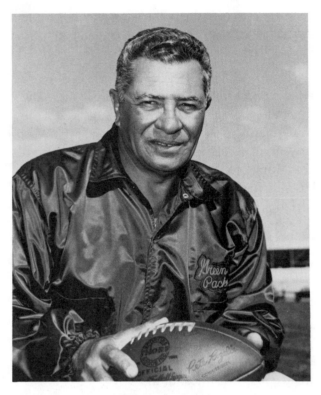

Vince Lombardi

Tom Landry

Football's Place in Society

Former football player General Douglas MacArthur said that football is the closest thing to war, that's why it would always be played at West Point. Football allows for a great deal more strategy than other games, because after each play the teams can regroup and, based on the situation, plan how to attack and how to defend the enemy.

Many former players testify that football has given them the means to be mentally tough. Successful programs emphasize the setting of both individual and team goals. Successful programs also give young men the hope and heart to accomplish their goals in life. In an effective football program, young people can experience the success that flowers from the combination of lofty goals and hard work. And many carry that lesson into their business, political, and family lives.

All-Pro linebacker Jack "Hacksaw" Reynolds recently said, "The players that I used to play with were a lot tougher mentally. The softer our country gets the softer our players get." Reynolds' observation

has been echoed by many coaches. The drift of so many people in society to "have pleasure now" sets up a psychological roadblock to a fundamental necessity of society — to defer immediate pleasure for a greater good in the future.

Former Dallas Cowboy coach Tom Landry concurred. He noted that "I came out of a Depression and was in a war and I think that affected how we looked at things. You could treat us almost any way you wanted. Coaches could've kicked us and it wouldn't have affected us. When I first started coaching, there was no excuse for a player not playing the best he could. But in my later years I had to learn to motivate people to become that way."

Today coaches must inspire young men to desire to succeed. For a football team or a society to flourish, there must be a commonality of purpose and a flaming desire to accomplish exalted goals.

It has been said that winners develop the habit of doing the things that losers don't like to do. The young people of our nation have to learn this lesson if our country is to continue to lead the world. There was drudgery in building the pyramids. Michelangelo spent many uncomfortable years lying on his back on a scaffold while painting the Sistine Chapel ceiling. There were cold, unhappy days spent by the Army of the Revolution at Valley Forge. There have been many thousands of miserable seasick people arriving at Ellis Island anticipating their arrival in this country. Nearly everything valuable has occurred because of discipline, often in spite of great pain or adversity.

Vince Lombardi felt very strongly that "the quality of a man's life is directly proportional to a man's commitment to excellence." Every human being who wants to live to his fullest potential needs high goals and a strong work ethic. The game of football has given millions of American men the opportunity to pursue, in game conditions, the achievement of their goal of success. Coaches universally have required a strong dedication to the work ethic.

Georgia Tech athletic director Homer Rice summarized the meaning of football for him. The lessons of football have taken him from success in high school, to success in college, success in coaching at every level, and now success as an athletic director — and most of all, success as a person.

Following is his complete letter to us on the meaning of football to him:

"It is my life. I actually began the game of football at a very early age. By age six, I was the mascot of my brother's high school team. I went to every practice. I was involved in some of the drills, wore a uniform — it was the beginning of my love affair with the game.

"As I think back through the years, football was directly responsible for my career and any successes I have had as a total person. I emphasize total person because football taught me all aspects of life; spiritual family, human relations, health and fitness, career and planning my finances so that I could retire financially independent. It helped me develop a self-image that produced confidence and self-assurance. My attitude became positive, and it was impressed upon me that I could face life with all of its problems and opportunities. I was convinced that I could succeed in anything I undertook.

Homer Rice

"Most importantly, it taught me to work with a group — the team. I began to realize the importance of having friends, my teammates my family and personal friends. As I look back I thank God that I had this association. It led me into a career in sports that has truly been a meaningful life.

"Football taught me the necessary ingredients to make it to the top. This game helps you become mentally tough, it equips you to do the things you already have the power to do, it helps you to maintain positive attitudes that lead to the winner's circle in all areas of life. We all experience troubles and problems in life, but more important than our troubles is how we react to them. People with positive attitudes still face disappointments, frustrations and pressures. It is their reaction that is different. Problems can cause reactions that defeat you, but if you never give up, you will eventually win.

"Football also taught me to set goals. I learned that because of the lack of goal-setters in America, only three percent of our population reach age 65 with any degree of financial security. The only way to establish a winning tradition is to win. The only

way to win is to set goals. Make plans to reach your goals, work the plans, expect the positive results and be grateful for the winning tradition that is to come.

"We program ourselves to be winners or losers, and winners through programming set goals. One of the most important ingredients I learned from Paul Brown when I visited his camp in Cleveland years ago was that he always had his players write down what they learned that day in practice. I witnessed Otto Graham, the great All-Pro quarterback, writing down how to take the snap from the center. At the time, I felt this was elementary, but I came to realize the importance of writing down my thoughts. Paul Brown explained this procedure by saying that he never assumed that his players know anything until he could see it in writing.

"When a goal is written down, it becomes crystallized. You understand exactly what you are trying to do. Writing it down will impress upon the subconscious mind. This will lead the subconscious mind to work 24 hours a day to help you obtain the goal. After the goal is written down, be sure to look at it as often as possible. I have my goals written on 3 x 5 cards that are covered in plastic that I carry with me. While waiting in airports, offices, riding in cabs, I read and re-read my goals. If you plan wisely, if you do it step by step, if you have small successes while reaching for your ultimate goal, good things will happen. A football team may have as its goal to win the national championship or the Super Bowl. However, each team must win that first game, the second, then the third, on their way to the ultimate goal.

"Hoping to do something will not get the job done. A burning desire to attain a goal is the greatest motivator. Strong desire creates strong habits. Strong habits create success. Success is not a touchdown on every play. Success is consistently picking up first downs every day. The individual who makes it to the top concentrates on moving the ball, avoiding the big mistake, preparing for that moment when the defense makes a mistake, preparing for that moment when the defense makes a mistake and the big play produces pay dirt! The principle to grasp is preparation. Be ready for the big play by picking up first downs every day.

"Football taught me that I must pay my dues in anything I undertake. I started off my coaching career in a very small high school, then advanced to a larger high school, on to the collegiate level and ultimately to the National Football League. From there I became Executive Assistant to the President at one of the leading institutions.

"I learned that I must be prepared to take advantage of the breaks and rely upon the law of averages — if you never quit, you will never lose. It is not a matter of attaining perfection but of striving for it. Positive results make life more enjoyable and self discipline leads to positive results. A successful person consistently does the things that need to be done to achieve positive results — results that give the highest possible quality to life. Don't try to do everything — just do something. If you don't learn to take life one wave at a time, it will overwhelm you. The only way to eat an elephant is one bite at a time.

If you are waiting for everything to be just right before you take action, you are in possession of a fool-proof excuse for failure. People who wait for the right time to do something are often emotionalizing the word hard and confusing it with the word impossible. It is not impossible to change occupations right now, just difficult. It is not impossible to move to another city right now, just difficult.

"Perseverance must win out. It is the most powerful success tool known to man. Perseverance is being able to handle massive disappointment, massive frustration. It is what makes you keep going long after the other person has given up. As a matter of fact, if you stop to think about it, no one can defeat you. Defeat can only occur when you decide to quit. The nice thing about life is that there are no limits to the number of times you can try. Perseverance is a trait so powerful that it can overcome any deficiency. Remember it is what you do with what you have. The choice is yours. You can spend your time hoping to find the mysterious secret to success or you can use your effort to cultivate the same simple habits all successful people routinely practice.

"The word is effort. Football taught me perseverance and effort.

3

Theories of Winning

Intelligent football coaches, like heads of state, generals, and business administrators, must have an overall theory on how they expect to win. Because practice time is limited, coaches must determine their general approach to the game so that the alignments, plays, and skills required can be designed and practiced.

Some emphasize their defensive talents, a few count on their knowledge of the kicking game, but most count on their offensive ideas to produce victories. Some believe that the best defense is a good offense. Others believe that the best offense is a good defense. Advocates of both positions have won national and professional championships.

Field Position Theory

The field position theory of winning is probably as old as the game. Whether it was Knute Rockne, General Bob Neyland, Red Saunders, or Darrell Royal, most of the legendary coaches of college football have been field position advocates. Those who emphasize position football generally want to keep their opponents bottled up in their own territory. It is their belief that it is extremely difficult to march a team 70 or 80 yards for a touchdown.

The odds are that somewhere during that march there will be a penalty, a fumble, an incomplete pass, or an interception that stalls or stops the drive. Field position advocates place their hopes in the old adage that to err is human, and hope that their op-

ponents are particularly human on game day. By emphasizing defense and kicking, they hope to be able to slow down their opponents and to force the miscue that results in a stalled drive or a turnover. These coaches generally put their best players on the defensive team. They also spend a great deal of time perfecting the kicking game, especially punting.

Victorious teams aren't necessarily those that win the game, they are those that avoid losing it. This is particularly true in close games. With the ball inside the 10-yard line, a team might punt the ball on first down. Inside the 20, it might punt on second down. And inside the 35, it might punt on third down. Of course, a team that spends a great deal of time on the kicking game may well surprise opponents with a fake punt on first, second, or third down. If the opponent sends back one or two safeties to field the punt, it is weakened against the run and the pass, so an occasional fake might get good yardage.

The quick kick is another important element in the field position general's arsenal. Because the idea is to keep the opponent deep in his own territory, and because a well-executed quick kick can gain 60 or more yards (compared to the 35 yards expected on a punt), the often orphaned quick kick is a favored son to a field position coach.

The field position coach generally divides the field into specific areas. As has been noted, inside a team's own 35-yard line is going to be an early kicking down. Between the 35 and the 50 is an area in which safe plays are called. Once past midfield, a team probably will open up and throw some passes. Once inside the opponent's 35-yard line, it generally assumes that it is in four-down territory so it only has to make an average of two-and-a-half yards per play in order to score. In that instance, it might revert to a more conservative running game.

Knute Rockne divided the field into five 20-yard areas. From his own goal line to the 20, he would kick on first down. From his 20 to his 40, he wouldn't pass, and would punt on second or third down. Between the 40s, he might pass and would punt only on fourth down. From the offensive 40 to the 20, he would use some trick plays or a field goal if his offense was stopped. From the 20 to the goal, he would use the plays most likely to score.

Darrell Royal, the former Texas coach, thought in terms of three zones. From his goal to the 35, he wanted to get the ball across the 50 in any way possible safe runs, passes, and if necessary, the punt. Between the 35s, which he called the alumni zone, he thought it was the duty of the coach to entertain the fans. From the offensive 35 on in, he believed it was four-down territory and his teams had to score.

Play it safe and avoid mistakes is the maxim that guides the thinking of the field position type of coach. His defensive ideas are geared to slowing the opponent. His offensive ideas tend to be conservative. He is likely to use an offensive attack based on power, with double-team blocking putting two of his players against one member of the opposition. He is football's answer to Aesop's tortoise: Slow and sure wins the race.

Don't lose the game is a philosophy that is often more effective than the average person realizes. A few years ago, Lawrence High School of Lawrence, Kansas won more than 50 straight games using the idea of playing for the tie. They were able to get other teams to lose the game rather than take the risk of losing it themselves. Because a college football game generally includes more than 130 plays, with 22 players in on each play, there are ample opportunities for errors. The old coaching adage that football is a game of inches indicates the small margin of error that can be the difference between winning and losing and the field position coaches don't want to lose.

Ball Control Theory

The ball control coaches are more interested in offense safe offense. They hope to make three-and-a-half yards on each of three running downs or five yards on two of their three passing downs so that they can get the first down. Naturally, they want to avoid any mistakes such as penalties (that would force them out of their short yardage theory) or turnovers (which would take away the ball.)

Their emphasis is on safe running and safe passing plays. The Oklahoma teams of the 1950s, under Bud Wilkinson, were masters of the ball control running attack. Most college and professional teams today are ball control teams. The conservative offenses of the Rams and Bears are good illustrations of running attacks, and the Brigham Young teams of LaVell Edwards or the recent San Francisco 49er teams are examples of ball control passing attacks.

When drawn on paper, every offensive play can easily gain four yards. On the blackboard, every lineman makes his block and the ball carrier never fumbles. The thing about football is that the players seldom perform as well as the O's on the chalkboard. On the chalkboard, the O's always beat the X's at least when the offensive coordinator has the chalk.

The Big Play Approach

While all teams have their safe runs and passes, a few occasionally stray from the ball control theory. Some coaches believe that striking for a touchdown on one play at well-timed moments improve the chance of winning. Whether it is the long bomb, the deep reverse, the trick play, or the middle distance pass that breaks through the defense, getting an immediate touchdown is always on the mind of the big play-oriented coach.

Although some coaches approach high-risk plays with more prayer than preparation, the true big play advocates plan for the event. Each long scoring play has been practiced and evaluated hundreds of times before it is used in a game. The advantages of big play thinking go beyond the chance of the quick score. The defensive coordinators and their teams know that a big play team may strike on any play. Opponents must always be alert to defend against a long quick score, and this detracts from their ability to stop a basic ball control game. The defensive backs may not support on the run quite as quickly because of their fear of the bomb. The defensive linemen or backers may not pursue quite as recklessly because of their fear of the reverse. If they rush the passer too aggressively, they may open up the draw or the screen pass. So the threat of the big play makes the ball control game more effective.

Most coaches use more than one approach during the season. If the opponent is physically superior, a big play approach might be viewed as the only way to win. The coach might use a fake punt or put in a few trick plays, figuring it is his only hope. Even the most die-hard field position coaches go for the big play sometimes, because it helps keep the defense honest. And the big play people use plenty of ball control plays. But the day that the big play coach punts on first down will be the day a million dollar quarterback refuses a pay raise.

Successful coaches look at the probabilities of success for a certain type of play. For example, a field position coach might throw long from his own end zone about once every 10 years. He knows that the opposing coach is aware of his conservative bent, so once in a while he may throw long, knowing that the opposition expects him to stick to a safe running play.

Winning with the Run or the Pass

The rule changes regarding the use of the hands in blocking over the past several years gives the offense a greater advantage than it once had over the defense. It also gives pass protectors much greater latitude than they had when their hands had to remain close to the chest. Both the running game and the passing game are enhanced by the current use of the hands in blocking.

Running attacks and passing attacks can be conservative or daring. Dive or power plays are safe especially if the runner carries the ball with both hands so he doesn't fumble. Safe passing attacks probably opt for several short passes to the backs away from the major pass defenders.

On the other hand, option football (such as the veer and wishbone) increases both the chance of fumbling and the chance for long gainers. Big play passing teams don't worry as much about the interception. When a long pass is intercepted, it is about the same as having punted the ball.

Running advocates say that three things can happen when you pass, and two of them are bad: the incomplete pass and the interception. So to avoid the incomplete pass or the interception, they stick to the run. Passing enthusiasts, however, believe that a good passing attack can be put together with less talented players than can a good running attack. Consequently, many coaches pass because of weakness, rather than strength.

A major fascination with the pass is that it is so much fun to design. Coaches are notorious for drawing plays on everything from tablecloths to menus. On paper, there are no incomplete passes, so every coach can theorize his way to the Super Bowl. Not only do coaches like to plan a passing attack, the players (at least the passers and receivers) like to practice it. Plenty of kids like to find an open field and throw the ball around. How many want to practice blocking?

Finally, there is the weather factor. Wind, rain and cold temperatures affect a passing attack more than a running attack. If you are guaranteed of playing every game on clear and windless 70- degree days, a passing attack makes more sense.

Pass-oriented offenses have become more popular in recent years, and many coaches believe that is the best way to win. While most coaches express their hope for a balanced attack that gains nearly equal amounts of yardage from the run and the pass, the running game has a lot going for it. In the college game, the 10 top running teams in the country generally win about 80 percent of their games, but the top 10 passing teams generally win only about 50 percent of their games. At the pro level, it has been found that teams that run 40 times in a game win 90 percent of the time. How many times does a team lose when one of its backs runs for over 100 yards in a game? Not often.

Intelligent coaches at all levels must do some hard thinking before deciding on a style of play. A coach must consider the players he has to work with (their toughness and their skills), the weather, and his own competencies and beliefs. At the college level, the coach can recruit for many of his needs, so he may not be as influenced by player inadequacies. Coaches at the professional level can draft to suit their style of play, but they are nearly precluded from choosing a pure field position approach because the fans come to see more offense.

The coach's decision on how his team can best win is essential in determining his theories of offense, defense, and kicking. It will also play an essential part in the development of his week-to-week strategy for upcoming opponents and in the types of decisions he will make during each game. When a coach decides to punt on fourth-and-one on his opponent's 45, that decision was probably made months, or even years before, as part of his overall theory of winning. The boos from the stands will not persuade him to do otherwise.

The Running Attack

Theories of running attacks can be categorized as the power theory, the quickness theory, or the finesse theory. Virtually all coaches use at least two of these theories, but most emphasize only one.

The power game is based on the idea of having more players than your opponent at the point of attack. This usually is accomplished with double-team blocks by the linemen and/or blocking backs, such as in the following examples.

A double-team block

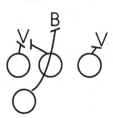

**A double-team block
with an isolated linebacker blocked by a fullback**

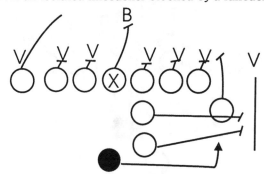

A power play with two double-team blocks

The quickness game advocates attempt to get the ball carrier to the line of scrimmage before the defense can react and pursue. The halfback dive, the fullback buck, and the quarterback sneak are examples of quickness plays.

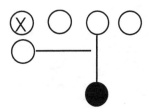

Split-T dive

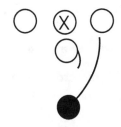

Fullback buck

Quarterback sneak

The finesse game utilizes deception or "reads" to fool the defense. Traps, counters, and reverses, as well as the various option series, fall into this category.

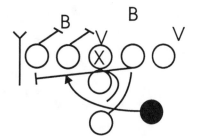

Halfback trap

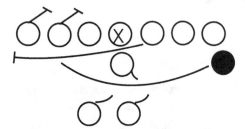

Wingback reverse

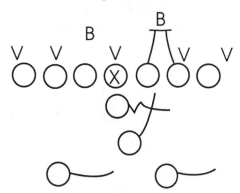

Wishbone triple option

Now for a bit more detail on these three approaches to the running attack.

The Power Game

Probably the best example of the power theory is the old Tennessee single-wing attack. The basic series was an off-tackle play in which the strong end and wingback double-teamed the defensive tackle, and the blocking back and fullback tandem blocked the defensive end (who was set up by the tailback faking to go wide, then cutting back behind the tandem block). Both guards would pull through the hole to block.

In the "good old days," plays were called attacking the defensive positions. The defensive tack-

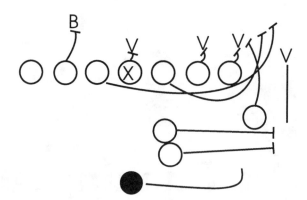

Single wing off-tackle power play

les always played in the area of the offensive ends. Today the plays are nearly always called over an offensive lineman, because so many types of defenses are used. The off-tackle play usually involves the end blocking with his tackle or a wingback. The opponent they block might be a defensive end, a linebacker, or even the defensive tackle.

(Today "off-tackle" seldom means "off" the defensive tackle. Coaches simply refused to change their old terminology although the defensive alignments and offensive numbering systems changed.)

If the defensive tackle played wider than normal or fought hard outside to stop the double-team, the blocking changed and the hole was moved inward one position — with the tackle being blocked out rather than double-teamed in. If the defensive end crashed or played close to the tackle, he was blocked in by the fullback and the tailback would run wide.

The favorite inside power play was the fullback buck with a wedge block, in which the linemen formed a shoulder-to-shoulder wedge and pushed aside anyone in their path.

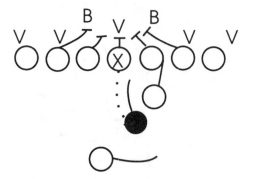

Wedge on the offensive center

Like any offense, however, the Tennessee wing had its weaknesses. The holes were hit slowly, and the center had to snap the ball backward before blocking, which is more difficult than the snap in a T-formation offense; also, many centers kept their heads down to make certain that they didn't make a bad snap.)

Another problem was that teams had to have a durable and outstanding triple-threat player at tailback. The 1950 UCLA team lost its four top tailbacks for the duration of the season before the first game. By the end of the season, its starting tailback was a former eighth-string tailback, a sophomore named Ted Narleski, who made the All-Coast team. For those who could survive the punishment, playing single-wing tailback was the ultimate football position. He was equivalent to a combination pro quarterback and an I-formation tailback.

The Maryland I-formation, developed by Tom Nugent, also was a powerful attack. In this attack, four backs lined up behind the center. Don Coryell, the former San Diego Charger coach, used a similar attack when he was coaching at Whittier College. During his last years with the Chargers, he brought back some of his old Whittier plays to reinforce the Charger running game.

Here is a sample of the power that can generated by such an attack. Note the similarities with the single wing power.

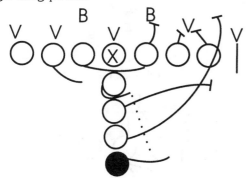

Off-tackle play

While at USC in the 1960s, John McKay combined the I-formation with pro style wide receivers. This helped his passing attack, but detracted from the running game. Following are two samples of power plays from the USC "I", the off-tackle play and an inside isolation play where the linebacker is not blocked by the linemen but is isolated, and then is blocked by the fullback — with the tailback having the option of running to either side of the fullback's block. The pro-style "I" attack is commonly used today at all levels of play.

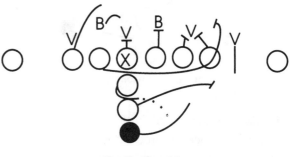

Pro-I off-tackle

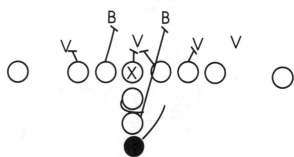

Pro-I isolation play

The disadvantages of the I-formation are that it inhibits outside running plays and it doesn't have the capability of crossing the backs in faking actions; therefore, it is easier for the linebackers to key. The power "I" is seldom used as the primary attack, but it is often used as part of a pro attack. In this play, the flanker is brought in to the halfback spot. From that point, he and the fullback can lead the tailback to his side of the line, or the fullback and tailback can lead the halfback to the other side of the line.

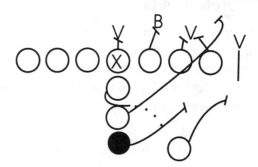

Power-I — halfback lead

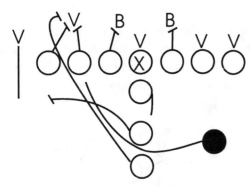

Power-I — tailback lead

The off-tackle power game from the T-formation was probably best emphasized by Vince Lombardi's attack at Green Bay. The Green Bay sweep could be cut off-tackle or continued as a wide sweep, depending on whether the outside linebacker was blocked out or in.

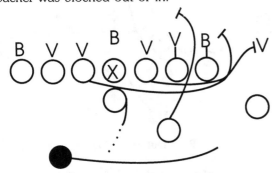

Lombardi's Green Bay sweep

It is easy to see how the T-formation attacks have taken the blocking patterns from the single-wing power play. However, each time that a back is flanked as a wide receiver, a potential blocker is lost. If the quarterback is not called on as a blocker to avoid the possibility of injury, another blocker is lost.

The Quickness Game

The quickness game is indigenous to the T-formation. Because the center hands the ball to the quarterback, he can hand off to any of his other backs — without them having to wait for the ball to get to them, as in the single wing.

In a quickness attack, power blocking schemes are not used. Most of the blocks are one-on-one, and don't have to be sustained as long because the back should reach the hole in about a half a second. If the play is to hit between the guards, the fullback prob-

ably carries the ball. If the play is to go just inside or outside the tackle, the halfback usually carries it. This halfback dive is the basic play of the split-T attack.

Fullback buck

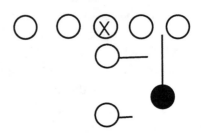

Halfback dive

From the I-formation, it is the fullback who is the quick hitter. He can go to the same side as the tailback or to the opposite side in a counter action.

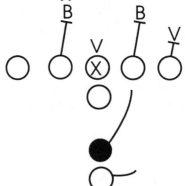

I fullback buck

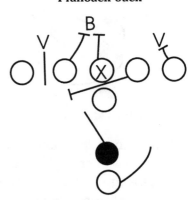

I fullback counter trap

A quick pitchout from the quarterback gets a play wide quickly. If the end plays close to the tackle, he can usually be flanked by the quick pitch. (Note: If there is a fullback, he usually runs toward the defensive end to threaten him with a block, making it easier for the ball carrier to outflank him.) For maximum effectiveness, the halfback should line up at least as wide as the offensive tackle.

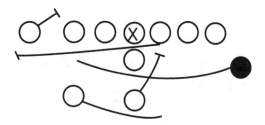

Wing T reverse

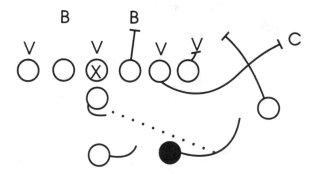

Quick pitch

The Finesse Game

All attacks should have some elements of the finesse game. At least one play should end up opposite the way it starts, to make the linebackers more cautious in their pursuit of the ball carrier. By keeping them aware of the countering action, they will be a bit less effective in stopping the team's primary power or quickness plays.

If the attack has a wingback, he should be the primary person used in the countering actions. When the wingback, end, or a wide receiver becomes the ball carrier, it is called a reverse. The following are examples of reverses:

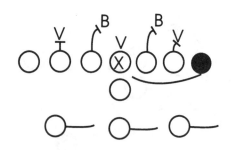

Inside reverse to a tight end

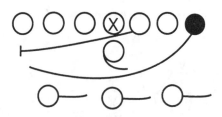

End around

Following are some examples of countering actions using the "set" backs:

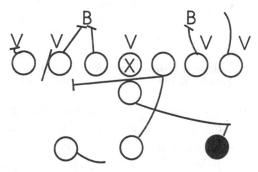

Cross buck

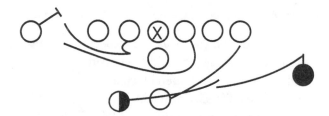

Reverse to wide receiver from a pro-set T

The counter "trey" (code word for trap) was developed by Joe Gibbs when he was the coach of the Washington Redskins. Many teams now use this power type of counter. It can be used out of a one-, two-, or three-back set.

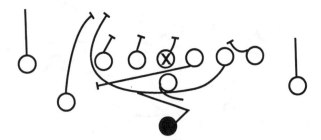

Counter trey from a one-back set

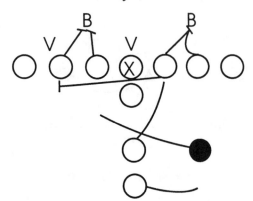

Cross buck from power-I

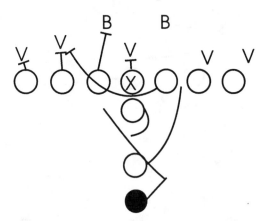

**Tailback counter from pro-I formation
(used if defense is keying the fullback)**

The quarterback must determine whether the end is going to tackle him (if so he should pitch the ball) or pursue the trailing halfback (if so he would keep it and run, perhaps pitching to the halfback further up the field). Coaches should give the quarterback a "key" to help him with his decision.

For example, if the quarterback can see the front numbers of the defensive end (indicating that the end is facing the quarterback and is probably going to tackle him) he should pitch. Or perhaps the key would be that if the end is less than one-and-a-half yards from the tackle, the quarterback should pitch. Or it might be that if the end is on the line of scrimmage he pitches, and if the end has penetrated into the backfield, he keeps it.

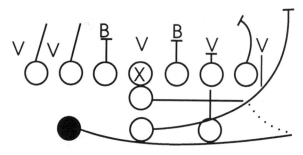

**Split-T option
(end playing tight, QB options to pitch)**

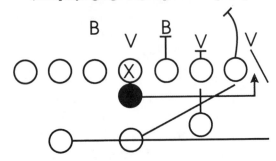

**Split-T option
(end playing loose, QB options to keep and run)**

Another part of the finesse game involves what has come to be known as "option" football. In this type of attack, the quarterback must determine whether to keep the ball and run with it or pitch it to a running back, depending on what the defense allows. On wide plays from the split-T attack, the quarterback fakes to the diving halfback, fakes to the fullback (who was running off tackle), and then, when he comes to the defensive end, he decides whether to keep the ball and cut upfield or pitch to the trailing halfback. The man who is being optioned (in this case, the defensive end) is not blocked.

In either of these plays, the fullback can be used as a lead blocker for the halfback or can run the slant at the defensive end, then block in on a linebacker or lead the halfback downfield. The "speed" option does not rely on an inside dive fake. This play is generally run from a two-back set. What it loses in the inside fake, it gains with the additional blocker.

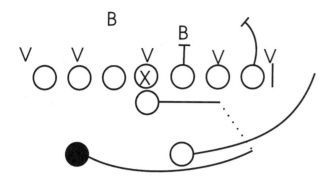

Speed option to halfback

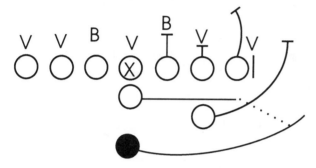

Speed option to fullback

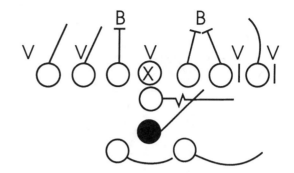

**Wishbone triple option
(defensive tackle has outside responsibility)**

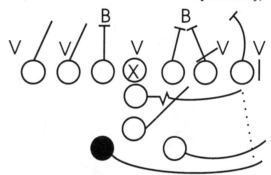

**Wishbone triple option
(defensive tackle has responsibility for the fullback)**

The ultimate in option football is the triple option. The wishbone and the veer are the major triple-option attacks, although some teams run a triple option from an I-formation. The invention of the triple option is credited to Georgia Tech athletic director Homer Rice when he was coaching in high school in the 1950s. He used it with the inside belly series. Bud Moore at Texas A&M used it from the I-formation in the 1960s, and Darrell Royal at Texas used it from the wishbone formation a bit later.

In a triple option, the defensive end and tackle are left unblocked. This enables extra offensive linemen to double-team the other defenders, especially the linebackers, giving this type of "finesse" attack some of the elements of a "power" attack.

In the wishbone (named for the shape of the alignment of the backs), the quarterback puts the ball in the fullback's belly as he looks and "reads" the defensive tackle. If the tackle has an outside responsibility, the ball is given to the fullback. If the tackle comes in to stop the fullback, the quarterback takes the ball back, while the fullback blocks the tackle. The quarterback then moves quickly down the line to option the defensive end. Here he "reads" the defensive end, just as he did in the split-T option.

The triple option has all of the elements: finesse, power (because of the double-team), and quickness. As such, it is very difficult to stop. The drawbacks are that with the quarterback having to make the two options in less than a half a second, there is ample opportunity for mistakes — the fullback may think he is keeping the ball, while the quarterback is trying to pull it away, the pitch may go astray, or the quarterback may make the wrong read. Also, because the true wishbone has three set backs, the threat of a pass is reduced.

Bill Yeoman, recently retired as the coach at Houston, attempted to rectify the passing weakness of the wishbone by substituting a wide receiver for the fullback and splitting one of his ends. This formation is called the "veer" or the "Houston veer." In the veer, the first option is to the diving halfback rather than to the plunging fullback. The second option is to the "off side" halfback. In the wishbone, both halfbacks run wide, so that if the ball is pitched to the ball carrier, he has a lead blocker. In the veer, the halfback must go it alone, hoping that his fleetness of foot and his keenly intelligent fakes help him elude the killer cornerback.

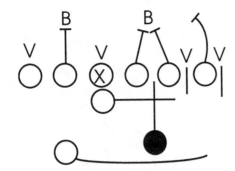

Veer option (give to halfback)

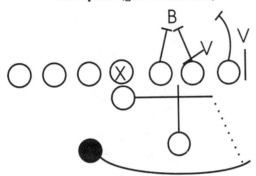

Option on the end

Developing a Running Threat

Every play, with the exception of the quarterback sneak, is part of a series. The play series is based on a power theory, a quickness theory, a finesse theory, or some combination of the three. In selecting a play series, the coach must be guided by his overall theory of what he expects to do from that series. If he wants maximum power or finesse, three backs in the backfield are probably more effective. Does he want to pass? If so, he probably wants three or more immediate receivers next to the line of scrimmage, and he probably wants his set backs wide so that they can get into the pass pattern quickly.

He might want his backfield action such that it yields a good faking action should he decide to pass. The split-T series would be a terrible series from which to pass, because the wide line splits make it difficult to hold out the pass rushers, and the only immediate receivers are the ends. Other series offer a good deal of faking and pass protection.

In theory, any back can hit any hole in the T-formation. However, in practice, the fullback is the tough running and blocking type of player while the

halfbacks are faster and more elusive. Some coaches want a total power game and go with all backs being fullback types. Others go with all backs being racehorse types. Once in a while the coach is lucky enough to get a back who can do it all. Such a back makes the coach look like a genius.

Plays Starting with the Fullback

Many coaches set up their basic attack with the fullback. He might buck at the guard and set up a cross buck or a belly series. In the cross buck series, the fullback goes toward one of the guards, then the halfback on that side comes back behind the quarterback or between the quarterback and the center. This is often done with the guard trap blocking.

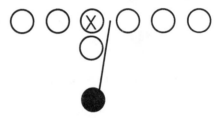

Fullback buck (straight blocking)

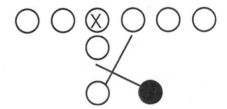

Cross buck (straight blocking)

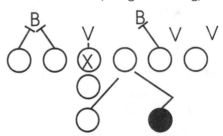

Cross buck (inside handoff, trap block)

Either method of cross buck can be done with straight-ahead blocking or with a guard trapping while the fullback blocks the guard's man.

The inside belly series is another type of buck. The quarterback reaches back and puts the ball in the belly of the fullback. If the fullback play has been called, the quarterback gives him the ball, then fakes to the opposite halfback. If the halfback's play has been called, the ball is pulled away from the fullback at the last second and given to the halfback.

The fullback buck is also the beginning of the I-formation isolation series, but the fullback is generally the lead blocker, not the primary ball carrier.

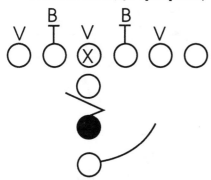

Buck from the I (QB open-pivots)

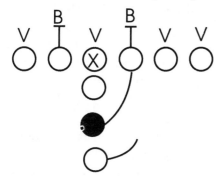

Fullback counter from the I (QB reverse-pivots)

Of course, when there is only one running back in the backfield, as in the A-formation popularized by former Washington Redskins' Coach Joe Gibbs, that lone runner had better be special.

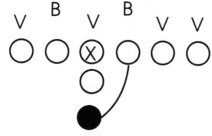

A-formation buck

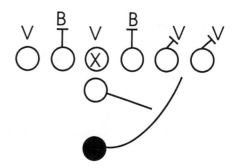

Slant

In the slant play, the fullback runs toward his tackle or end. This action is generally used as part of an outside play; the fullback either gets the ball as the primary runner or he fakes and blocks while the halfback or quarterback goes wide. As part of the split-T series, the fullback might get a cross block between the end and tackle or a double team by the end and tackle and an outside block by the diving halfback. As part of the quick pitch (or fly) series, the quarterback fakes the pitch to the flying halfback, but gives to the fullback. A third series, which incorporates the fullback starting wide, is called the "outside belly." In this, the quarterback moves wider and puts the ball in the fullback's belly ("rides" him). If the fullback's play is called, the quarterback gives it to him. If the wide play is called, he pulls the ball from the fullback and then options the defensive end.

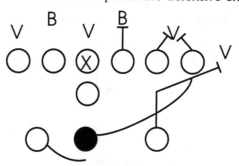

Split-T slant

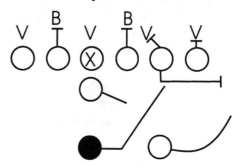

Fly series (quick-pitch slant)

Plays with the Halfback

The quick-hitting halfback play is the dive. If the halfback is set behind the tackle, he generally has the option of attacking just inside or outside the tackle, depending how his tackle has blocked the opposing lineman. If he is set behind the guard (as in the veer), he can attack from inside the guard to outside the tackle (the outside veer series).

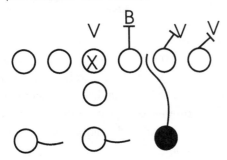

Dive play (defensive lineman blocked out)

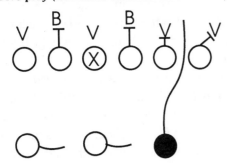

Dive play (defensive lineman blocked in)

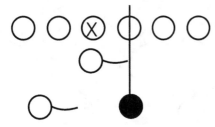

Inside veer (at guard)

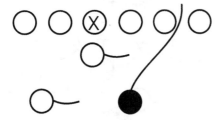

Inside veer (at tackle)

Plays with the Tailback

When the coach calls the halfback a "tailback," look out! It means he is the primary ball carrier. Whether it is the single wing, the double wing, or the "I," there's a stud back there who is either very fast, very powerful or very tricky — perhaps all three.

Some coaches believe in letting two or three running backs carry the ball in equal amounts, a theory that balances the attack, but other coaches want their best man to carry the ball 80 or 90 percent of the time. In 1984, Auburn ran a wishbone with all the backs getting a chance to run the ball. One of those backs was Bo Jackson. When the 1985 season opened, Auburn had changed its basic formation to the "I" and Bo, as the tailback, ran the ball far more often — all the way to the Heisman Trophy.

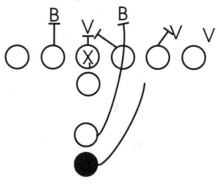

Tailback blast

Tailback power

As earlier noted, the seldom-used Tennessee single wing is the most powerful running offense. When running to the wingback side, the tailback starts as the ball is snapped. When running to the weak side, the tailback stands up and fakes the pass while the fullback and blocking back run in front of him, then he starts his run.

The type of running attack a coach chooses influences the type of formation he uses. (Formations will be discussed in the next chapter.) But the theory of the play (power, quickness, or finesse) and the primary running threat (fullback, halfback, or tailback) can usually be incorporated into a different formation than that in which it originally was used. So the off-tackle power play or the run-pass option of the single wing series have been adapted to the T-formation. The shotgun adjustment most "T" teams use is really an offshoot of single- or double-wing football. Similarly, teams that still use the single-wing attack often split wide receivers, an idea borrowed from the T-formation teams.

Coaches borrow from each other continually. They borrow, invent, and adjust in order to make their offenses as effective as they can possibly be. Here are some of the most influential running series in football.

The Tennessee single-wing power series includes the basic power play off tackle, the fullback buck, and the fullback spinner series (with a possible reverse to the wingback or a handoff to the tailback.) Elements of this attack can be seen in some of the power series in the "T" or "I" formations.

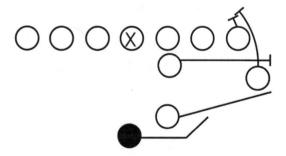

Off-tackle power play (power)

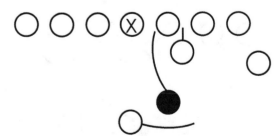

Fullback buck (power and quickness)

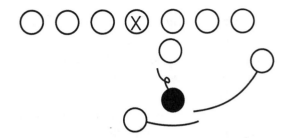

Spinner series (finesse)

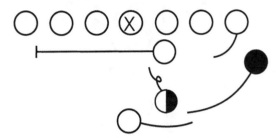

Reverse from spinner (finesse)

The buck-lateral series was probably the best "finesse" series in football. The series started with the ball being snapped to the fullback who would buck up the middle. The blocking back, instead of leading the play, would turn around to face the fullback. The fullback might hand to the blocking back, who might then turn and run into the line, or he might drop back and pass, or he might hand to the wingback for a reverse, or most often he would lateral to the tailback who might then run wide or pass. This series threatened every hole.

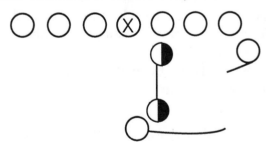

Buck lateral, possible reverse (finesse)

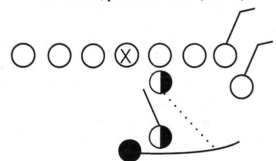

Buck lateral, run-pass option (finesse)

The traditional "tight T" or "full house" formation made quicker plays possible than did the single wing. The opportunity for faking and for quicker countering also is greater than in the offenses that feature the direct snap, such as the single wing. The quick dives and bucks, along with the threat of the immediate quick pass, made this formation almost universal by the early 1950s.

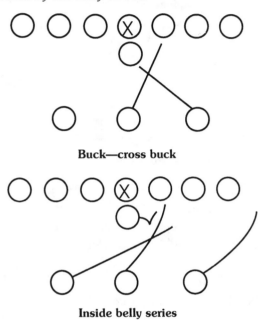

Buck—cross buck

Inside belly series

The inside belly series was probably first initiated by Eddie LeBaron, a diminutive quarterback from College of the Pacific in the 1940s. His uncanny faking ability caused many long runs to be called back because the referee blew the whistle when the fullback was tackled, although the halfback was carrying the ball. Bobby Dodd, the legendary Georgia Tech coach, perfected it and developed it into a major series.

In the inside belly series, the quarterback calls for either the fullback or the halfback to get the ball. It is not an option. The quarterback puts the ball into the belly of the fullback as he attacks the area of the offensive guard. The quarterback "rides" the fullback as he goes into the line. If the fullback is to be the ball carrier, the quarterback leaves the ball with him. If the halfback is to carry it, the quarterback rides the fullback as long as possible and then pulls the ball out and hands it to the halfback.

The outside belly series starts with the fullback attacking the tackle-end area. The quarterback rides the fullback and hands off the ball if that is the play called. If the halfback's number has been called, the quarterback takes the ball away from the fullback and then either pitches directly to the halfback or runs an option at the end with a possible quarterback keep or a pitch to the halfback.

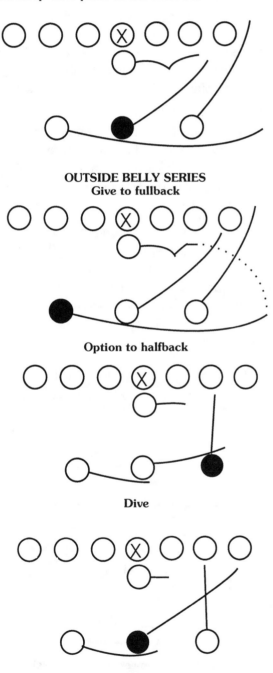

OUTSIDE BELLY SERIES
Give to fullback

Option to halfback

Dive

Fullback off tackle

The split-T dive-option series was developed by Don Faurot, coach of the University of Missouri. It was popularized by Jim Tatum, at Oklahoma and Maryland, and reached its pinnacle under Bud Wilkinson at Oklahoma.

This attack was a combination of quickness and finesse that threatened every offensive hole. By splitting the linemen up to eight feet, large holes were developed in the defensive front. Also, the large splits put the defenders on the side away from the play (the "off" side), a great distance from the attack point. Nearly all teams in that era (the 1940s and 1950s) used eight-man defensive fronts, which made it easier to split them. (Ironically, it was Wilkinson who developed the 5-2 Oklahoma defense that greatly reduced the effectiveness of the attack. That same 5-2 defense is the most universally used defensive alignment in football and is the father of the 3-4 defense that also is commonly used.)

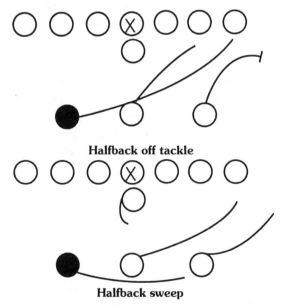

Halfback off tackle

Halfback sweep

The split-T attack is based almost entirely on quickness, with only the fullback counter as a finesse variation. The quarterback sneak is also an important part of the attack. The guard can split from one foot to six feet, the tackles two to eight feet, and the ends three to eight feet. The split depends on how far the defensive linemen split with the offensive line. When a defensive lineman plays "head up" on any split, some coaches say "take them to the sidelines with your split."

Another advantage of the split-T quickness attack is that the fakes are made at the line of scrimmage. Each defender has to commit to the play in his area and cannot pursue the play as quickly as when the fakes are deeper in the backfield.

The split-T series is based on the principle of creating lateral holes along the line of scrimmage by the split of the linemen, with vertical holes resulting at every spot where there is a linebacker. Because the holes are already present when the teams line up, the offensive lineman only has to keep his defender in the same spot. He doesn't have to move him away from the hole as in the single wing.

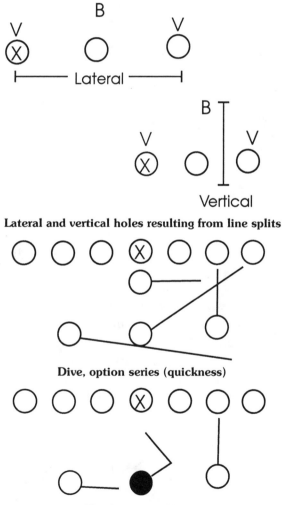

Lateral and vertical holes resulting from line splits

Dive, option series (quickness)

Fullback counter (finesse)

The wing-T, developed by Dave Nelson at Delaware and made famous by Forest Evashevski at Iowa, attempts to use much of the power and the wide reverse counter play of the single wing, with the speed of the T or split-T.

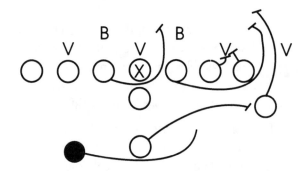

Off-tackle power (backfield balanced)

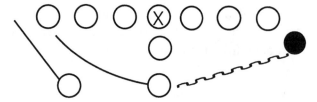

Off-tackle power to wingback who started in motion

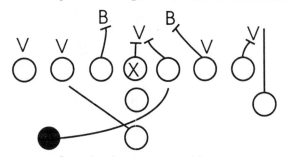

Cross buck action or tackle trap

The pro I-formation of John McKay incorporates much of the power of the single wing with some of the quickness of the "T," and the passing potential of the professional wide formation. Although the fullback buck and the outside belly series are integral parts of the attack, he added the isolation play for power and a new idea of "option running" for his talented tailbacks. If the linemen just stay with the defenders, the tailback can pick his holes.

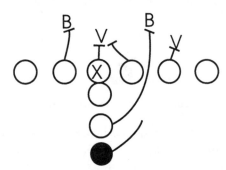

Pro-I isolation

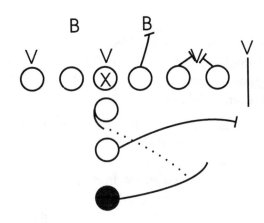

Pro-I off-tackle (power)

KISS the Defense Goodbye

Coaches have a great many options from which to choose in developing a running attack, but they can't have it all. Each coach must choose whether to emphasize a power, quickness, or finesse attack. He must then decide whether he is going to feature one primary ball carrier or spread the ball carrying responsibilities and balance his attack. He must decide whether to fit the players to his system (making small changes each year to accommodate the abilities of his players) or to fit a system to his players — possibly making great changes every year or so. In doing this, he might emphasize a tough fullback one year and a fast halfback the next.

A countless number of running plays are available, but there isn't nearly enough time to teach all possible plays to each team. The general theory of most successful coaches is the "KISS" approach. (KISS is an acronym meaning "Keep It Simple, Stupid.") A team is generally better served by doing fewer things well than by doing many things poorly. Consequently, most teams have three or fewer basic running series. Many very successful teams, particularly at the high school level, use only one series.

One of the most fascinating aspects of coaching is drawing the X's and O's. Have you ever thought of designing your own offense? All of our current offenses started with the imagination of a coach scribbling on a piece of paper. Undoubtedly, many new attacks are just waiting to be discovered. Will you be the next offensive genius?

5
Blocking for Running Plays

It is much easier to draw up a play than it is to make it work on the field. What makes a series work are the blocking patterns and the skill of the blockers. Coaches often argue what is the most important segment of a football team. Some claim that it is the defensive cornerbacks. The media hype the so-called "skill positions" — the quarterback, running backs, receivers and defensive backs. But most coaches believe that a good offensive line can make a team. A great offensive line can open holes for a mediocre running back, but a poor offensive line cannot open holes for the greatest of running backs.

You may have heard about the time Knute Rockne's famous backfield, the Four Horsemen, was getting a bit cocky because of all the publicity it had received. So in one game Rockne took out the Seven Mules, the nickname for the starting Notre Dame line. To the surprise of the "Horsemen," they were totally ineffective. Only when the "mules" were inserted in the game did the backs start to run with abandon. The old coach had taught a major lesson in humility.

No wonder great backs appreciate their offensive lines. Eric Dickerson, O.J. Simpson and other great backs have taken good care of the men who have taken care of them. Expensive gifts and sumptuous dinners are a small price to pay to the linemen who make them look so good.

The Types of Blocks

There are several types of blocks, and several techniques for executing each block.

Techniques of blocking are varied. For example, a one-on-one block might be executed by stepping into the opponent, getting under his shoulder pads, getting the blocker's head on the same side of the defender as the hole where the back will run, and lifting him while driving him backward. It also might be done as a scramble block in which the blocker stays low (possibly on all fours) and drives at the defender with little or no lift. It might also be done by working the defender up without trying to drive him anywhere, just maintaining contact. Each type of block has its place, depending on the type of attack and the size and skill of the blocker. (These will be discussed fully in the chapter on fundamentals.)

Individual blocking assignments also can take several approaches, as follows:

- The straight one-on-one drive block has the lineman taking the man nearest him away from the hole.
- A reach block has the lineman blocking one-on-one on the next man out.
- A reverse shoulder block has the lineman blocking the next man on the line with the blocker's shoulder which is farthest from the defender being the point of contact. This type

of block gives the offensive man an angle on the defender so he should be in a more advantageous position to make the block.

- A cross block has the two adjacent linemen blocking the defenders near the other. If the two defenders are both on the line of scrimmage, the outside offensive lineman blocks first and the inside lineman moves slightly behind to block his man. This block is often used when a linebacker is on the inside man. The outside lineman moves first and blocks the linebacker while the inside offensive lineman moves behind and blocks the "down" lineman.

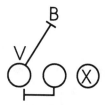

Cross block vs. linebacker

- A fold block is like a cross block, but the lineman blocking the "down" lineman goes first while the blocker who is assigned to block the backer goes behind his teammate then blocks the backer

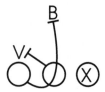

Fold block

- A scoop block is another combination used on a down lineman and a backer. The man on the down defensive lineman hits him while the man to his inside moves to help him. After the inside man has made contact, the outside man releases and blocks the backer. If a backer is "reading" the block of the man on him and sees him blocking, the backer probably "fills" into that area rather than pursuing the play. This makes it easier for the outside blocker to seal him away from the play.

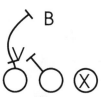

Scoop block

- A trap block has a blocker, usually one who was lined up inside, to run outside and block a defender, who has probably penetrated into the backfield.

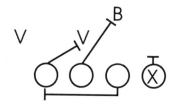

Trap block

- A lead block has a player running through the hole to block the most dangerous defender.

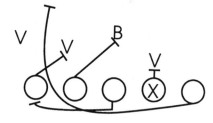

Lead block

- A double-team block puts two offensive players, usually linemen, against one defender.

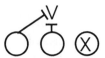

Double-team block

- A wedge block has three or more players blocking an area. They must get under the defenders and move them backward. In a wedge block, the offensive linemen are not assigned specific players to block.

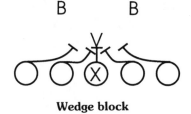

Wedge block

Designing the Blocking Schemes

Every running and passing play has blocking rules for *every* lineman, and usually for some of the backs too. The coach who develops the rules for each play must take into consideration the multitude of possibilities in defensive alignments. Here are some common defensive alignments:

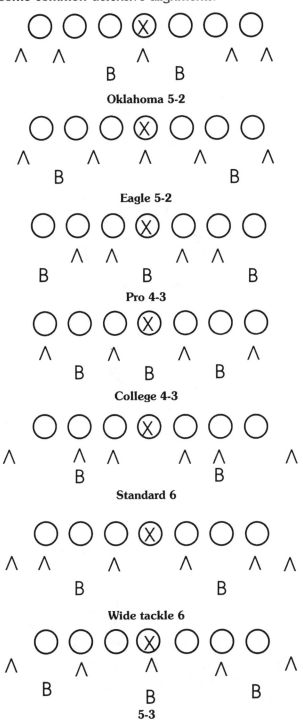

Oklahoma 5-2

Eagle 5-2

Pro 4-3

College 4-3

Standard 6

Wide tackle 6

5-3

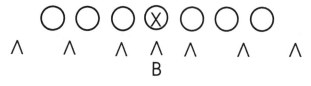

7 diamond

Sometimes linebackers are stacked behind a lineman (as in the 5-3 or 7 diamond above). Other times they are stacked in a gap. A "gap stack" presents some real problems in blocking, especially with a one-on-one blocking scheme, where one offensive player must block one defensive player without the help of a teammate in a double-team block.

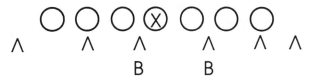

A defense using two gap stacks

Many defenses put linemen or linebackers in the gaps, or put them on the inside or outside shoulder of an offensive lineman, giving the defender the gap responsibility. The gap placement or gap responsibility reduces the splits of the offensive linemen.

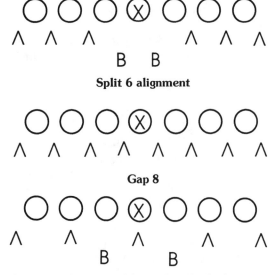

Split 6 alignment

Gap 8

Oklahoma 5-2 with tackles and ends shading outside

Blocking Rules

Base blocking rules (meaning the "basic" rules) are an essential part of planning the blocking scheme. Some teams use their "base" rules on all plays. Some have special rules that supplement the basic rules and add variation to the blocking scheme.

Quickness plays often have very simple rules. Here are some simple systems:

Number blocking rule. The center takes the 0 man (the man over him). The guard takes the number 1 man (first man away from the center on his side. The tackle takes the number 2 man. The end takes the number 3 man. Perhaps the first back out of the backfield would take the 4th man. Against an Oklahoma 5-2, it works very simply. Against a "man stack" you just assume that the stacked linebacker is one hole closer to the play. Against a gap stack, this type of rule has some problems.

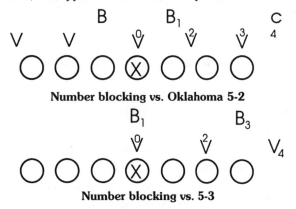

Number blocking vs. Oklahoma 5-2

Number blocking vs. 5-3

Against a gap stack, a coach might assume that the stack is lined up on the man inside or outside.

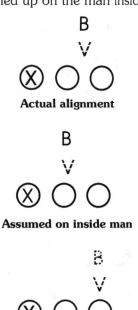

Actual alignment

Assumed on inside man

Assumed on outside man

Simple sentence rule. Another type of rule, which is more applicable when a team is trapping the outside of the hole is "take the man on or the first man away from the hole." If there is a gap stack, assume that the stack is on the next man in.

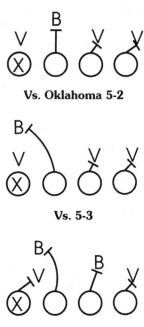

Vs. Oklahoma 5-2

Vs. 5-3

Vs. gap stack

For wide plays, this rule can be changed to "take the man on or the first man toward the hole."

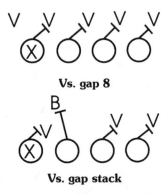

Vs. gap 8

Vs. gap stack

Priority rule with the same rule for each lineman. Here is a typical "base blocking" rule that is applicable on most plays for the center, and the playside guard, tackle, and end. The rule is, "inside gap, man on, first man downfield." This means that the lineman must first check the gap to the inside. If a man is there, the lineman blocks him. His next responsibility is to block a man on him. If neither of these situations applies, he should block the first man downfield (possibly a linebacker or defensive back).

Priority rule with different rules for each lineman. A very common approach to making blocking rules is giving a priority of assignments that can take care of every situation. Each play has a different rule. Following is a sample of the rules used by many wishbone teams.

- Center — man on, play-side gap, first man downfield
- Guard to play side — block first man on the line of scrimmage who is inside your tackle
- Play-side tackle — block first man head up or to your inside (whether he is on of off the line of scrimmage)
- Play-side end — block safety in four-deep, defensive halfback (corner back) in a three-deep secondary alignment
- Off-side guard — block first man to your side of the center (whether he is on or off the line of scrimmage)
- Off-side tackle — seal first man outside guard and block the second man on your side of the center. (Seal means get in front of him so that he has to go behind you, before you make your block.)

Making Adjustments to Unexpected Defenses

When the defense aligns in a manner that was not expected by the offense, the quarterback or the linemen must make adjustments to avoid a bad play. The quarterback can change the play at the line of scrimmage. These plays are called "automatics" or "audibles." This adjustment is more often used by teams that use very simple blocking rules. This will be more fully discussed later in the book.

For teams that allow the linemen to adjust their blocking on every play, the "call" blocking might give the advantage back to the offense. Linemen usually like to have the option of calling their blocks. After all, they know better than anyone else what is working well in the game. Additionally, the offensive linemen are often very intelligent. The intelligence

tests given by the professional teams indicate that the offensive linemen are generally the smartest players on the team.

Calling Blocks at the Line

When the linemen are allowed to call how they will block on a given play, they use code words or letters. Usually every man on the line calls out a word, but the only one that counts is the key man on that particular play. The key man may be the man on the inside or the outside of the hole.

Some teams label each block with a letter. Here is a traditional use of letters for calling the blocking:

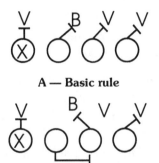

A — Basic rule

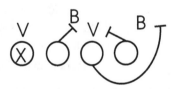

B — Cross block (outside man goes first)

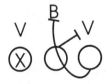

B — Fold block (inside man blocks a linebacker)

C — Cross block (inside man goes first)

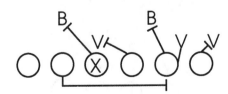

D — Trap block, with linemen blocking down

D — Trap block, with double-team

"You" call

The trap block was first called the "mouse trap." In the old days, when all linemen charged hard into the backfield, one man would often be unblocked and coaxed into a "mousetrap" where the pulling guard could easily block him. Modern defensive techniques have made this a more difficult block to execute; however, it is still often used.

In the trap block, the off-side guard pulls to make the block. This might be done with all other men blocking down one man or with a double-team at the inside of the hole.

Some teams have a code word when they want to exchange blocking assignments. Only the two men at the hole are involved. Perhaps the inside man says "me," meaning that he goes first. Or he may say "you," meaning that his partner blocks first while he goes behind. If the key man doesn't want to exchange assignments, he might say "go," meaning to go ahead with the basic rule for that play. (Remember that all the linemen are saying "me," "you," or "go" so the defensive linemen are not aware as to which lineman is calling the "live" word.)

One-on-one blocking at the hole between the guard and tackle versus an Oklahoma 5-2 could be done these three ways if only the guard and tackle are involved. The guard is calling the block in the following illustrations:

"Go" call

"Me" call

Instead of a "me" or "you" call, the coach might decide to use a more variable code. An example might be for the inside man to call any city, meaning that he goes first. So whether he says Dallas, Baltimore, San Francisco, or Paris, it all means the same thing. Similarly, if he wants the outside man to go first he might call any color. So whenever a coach refers to a cross block with the inside man going first (whether in a practice, chalk talk, play book or game), he refers to it as a "city" block.

Whenever he refers to a cross block with the outside man going first, he calls it a "color" block. Most coaches use codes for blocking rules, formations, play patterns, pass defense coverages, defensive stunts, and automatics. Often they develop their own secret codes. Other times they borrow codes from famous coaches. In football, you can't keep everything secret for long. Today's blocking schemes have become more and more complicated. No longer are the guards the only linemen who pull and trap. No longer are traps only from the inside of the formation to the outside.

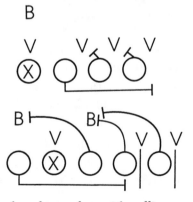

Examples of trap plays with pulling guards

Although the guard is still the primary pulling and "trapping" lineman on most teams, and although the inside-out trap is the most common type of trap, today the center, tackles, ends, wingbacks, or the man in motion can all pull, and perhaps trap.

The following illustrations offer examples:

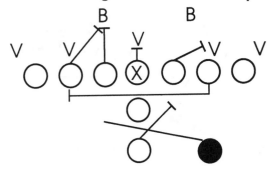

Tackle trapping in a counter

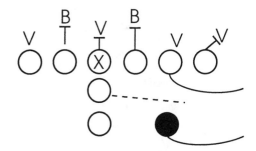

Tackle pulling on a quick pitch

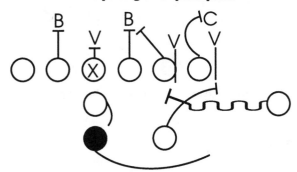

Back in motion trapping defensive tackle in

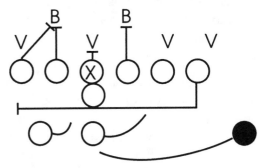

End trapping on reverse

Using the backs to block is an integral part of most offenses today. In earlier days 10 blockers and a tailback got all the glory. The single wing series was the ultimate in using the backs as blockers.

The old T-formation plays and the split-T attacks relied more on quickness and finesse rather than power blocking, so the backs were not often used as primary blockers. Today, with the "I" pro, the power "I", the wing-T running attacks, and with the emphasis on pass protection for the quarterback, it is imperative that the backs (especially the I-formation fullback) be effective blockers.

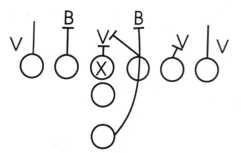

Pro-I isolation block

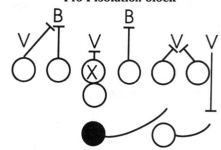

Off-tackle with the halfback lead

Downfield Blocking

It isn't enough to block the defenders near the point of attack. Nearly every play in modern football is designed to score a touchdown. This requires that some linemen be released downfield to block.

If the play is in the center of the line, both ends usually are released. It is possible that one or both tackles also releases downfield.

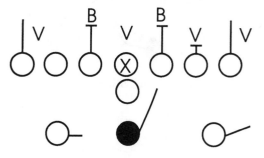

Fullback buck with ends releasing

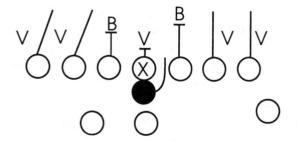

Quarterback sneak with tackles and ends releasing

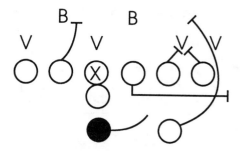

Double team with on-side guard trapping

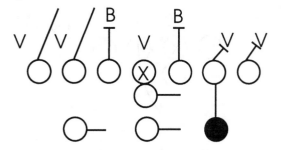

A dive right with left tackle and end releasing

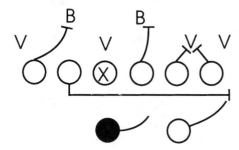

Double team with off-side guard trapping

Total Blocking Patterns

A fullback slant can be blocked against an Okla-homa 5-2 in one of several ways, such as the fol-lowing:

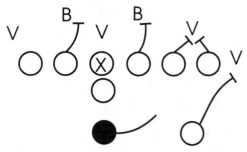

Double team with halfback blocking out

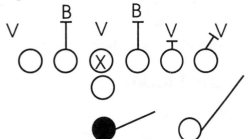

Straight blocking

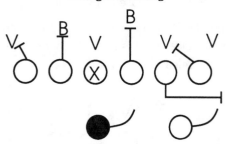

A "you" block

With these five simple ways to block one play against one defense, imagine the possibilities for blocking this play against the nine defenses illustrated earlier. Remember, there are many more defensive alignments than illustrated and there are many ways to block any one play. This is why the X's and O's become so complicated.

In fact, one of the coach's major jobs is to determine which blocking schemes probably will work best against the next opponent's probable defenses. Because teams don't have 50 hours a day to practice, coaches are greatly limited in their ability to meet every possibility that the next opponent might use. That's why every play doesn't work on the field like it does in the playbooks. This is also why we must have a "base blocking" rule to use so that any unusual defensive alignments won't confuse the offense and create a big play for the defense.

6

Offensive Formations

Obviously a coach chooses a formation that enables him to attack most effectively according to his system. Today's pro teams nearly always use formations that send three immediate pass receivers into the defensive secondary. Often they set up to allow four or even five men to attack the pass defense. College or high school wishbone offenses might keep both ends tight and all three backs in the backfield to enhance their running games.

Nearly everyone is familiar with the variations of the T-formation which we see in most present-day football games. But let's look at some of the formations that were popular in past years, some of which are still used by high school and college coaches. Most of these were in use in the 1920s and '30s. But note how modern formations have evolved from ideas in existence more than 50 years ago.

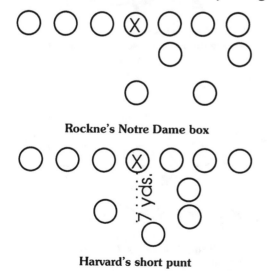

4 1/2 yds.

Pop Warner's single wing

Warner's double wing

A Rockne passing formation

Rockne's Notre Dame box

Harvard's short punt

7 yds.

10 yds.

Minnesota's spread

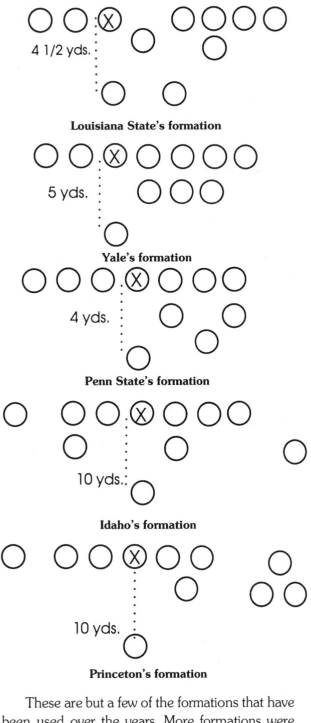

Louisiana State's formation

4 1/2 yds.

Yale's formation

5 yds.

Penn State's formation

4 yds.

Idaho's formation

10 yds.

Princeton's formation

10 yds.

These are but a few of the formations that have been used over the years. More formations were used in the early days of the game than now. Does that mean we are all copycats now, or have we reached the "ultimate" in offensive alignment? Probably neither, because the offense must align itself to attack the defense. As the defense adjusts to strength, so must the offense change its strength.

When the "nickel" defense (using five rather than four defensive backs) came into play to stop the pass on an obvious passing down, many offensive teams adjusted by using a running formation and a running play. And when the defense substitutes an additional lineman to stop the run in a short yardage situation, many teams exploit it with a the pass.

Selecting the Offensive Formation

Before starting an offensive play, the coach or signal caller must decide which formation to use. He might choose a formation because it is especially advantageous for that play , or he might choose a formation just to see how the defense adjusts so that any weakness can be exploited on an ensuing play. For example, on an off-tackle power play, there is an obvious advantage to having a tight wingback next to the end to double team the defender. If this is done, the defense bunches up to stop the obvious power of the formation, but perhaps it also opens itself to a pass from that formation.

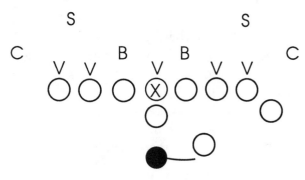

Wingback set vs. Okie 5-2
(no defensive adjustment, so it is open to the run)

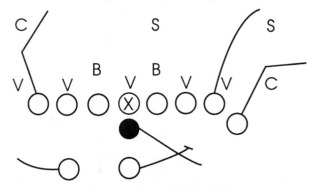

Wingback set vs. Okie 5-2
(defense adjusts by rotating its backfield, exposing it to a quick pass to the strongside end or wingback)

A tight formation ("T," wing-T, single-wing) has the advantage of running power, good faking, and quick counters, but lacks the quick pass threat. Teams with good passers and receivers are more likely to want at least three immediate receivers threatening the defense. They also want to spread the defense from sideline to sideline so that the defense has more area to defend. With the defense spread wide, there are more possible openings between the defenders for the receivers to exploit.

It is more difficult for a back than a lineman to block a defensive lineman, so most coaches prefer to have at least six linemen near the ball. They therefore split one end and flank a back. Other coaches want to keep three backs close to the quarterback so they split both ends and set one back as a wingback. They lose a little blocking, but gain on the faking and countering aspects of their attacks.

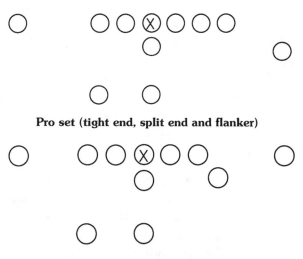

Pro set (tight end, split end and flanker)

Two split ends and a wingback

Coaches set flankers to create opportunities for pass plays and to spread the defense. If you can get the opponent to put a cornerback and a linebacker far to one side of the field to stop your pass threat, it is difficult for those defenders to stop a run up the middle or a play to the opposite side of the field.

Today, more and more often we are seeing four immediate receivers. When a coach wants four immediate receivers he has the choice of putting two on each side of the center or of "going trips," with a corps of triple receivers on one side. The flanking of two backs leaves one, the "Ace" back. Some teams occasionally flank all three running backs.

Following are examples of balanced four receiver sets:

Two split ends and two wingbacks

Two tight ends, two flankers

Double slot

Pro set right, slot left

The following are examples of 'trips" sets:

Slot, split end, flanker

Two slots and a split end

You also can use five immediate receivers — putting the quarterback under the center or in a shotgun set, as follows:

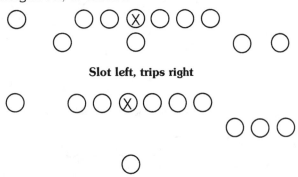

Slot left, trips right

Shotgun — three backs right

Placement of the Linemen

The rules say that the offensive team must have at least seven men on the line of scrimmage and that the end men on the line are eligible for passes. Today most teams use balanced lines, with a guard, tackle, and an end on each side of the center. When a team occasionally goes unbalanced, it often catches the defense off guard.

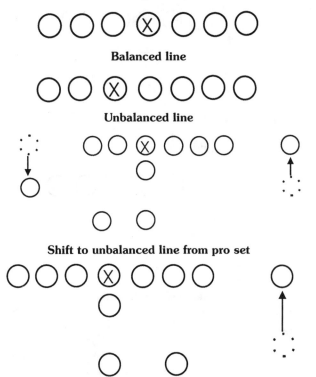

Balanced line

Unbalanced line

Shift to unbalanced line from pro set

Shift to eight-man line
(wingback moves up so that he can block better)

Unbalanced line with guards and tackles over

Unbalanced line with snapper as the end

The spacing of the linemen is another factor for a coach to consider. If the linemen are close to each other (a tight line), they can pass protect, double team block, and cross block more effectively. Also, it is more difficult for the defenders to penetrate the offensive line of scrimmage. The backs can also get around the end faster on sweep plays. On the other hand, the defenders are all closer to the point of attack. If one of them penetrates, he is likely to be in position to stop the quarterback or ball carrier.

If the offensive linemen are split wider, they spread the defense better and create either holes or blocking angles. If the defensive lineman moves out with the offensive man, a hole is created. If the defender splits only part way, perhaps playing on the inside shoulder of the offensive man, a blocking angle is created. Most offensive linemen are taught to be creative in their splits — often splitting wider on the side away from the play, to put the defender farther from the hole.

In the early days of football, the line splits were only a few inches. The split-T spacing of up to eight feet between linemen reached the opposite extreme. Today most teams split one to two feet between the tackles with the tight ends splitting two to four feet.

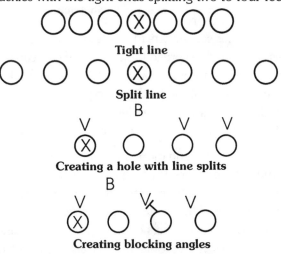

Tight line

Split line

Creating a hole with line splits

Creating blocking angles

Another factor in determining the placement of the linemen is their strength and abilities. In a basic T-formation, the linemen generally have the same assignments on either side of the center. In some attacks, however, such as the single wing, power "I" and some pro attacks, the assignments might be quite varied from one side to the other.

On one team, the strong side of the line might emphasize double-team blocks, while the "weak" or "quick" side of the line specializes in pulling, one-on-one blocks, cross blocking, downfield blocking, or other such skills. When the two sides of the line have different types of blocking responsibilities they "flip-flop." A flip-flopping team always has its "strong side" linemen on the side of its basic power plays and its "quick side" linemen on the side to which it counters or runs quick plays. Teams that flop their line do so by crossing their linemen as they break the huddle or by snaking them, in which the strong end or wing back leads the team in a motion that looks like a serpent's path.

Setting the Backs in a Formation

It is obvious that if all three backs are set in the normal T-formation, the defense is vulnerable to quickness and countering. Each back removed from the three-back formation reduces the running attack while adding to the passing threat. When a coach decides to remove a fullback, he gives up the buck, the fullback trap, the fullback counter, and the full-back slant. When he removes a halfback, he gives up the dive threat, the quick pitch to that side, and the halfback traps and counters to the other side. The defense knows this and can afford to reduce its defense in the areas where it is not threatened.

After the coach decides where he wants to set the backs, he might have to adjust their position somewhat according to what he wants the back to do. For example, a very fast back in a split-T formation might beat the quarterback to the hole, so the coach might have to set him a foot or two deeper than normal. In most offensive running attacks the timing of the backs is very important, so backfield coaches often use "cheats" to improve the timing.

Examples of "cheating" the backs are setting a halfback wider or deeper when the quick pitch is used to his side, moving a halfback up or in for certain trap plays or for pass blocking, and moving the fullback up when he is faking and blocking.

The way the backs set their feet and place their hands is also a factor in their effectiveness as blockers or runners. In a "two-point" stance, the back does not have a hand on the ground. This enables him to see the defense better and to get wide fast, but he can't go forward as fast, so he may have to line up closer to the line of scrimmage. One of the problems with the two-point stance is that the back often is eager to move and goes in motion early, causing an unnecessary penalty.

If the back is expected to go forward, right, and left, the toes should be an equal distance from the line of scrimmage, so that an imaginary line drawn between the toes of his two feet should be parallel to the line of scrimmage. If he is expected to go only forward or to his right, he can have his right foot back. (It is slower to go to his left from this stance.) If he is goes laterally much of the time, he would not want much weight on his hands. If the back is going forward, he could get into a sprinter's stance.

Defenders, of course, look for keys from the backs. Does he have extra weight forward (indicating he will dive), is he cheated wide (for a possible pitch), is he tipping off where he is going by his eyes or by his body lean? Coaches, in scouting or in evaluating films, look for such tips.

In the mid 1950s, Coach Red Sanders at UCLA noticed that John Brodie, the Stanford quarterback, kept his feet parallel when he was going to pivot to hand off for a running play, but had one foot back when he was going to pass so he could drop back faster. Each time that the defense saw his feet staggered they yelled "Omaha" to attack him with an eight-man rush. Stanford, which had beaten UCLA the year before, 21-18, went down to a devastating 72-0 defeat, largely because of the tip-off.

When a coach is running an "I" pro attack, he might put his tailback from four-and-a-half to seven or eight yards back. If he wants the back to hit a certain hole, he will set him closer. If he wants him to pick his hole, depending on how the defense adjusts to the play, he will be deeper. The USC attack under John McKay and John Robinson used a deep set that enabled the skilled back to improvise, thus freeing players such as Mike Garrett, O.J. Simpson or Marcus Allen to utilize their talents.

Shifting the Offense

Knute Rockne is credited with developing the backfield shift. After lining up in a T-formation, the backs would shift right or left into a box formation. The ball would be snapped as they finished the shift. This put a great strain on the defense to adjust in time for the play. (The rule now is that after a shift a player has to remain motionless for a full second so the defense can adjust to the new formation.)

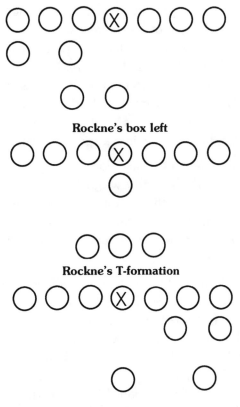

Rockne's box left

Rockne's T-formation

Rockne's box right

Bob Zuppke, at Illinois, used a line shift to help spring Red Grange to his legendary running exploits. The guards were set behind the line, then shifted into the right or left gap together to give an unbalanced line for Grange to run behind.

Iowa's Howard Jones, who later coached at USC, also had some interesting ideas on shifting his offensive people, as follows:

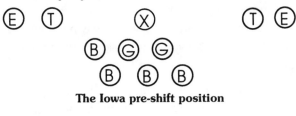

The Iowa pre-shift position

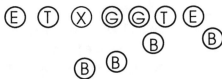

Shift to unbalanced line — single wing

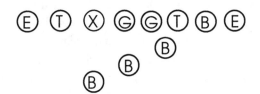

Shift to eight-man unbalanced line

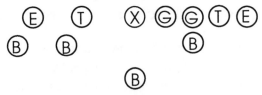

Shift to unbalanced line — backs opposite

Today, many teams use backfield shifts to upset the defensive strategy, as follows:

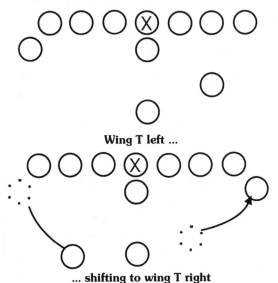

Wing T left ...

... shifting to wing T right

Perhaps no modern team has exploited the shift as much as the Dallas Cowboys did under Tom Landry. They would line up in one set, then everybody would move. The linemen adjusted their splits and the backs moved to another position. They knew where they were going, but the defense didn't. They might shift to a split back, pro set, one back or any other set they could devise. The defense had to prepare for a play from the original set, then adjust to whatever plays might be run from the final set.

As defenses became more specialized, with a strong safety, strong cornerback, strong and weak linebackers, and perhaps strong and weak defensive linemen, it was inevitable that someone would shift to upset such defenses. Defenders declare the offense "strong" to the side of the tight end, so many teams set the tight end to one side, let the defense set, then move the tight end to the other side. Moving one offensive man forces the defense to move at least two defenders, and perhaps six or more.

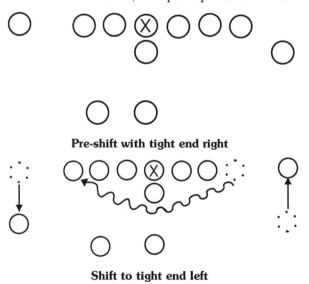

Pre-shift with tight end right

Shift to tight end left

This shift might force the movement of the strong and free safeties, the strong and weak side inside and outside backers, a "rover back" (if one is used), and perhaps the cornerbacks.

The Use of Motion

American football teams are allowed to have one back in motion parallel to the line of scrimmage or moving backward. (Canadian rules permit more than one player to go in motion at the same time.)

Motion changes the strength of the formation, such as by changing from a flanker to a slot or a slot to a flanker formation.

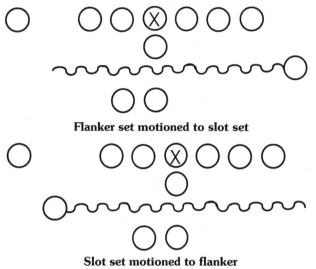

Flanker set motioned to slot set

Slot set motioned to flanker

Motion can be used to stretch the formation from a tight to a wide set, or to reduce the formation from a flanker set to a tight set, as follows:

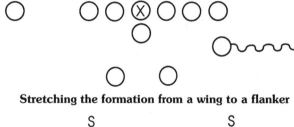

Stretching the formation from a wing to a flanker

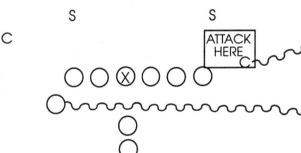

Reducing the formation from a flanker to a wing

Teams that don't adjust to the motion become vulnerable to the offense's new strength. Defenses often disregard these changes.

A balanced defense that doesn't adjust to a change in formation strength (attack toward the motion)

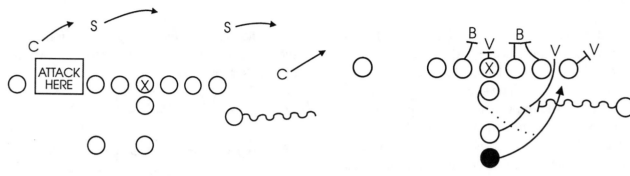

A defense adjusting to motion, which doesn't change the formation strength (attack away from motion)

Outside in motion, with trap block

Sometimes "short motion" is used. This is almost like a shift. Examples of the types of motion a wingback can use are as follows:

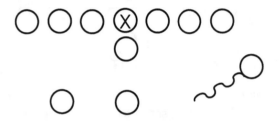

Short motion to the halfback position

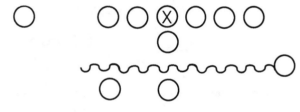

Motion to the slot area

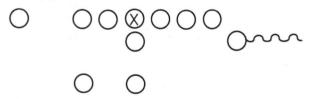

Motion to the flanker area

While a back in short motion cannot run a dive play, he can run a trap or counter to the other side and can certainly run a sweep. This type of motion is used extensively by wing-T teams.

Motion can also be used to bring a slot back or flanker into a position where he can execute an outside-in trap block. This is often a great surprise to the lineman being trapped, and often a greater surprise to the flanker who learns that he can block as well as catch passes.

Another major use of motion is to determine whether the defense is playing man-to-man or zone on that play. This makes it easier for the quarterback and the receivers to determine which patterns will work best. If a zone defense is exposed (the motion back is not followed by a defender) perhaps a deep curl would be run. If a man-to-man defense shows (a defender follows the motion man) perhaps a crossing pattern or a comeback would work best.

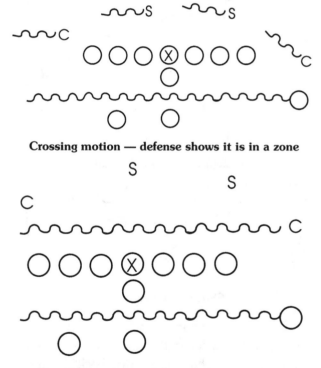

Crossing motion — defense shows it is in a zone

Crossing motion — defense is in man-to-man

Modern day teams are usually multiple formation teams that use a good deal of motion. A good part of the "chess match" element of the game is involved in setting one's formations, evaluating the opponents' adjustments to them and exploiting the weaknesses they expose.

7

Passing Theory

The forward pass is the heart of the pro attack and the delight of the fans. This present-day phenomenon was once a lowly orphan in the game. It wasn't even legal until 36 years after the game was invented. Some pressure on the rules committee by such coaches as Eddie Cochems of St. Louis University and John Heisman at Clemson College finally influenced Walter Camp, the head of the football rules committee, to legalize the forward pass in 1906. A few years later, Camp tried to have it again ruled illegal because he wanted to increase the running game's effectiveness.

In the movie "Knute Rockne, All-American," Pat O'Brien as Rockne is shown practicing the pass during the summer months at Cedar Point, Ohio. Several months later, he springs the surprise of all time on the heavily favored Army team, as little Notre Dame from the "West" defeated the Cadets in their 1913 game. It really did happen that way, but the forward pass had been used by teams in the Midwest since St. Louis completed the first pass against Carroll College in September of 1906. Still the big roughhouse teams of the East weren't ready for the "sissy" pass, so it remained for the teams from the Midwest and the South to develop it.

In those days the ball was shaped more like a blimp, similar to a rugby ball, and was very hard to throw. The first passes were executed more like basketball chest passes or by throwing the ball underhand, end over end. It didn't take players long to learn how to throw the overhand spiral. In fact,

Bradbury Robinson of St. Louis University was credited with several 50-yard pass completions in 1906.

While Eddie Cochems is generally credited with the earliest development of many aspects of the passing game, Pop Warner (Carlisle), Amos Alonzo Stagg (Chicago), and Jesse Harper, Rockne's coach at Notre Dame, are all considered among the pioneers in the development of the forward pass.

The rules relating to the pass have changed a bit over the years. At first, the passer had to throw from a spot at least five yards deep and five yards to the side of where the ball was snapped, and an incomplete pass cost the throwing team a 15-yard penalty. In 1910, it became illegal to pass more than 20 yards downfield, because the pass was taking away from the "real game" of football. This rule lasted only two years. Beginning in 1910, the passer was no longer required to pass from five yards wide of the center, but he still had to be five yards deep when he threw.

By 1931, the shape of the ball was changed to make it easier to throw, and in 1934, the rule requiring a five-yard penalty for the second incomplete pass in a series was eliminated. In 1941, the rule stating that a pass that fell incomplete in the end zone was ruled as a touchback and went over to the other team was eliminated. In 1945, it was made legal to pass from anywhere behind the line of scrimmage. The last major change (in 1963) was to allow any back less than a yard behind the line (such as the T-formation quarterback) to be an eligible receiver.

It might appear as if all the coach has to worry about is getting the receivers open — just like in the park, where Charlie tells Joey to "go out and cut behind the tree, and I'll hit you long." In today's game, it's much more complicated than that.

The passing game is an essential part of any offensive attack. While the running game enables a team to attack the width of the field, the passing game enables it to attack both the width and the depth. For a run-oriented team, the formations tend to be tight — four backs and two tight ends.

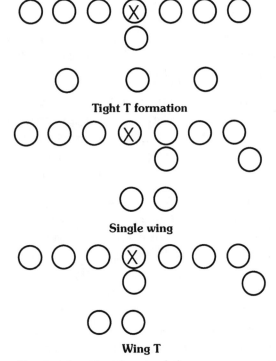

Tight T formation

Single wing

Wing T

To develop the threat of the pass, a running team may split one end or flank one back to widen the area which the defense must protect.

Split end

Double tight with a flanker

Teams looking for a balanced attack are more likely to split two people to develop a more immediate passing threat.

Split end and flanker (pro set)

Split end and slot back

The teams that rely largely on the pass often place three, four, or even five people in positions where they can release immediately for the pass.

Two split ends and a slot right (shotgun)

Slot set left, flanker right

Double tight, double flanker

Split left, "trips" (triple receivers) right

Slot left, "trips" right

For some teams, the pass is primary. Brigham Young University has achieved a great deal of fame and a national title with a pass-oriented offense. The San Diego Chargers under Don Coryell and the San Francisco 49ers since Bill Walsh became coach also have thought of the pass as all-important. More recently, the "run and shoot" offense, developed by Glenn "Tiger" Ellison and popularized by Mouse Davis when at Portland State, has centered the offense around the pass. Both college and professional teams have used it successfully.

Teams using the forward pass want to "stretch" the defense vertically and horizontally. They want to be able to hit "out" patterns right on the sidelines (a horizontal stretch) and they want to be able to throw the 60-yard pass deep (a vertical stretch). After they have proven they can do both of these, the defensive team must be prepared to defend the entire field.

While the Great Wall of China might have stopped an infantry and cavalry in its day, it would not be able to stop an attack from the air. So while the gap-eight or goal line defenses may have been effective against a pure running team, they are very vulnerable to the pass. Today every offensive team must have a passing attack, just as every army needs an air force. And every defense must be constantly on guard against the pass, which often opens up the possibility that a running play will be successful.

The Action of the Passer

The most common type of pass is the "drop back" pass. The quarterback either backpedals or turns and runs to a set depth before setting up to pass. Dropback passes are designed for the quarterback to drop one, three, five, seven and sometimes nine steps. The depth of the dropback depends on the depth that the receiver is to run in his route. When the Miami Dolphins upset the Bears in 1985, they did it primarily with one-step and three-step drop patterns. Dan Marino was able to get his passes away before the vaunted Bears defenders could get to him.

The passer who turns and runs to his passing spot can get back more quickly. On the other hand, the passer who backpedals is better able to see what

the defense is doing and "read the defense" more effectively. While many coaches employ only one or the other type of drop, many pro teams use both. For these teams, the "pre-snap read" (how the defense is aligned) might be the key to which type of drop the quarterback may use.

Most teams also use *play-action passes*, in which the quarterback first fakes a running play and then sets to pass. This action usually holds the linebackers and opens the underneath zones. If the linemen block aggressively, as they would do on a running play, the defensive backs also might be fooled. However, with this aggressive blocking, they might not be able to give the quarterback effective protection. And if they pass protect block, (stand up and retreat) they generally do not fool the defensive backs.

In a *roll-out action*, the quarterback runs deep behind the protection of his backs. He may pass from 10 to 20 yards wider than from where he lined up. This rolling action puts a great deal of pressure on the defensive player who is assigned to cover the short wide area and to support on a wide running play. If the defender drops to protect for the pass, the quarterback might be able to run; if the defender comes up to support the run, the pass is open.

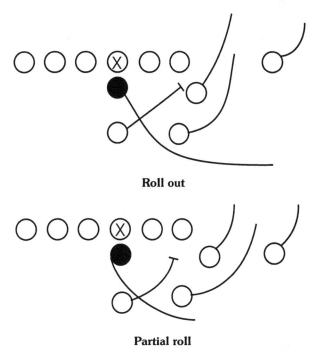

Roll out

Partial roll

In the *partial roll out*, the movement of the quarterback past the offensive tackle often signals the defense to change their assignments with a wide pass defender having to move up to support the possible run. This might leave another man open in the pass pattern. As the defenders rotate their pass coverage and change their zone responsibilities, the throwback pass might become available.

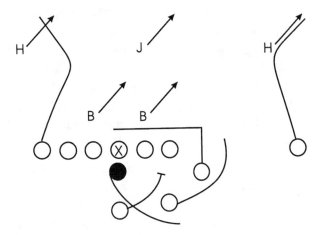

Partial roll with throwback open

The *sprint out* is similar to the roll, but the sprint out is faster and more shallow to put quicker pressure on the defensive cornerback to make up his mind as to whether to play the run or the pass. The sprint out is similar to the option play discussed in the chapter on running theory. But unlike the option play in which the quarterback can only run or pitch back, in the sprint out he can run or pitch forward.

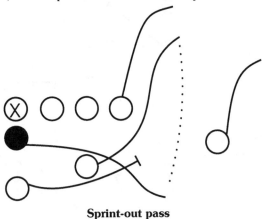

Sprint-out pass

The *moving pocket* ("rove," "dash," or "controlled scramble") is a recent development. Joe Gibbs, recently retired coach of the Redskins, de-

veloped an action that started as a drop back pass, then it looked as if the quarterback was scrambling out of the pocket — but the entire action was planned.

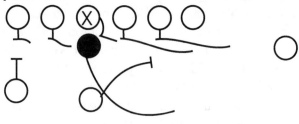

Moving pocket

The *waggle* is a type of short roll out. Some coaches call it a waggle if the quarterback moves behind the running backs on a running fake. Other coaches call it a waggle if the quarterback runs opposite the backs in a short bootleg action. (Every coach is entitled to develop his own terminology and numbering system.)

The *bootleg* is like a roll out, but it is away from the flow of the backs. The quarterback fakes to a back, then runs with the ball in the opposite direction. He may or may not have a pulling lineman to block for him. This play is effective on the goal line or in short yardage situations in which everybody but the quarterback has a man assigned to guard him.

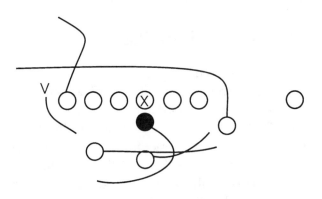

Boot with flood pattern

Play action passes are especially important to teams that rely on the run. Some teams have the linemen perform the normal "retreat" pass protection, others block aggressively as if the play is a run.

Aggressive blocking is more likely to fool the defensive backs who are often keying the linemen, but the passer probably will not be protected as long.

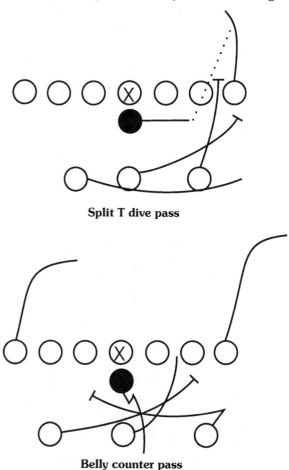

Split T dive pass

Belly counter pass

Protecting the Passer

A team cannot have an effective passing attack unless the passer can release the ball. The more time he has, the more effective he will be. Consequently, the blocking schemes that an offensive line must learn in a sophisticated passing attack are quite complicated. There is an old coaching maxim that states, "Rush the good passer, but cover the poor passer."

The better the passer, the more a coach must teach pass protection. As an example, let's take a simple "man" blocking scheme. The player is responsible for the defensive man who lines up on him. Here is how it would look in an Oklahoma 5-2 or the "pro" 3-4 with the linebackers reacting back as the passer "shows" pass by dropping back.

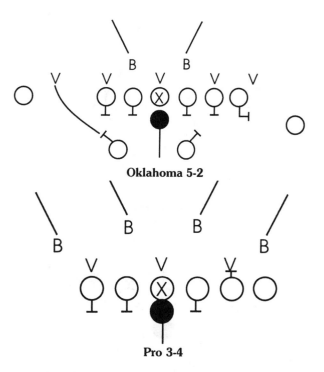

Oklahoma 5-2

Pro 3-4

If the linebackers rush, which they seldom do, it would look like this in a "pro" 3-4 and "pro" 4-3:

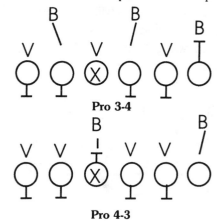

Pro 3-4

Pro 4-3

Another blocking scheme is to have the linemen responsible for the defensive linemen rather than the "man on." This is termed "big on big." The center takes the "0" man, the guard the "1" man and the tackle the "2" man. In a pro 4-3 it is quite simple: the guards and tackles take the men on them and the center drops back to help where needed, assuming that his linebacker doesn't rush.

Against the old Oklahoma 5-2, the guards blocked the defensive tackles and the offensive tackles blocked the defensive ends. The backs in this scheme would be responsible for the linebackers should they rush the passer.

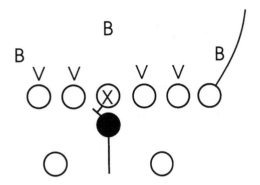

Pro 4-3, linebackers drop

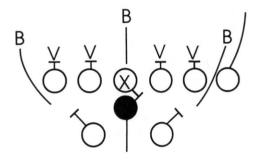

Pro 4-3, linebackers rush

Generally, the backs will be assigned to block if they see the linebackers rushing, but they may be allowed to swing to the outside if the linebackers drop back.

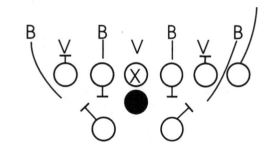

Pro 3-4, linebackers rush

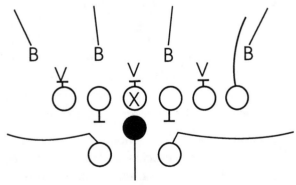

Pro 3-4, linebackers drop

Here is what is more likely to happen in a pass rush when the defense decides it wants to "sack" the passer. When the quarterback lines up in a shotgun formation, he is better able to read the stunts and blitzes and has more time to unload the ball.

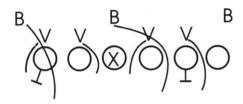

Possible stunt from pro 4-3

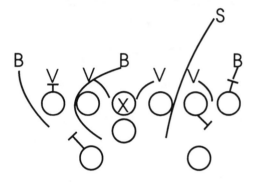

Full rush with safety blitz

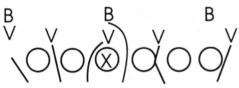

Possible stunt from a 5-3

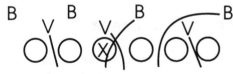

A stunt from a 3-4

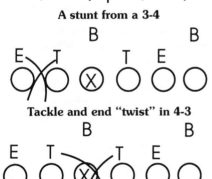

Tackle and end "twist" in 4-3

Tackles "twist"

It looks relatively simple on paper, but on the field it is murder.

Another type of blocking scheme is called "slide" protection. If an offensive lineman is having trouble blocking his man, he might get help by sliding another man over to help him. In the following diagram, the protection is "slide left." The right guard checks to make certain that his linebacker is not rushing. If the linebacker is free, he slides to his left and helps the center on the nose guard. The following is a Raider "slide" blocking scheme that was used against Chicago's Richard Dent in the Bear 46 defensive alignment:

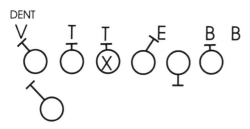

Slide blocking scheme

To take away the advantage of the defenders switching positions in a stunt or a twist, one blocking scheme that can be used is a "zone." In a "zone" scheme, the blocker sets up and waits to see who comes into his area. It might be the man who lined up on him, but it might well be somebody else. Here are some possibilities:

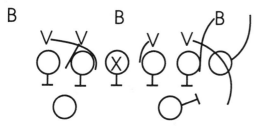

Stunt from a 4-3

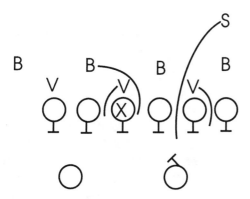

Stunt from a 3-4 with a safety blitz

You always hope that your quarterback can see this all happening and dump off the ball to a tight end or a back. However, quarterbacks have many other things to worry about, like "Are they going to knock me down and get my uniform dirty?" or "How much should I ask for in my next contract negotiation?" or "Where does my girlfriend want to eat tonight — Ma Maison or La Scala?"

Pass Patterns

Pass patterns can be individual routes or team patterns. They may have names or numbers. Most coaches develop a "passing tree" in which the most common patterns are numbered. Commonly, the patterns are designed to break from the line of scrimmage at five and 10 yards. As coaches have become more adept at designing patterns to beat the defenders to where they were most likely to go, the depth of the patterns has changed.

In high school, most linebackers are taught to drop back to a 10-yard depth. Consequently, passing coaches often have their patterns break at seven yards (in front of the backers), at 13 yards (just behind the backers, where the receivers can easily slide between the backers), and at 18 yards (safely behind the backers). At the college and professional levels, the routes may break deeper than 20 yards.

The types of patterns that the coach chooses to run should be determined by the expected defenses. (These defenses are discussed in more detail in following chapters.)

Theoretically, there are six short zones and three deep zones, but no coach is going to consistently commit nine players to these zones and rush only two defenders. Therefore, it is common to think in terms of three deep and four shallow zones or two deep and five shallow zones.

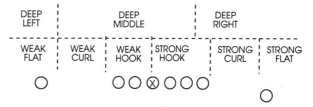

Model of six shallow and three deep zones

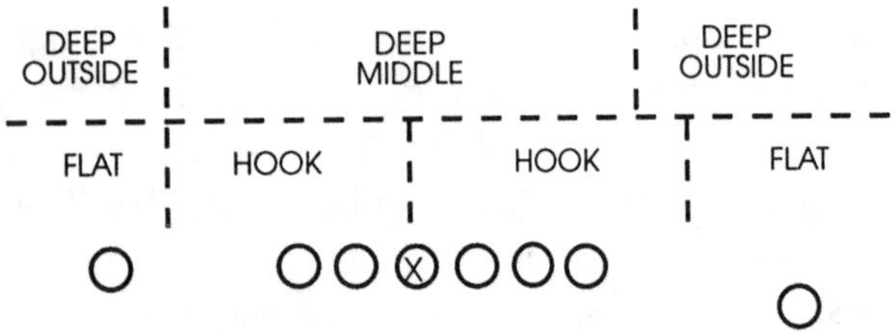

DEEP
OUTSIDE | DEEP MIDDLE | DEEP OUTSIDE

FLAT | HOOK | HOOK | FLAT

Commonly used three deep-four shallow zones

With today's great passers and receivers, teams that play only these seven zones would be easier to attack, so coaches frequently change the pass coverage from down to down. Among the common coverages are a five-under zone with two deep backs (four-man rush), a five-under man-to-man coverage with two deep safeties (four-man rush), a five-under three deep zone (three-man rush), a man-to-man defense with one safety (five-man rush), and a pure man-to-man coverage (six-man rush).

Teams might occasionally leave one or more zones open and commit the man from that zone into the rush, so sometimes there is an eight-man rush. At other times teams add zones using as many as nine men in coverage, leaving only two rushers.

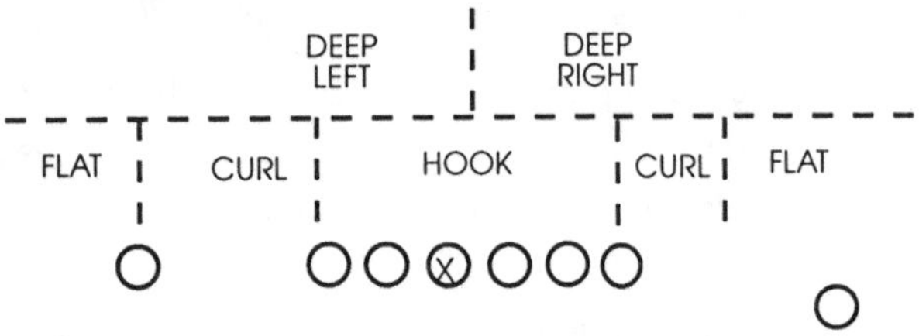

DEEP LEFT | DEEP RIGHT

FLAT | CURL | HOOK | CURL | FLAT

Five under-two deep zones

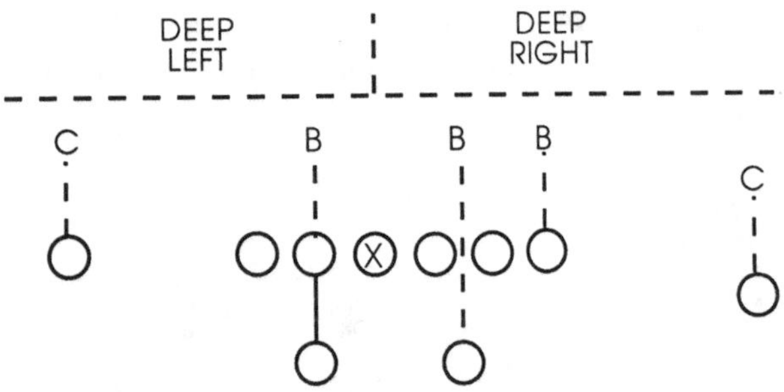

DEEP LEFT | DEEP RIGHT

Five-under man-two deep safeties

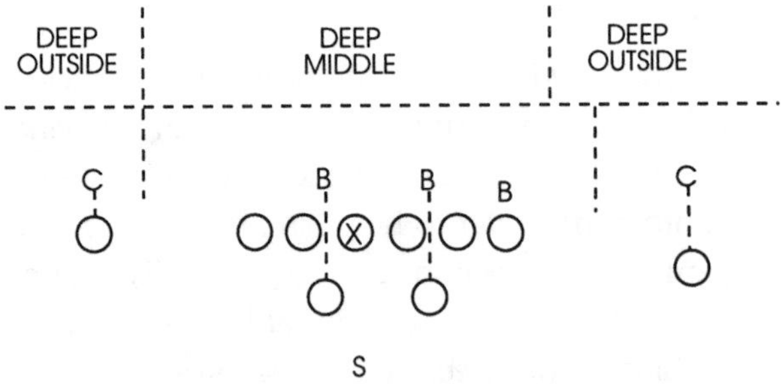

DEEP OUTSIDE | DEEP MIDDLE | DEEP OUTSIDE

Five under man-three deep zones

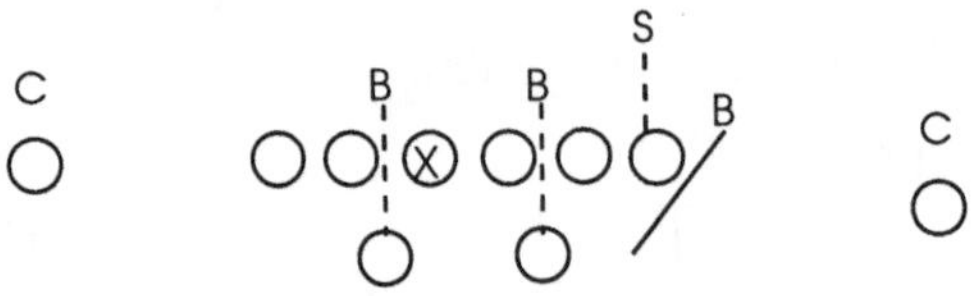

Man under-single safety

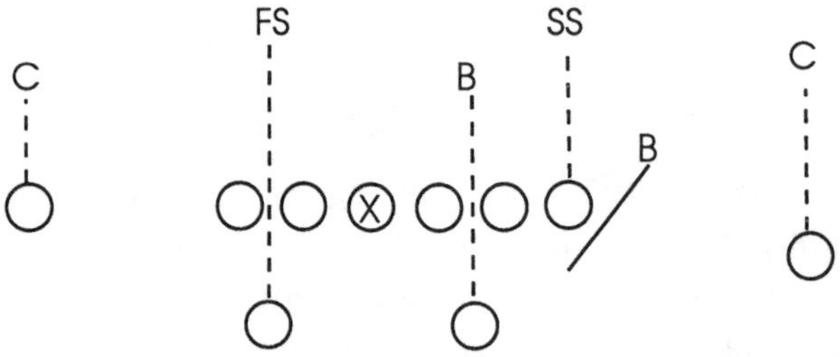

Pure man-loose coverage

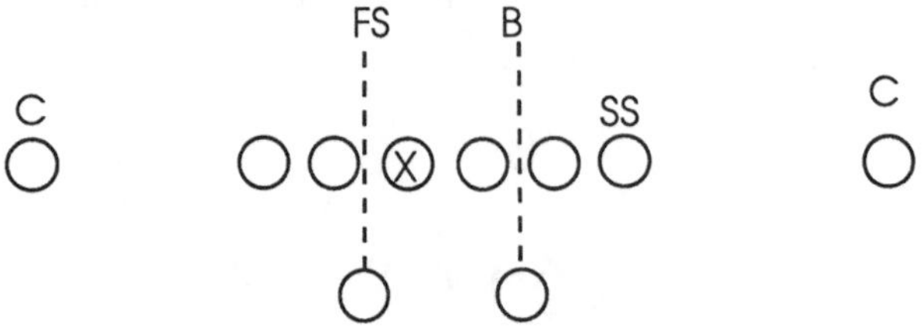

Pure man-tight coverage

Calling the Routes

Pass patterns have names that describe their actions. In a "flag" or "corner" route, the receiver goes deep and out toward the marker (which used to be a flag) at the front corner of the end zone. A "post" is the designation of the pattern designed to go long and in — toward the goal posts. A "buttonhook" or "hook" pattern's name comes from the way it looks when drawn on the blackboard. A "spot" pass has the receiver staying in the same spot he lined up, and an "out" or "sideline" pattern has the receiver going toward the sideline — and usually coming back slightly toward the line of scrimmage, to get away from the defensive back.

As more patterns were developed and passing offenses became more sophisticated, many coaches numbered the patterns. If the patterns were overlaid upon each other, they looked something like a tree. By using numbers in progression from short to long passes, coaches could easily teach more patterns.

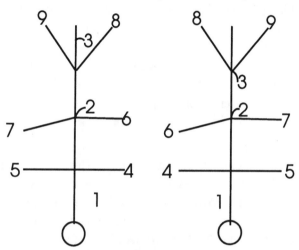

Left side patterns   Right side patterns
SAMPLE OF A PASSING TREE
(even numbers are inside patterns, odds are outside)

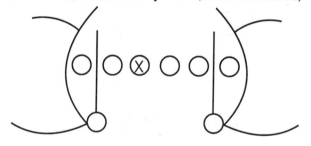

Some backfield patterns

If the coach is using the "passing tree" numbers, he might call the split end (usually called the X receiver), the tight end (the Y man), or the flanker or slot (the Z man) as the primary pass receiver. The other receivers run "complementary" patterns.

For example, if the coach called a "Y 9" or a "Y corner," the tight end would run a corner pattern and the other two receivers should know which complementary patterns to run. Perhaps the nearest receiver knows that he should run an intermediate level pattern in the same line of sight as the Y receiver, and the other receiver might run a short pattern in the line of sight area.

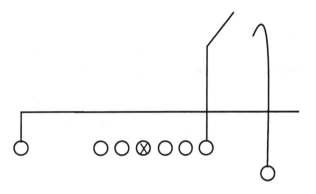

Y-9 (or "corner")
with X and Z running complementary patterns

Coaches often want to totally control the pattern and take the guesswork out of the minds of the players, so they might call "483" — meaning the X runs a 4, the Y runs an 8, and the Z runs a 3. This is the same as the pattern explained in the previous paragraph, but would be more explicit.

But the quarterback might not be as aware of his primary receiver when the coach calls a 483, so he has to look for the open receiver. When the quarterback called "Y 8" he had a pretty good idea of who the coach thought would be open.

Another type of complementary pattern would have all receivers running hooks (two patterns) or curls (three patterns).

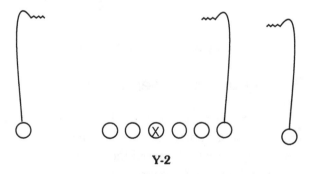

Y-2

Obviously some patterns work better against some defenses. If the coverage is man-to-man, a fast halfback has the advantage over a slower linebacker. Deep curl patterns (at 18 to 23 yards) would work against most zone coverages, and sending three players deep against a two-deep zone might work. Because coverages are generally disguised, the offensive team is never quite sure what defense will develop as the quarterback drops to pass.

Team patterns are often called to put some special pressure on the defense. In a "flood" pattern, the offense tries to flood one area with more receivers than can be covered by the defense.

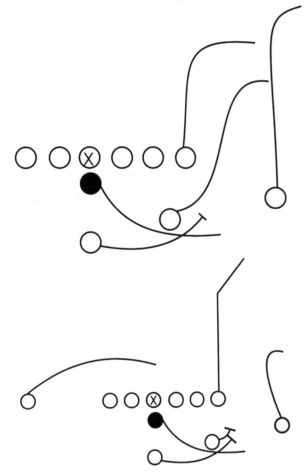

Two roll out passes flooding the right zones

Getting the Receiver Open

Many coaches attempt to get their best receiver against the poorest defender on the defense. This is called a "match up." They put their best or fastest "wide outs" against the poorest or slowest cornerbacks and their fastest running back against the slowest linebacker. This certainly gives the offense a "leg up" on getting a man open. Every game plan should have a few ways to make big plays for each receiver.

If the receiver is being bumped by a defender, he must first get free of him. He might use any of several tactics: a head fake, fake a block on the defender then get into his pattern, spin away from the defender, or use his arms to knock the arms of the defender away.

After the receiver is free of the defender's bumping, he may attack a defensive back. Some coaches teach the receiver to run a straight line to the place where he will make his cut, others tell their receivers to approach the defender in a weave or at a hard right-angle cut. A receiver who wants to cut right will plant his left foot and drive hard to the right. Sometimes, especially on deeper routes, the receiver will make a double cut.

Some coaches prefer a rounded cut. The rounded cut gets the player wider faster, but doesn't fool the defender as much. However, if the receiver can get close to the defender and make the defender turn and run with him, then make his cut when the defender has his legs crossed, he can increase the distance between himself and the defender.

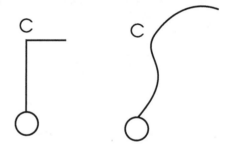

Square cut   Weave and rounded cut

Making good cuts and making the cut at the proper time are particularly important against man-to-man coverage. In a zone, defenders should be paying more attention to being in the proper place on the field in relation to the ball than to the cut of the receivers, so receivers are often less concerned about faking a defender than they are about getting to an open area between the zones.

Designing a Passing Attack

The forward pass is an integral part of many offenses. Usually the more skilled the players, the more likely the pass is to be successful. On paper, the passing coach can always beat the defense, but doing it on the field takes a great deal of planning and practicing. Because most skilled players like to pass and catch, practice is likely to be fun for them.

At present, three theories of passing are prevalent in the National Football League. Most teams still use the "old school" approach of a seven- to nine-step drop, with most of the patterns breaking fairly deep — 15 yards or longer.

A few teams, stimulated by the success of Bill Walsh when he guided the 49ers to successive Super Bowl wins, opt for the shorter passing attack. This is sometimes called the "graduate school" of passing. The receivers must run disciplined routes and the quarterback makes his reads in a definite progression. The quarterbacks are more likely to use three- and five-step drops.

The "new school" is the run-and-shoot approach. Here, the receivers are given more leeway in where they will get clear. The quarterback must see what is happening and make the delivery to the open receiver.

There are many different ways a defense can cover a pass, therefore the quarterback and receivers must learn to "read" the defenses. This is the heart of the modern passing offense, and the most technical area of modern football.

The first question to be answered by the quarterback and receivers is whether the coverage is a regular man-to-man (with the defensive backs five to 10 yards off the line), a bump and run man-to-man, or a zone defense.

If it is a regular man-to-man, the best patterns are comebacks (sidelines, hooks, curls), fakes, especially double fakes (Z out or in, hook and go, out and up), or patterns in which the receiver gets the defender to turn and run one way and then, just as the defender crosses his legs, cuts behind him. This makes it very difficult for the defender to recover in time to stop the pass. When playing against bump-and-run coverage, the receiver may lean into the defender and then make a break, he may run some sort of a comeback pattern, or he may simply try to outrun him.

Attacking Man-to-Man Coverage

When it is obvious that the defense is using man-to-man coverage, crossing receivers is often effective in screening out the defenders. One such type of pattern often used is a "pick" play similar to those common in basketball. Just as in basketball, moving picks are illegal. However, if a potential receiver hooks and stops and somehow gets in the way of a defender covering another player, it is legal. Such plays are often used on the goal line where man-to-man coverage is common.

Patterns that are effective against a man defense include the following:

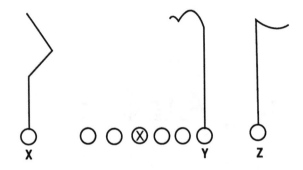

X running a z-out pattern, Y a hook and Z a sideline

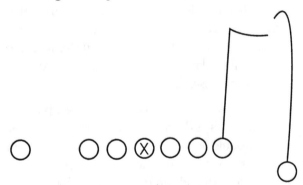

Z hook, Y out (a pick play)

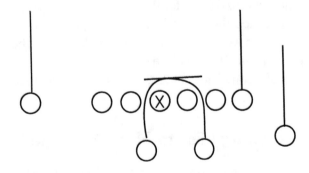

Backs crossing (a pick play)

Attacking Zone Coverage

When a defense uses a lot of zone coverages, as most teams do, patterns can be called in the huddle and the "read" is relatively simple. Quite often the coach designs patterns that stretch the defense either horizontally (across the field) or vertically (up the field).

An example of a horizontal stretch would be to have all the receivers doing hooks (going to 10 to 12 yards and then coming back two or three yards) with each receiver trying to get between and "under" the defenders in the short zones. The quarterback merely looks for the open receiver. He can usually see who will be open if he watches the retreat of the linebackers into their zones.

A vertical stretch would have two or three receivers at different depths up the field. One might run a very long pattern, another breaking at about 18 yards (between the deep and the underneath covers, and another staying close to the line of scrimmage. The passer looks at the defenders on that side of the field and determines which receiver will be the deepest open target.

Following are vertical stretch patterns using two receivers in a pattern that reads only one defender. This pattern is often called an "orbit" because the two receivers are in a partial orbit around the defender. The defender being "read" is the man responsible for the flat area. If he chooses to cover the deeper receiver, the quarterback throws to the shallow man; if he covers the shallow man, the pass is thrown to the man running the deep curl.

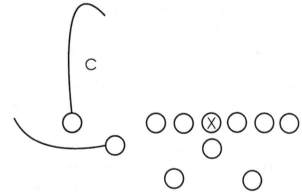

Orbit pattern with split end and slot back

Orbit pattern with tight end and running back

This same principle can be used on any short zone defender with a man curling deep and another at about a five-yard depth.

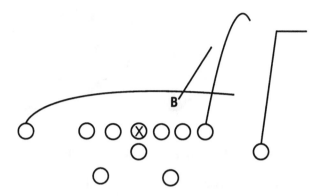

Two tight ends in one inside backer's zone

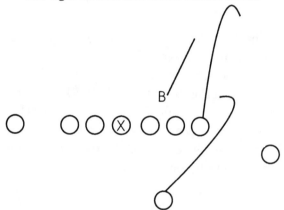

A tight end and a back in an inside backer's zone

Another type of pattern against a zone is a flood pattern in which two or three receivers are sent into one or two zones. The passer is expected to determine which is the open receiver and then fire the ball to him.

Most teams play four defensive backs, but need to cover only three deep zones. One of the defenders can be freed to cover a flat zone to the strong side. (The strong side can be the side to which the ball rolls, the wide side of the field, or the side of the two receivers.)

If the cornerback is assigned to cover the flat, it is often called "cloud" coverage. If the safety is assigned the flat for that play, it is often called "sky" coverage. "C" is the common beginning letter in corner and cloud, "S" is the common letter in safety and sky.

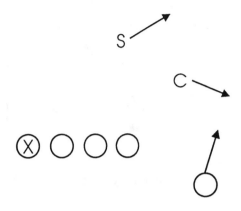

"Cloud cover" to two-receiver side

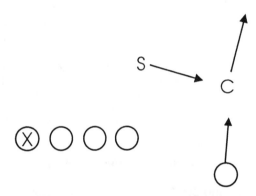

"Sky cover" to two-receiver side

Following is a common "read" used against teams that use "cloud" and "sky" covers. (Only one defender is "read" and there is only one receiver who is the major concern of the passer.) It is called a "post-read" pattern.

The wide receiver starts to run a post pattern, and both he and the quarterback watch the safety. If the safety starts wider and deep, the receiver changes his pattern to a corner and is ahead of the safety. If the safety starts wide but does not get depth, it means that he will be covering the flat so the cornerback has the deep third of the field. In this case, the receiver breaks inside the cornerback and runs a post pattern. The passer must get the ball to him quickly so that the other safety, who is now moving to the deep middle zone, cannot react to the ball. If it turns out that the defense is in man-to-man coverage, the receiver breaks back toward the passer after he has run about 15 yards downfield.

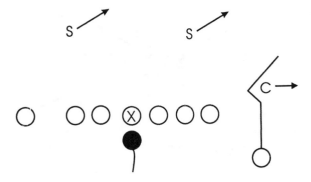

Post-read, safety has deep outside zone (cloud)

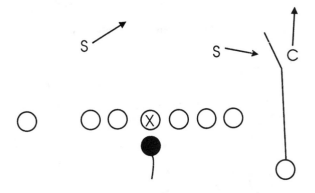

Post-read, safety covers flat (sky)

Still another type of "read" occurs when an offensive receiver is assigned to watch a linebacker to see if he will blitz the passer. If he sees the backer stunting, it means the backer's zone has been vacated. If he sees the backer stunt, the receiver yells "hot" and runs to the vacated area. The quarterback passes immediately — no matter what pattern had been called in the huddle. Some teams make the strong linebacker the first "read." The linebackers don't have to yell "hot" in that situation, the quarterbacks just "read" it.

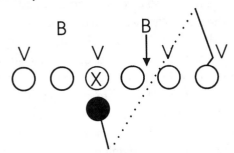

Tight end as hot receiver

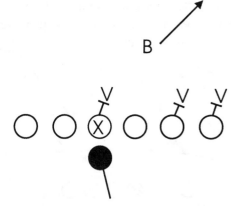

Tight end blocking if linebacker plays "honest"

More complicated reads can involve looking at two or three defenders to determine the coverage. Usually there is an "alignment" key and a "movement" key.

The following is an example of a "mirrored" pattern — the routes are the same on both sides of the line of scrimmage — from Leon Burtnett's passing offense at Purdue in the early 1980s. The prime targets are the X and Z men. If the "outs" are covered, the running backs should be open in the wide areas. If the defense blitzes, the Y end and the running backs become prime receivers.

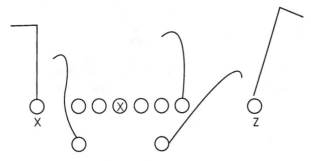

The basic pattern for the 60-80 pass

Following are the rules and keys for this pass, in simplified form.

Flanker (Z): Look at the near cornerback and safety. If the corner is five to 10 yards deep, it could be a man-to-man or a zone. If the safety is closer to the line of scrimmage than the corner, it is probably a zone. In any case, run a 10-yard out pattern (the basic pattern shown above). If the cornerback is up close, he probably will try to bump and run (a tight man-to-man) or bump and play the short flat zone. In either case, run a fade pattern (angling for a spot 18 yards deep and four yards from the sideline.

Split end (X): The motion is similar to the flanker, but he must also look at the near linebacker for additional keys. The weak safety also might give him a key. His primary responsibilities are the same (run a 10-yard out or a fade pattern if defenders are up close), but he may also get to the 10-yard out area (two yards from the sideline) by splitting wider then hooking out at the 10-yard area.

Tight end (Y): Looks first at the strong safety to determine whether he is in a zone or man coverage. On the snap of the ball, he concentrates on the nearest linebacker. The tight end tries to run an eight-yard hook over the middle, but if the linebacker won't let him inside he breaks to the outside. If the defense is blitzing, he can break wherever there is an opening. If he gets man coverage from the free safety, he works upfield and comes back for the ball.

Running backs: Check to see if they are needed in pass protection, and then release to an area four yards deep and between the offensive tackle and the wide receiver. Against an excellent pass rusher, the back may be assigned to bump the rusher before releasing. This is a good way to hide prior to releasing on short check-off or check-through routes.

Quarterback: Looks at the secondary first. He will have called for the flanker side or the split end side to be the primary target area. He concentrates on that side first in his read. If the safeties are closer than normal (inverted), there is probably strong run support or man-to-man coverage, and he should throw the out pattern to the wide receiver. If it is covered, he should look at the halfback and tight end to see who is open. If the alignment shows that the wideouts are tightly covered, he should look at the defensive end or outside linebacker to the primary side to see if he has dropped off in pass coverage. If he hasn't, one of the backs or the tight end should be open.

Remember, this is just one of many patterns, each with its own set of reads — and each read is more complicated than the above description be-

cause the keys can cover three and four deep alignments, regular formations and inverted formations, tight and normal zones and man-to-man defenses, as well as situations in which the blitz occurs.

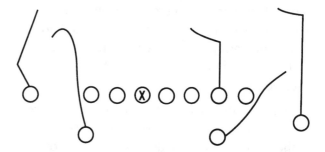

An option of alignment and pattern for the 60-80

Here is a BYU pattern in which the halfback is the primary receiver. The split end runs a "fly" pattern to clear the area and "stretch" the defense vertically. The tight end comes across the field working to a depth of 15 to 18 yards in the zone vacated by the defensive back who is covering the split end. The halfback runs into the short zone area to the same side. This is a type of "flood" pattern.

Meanwhile, the flanker is running a 20-yard "in" pattern that should be open if the defense is in a man-to-man cover. If the quarterback reads the defense as a zone, he looks first to the halfback, then the tight end, then the deep man — the split end. If it is a man-to-man, he can start with the same read but can figure that the flanker will eventually get free.

The halfback, as the prime receiver, looks at the linebackers. If the two near linebackers drop back for the pass, the halfback should get about six yards past the line of scrimmage and split them (get between them) and then turn to catch the ball.

BYU pattern with halfback as primary receiver

Following is another pattern in which the half-back is the primary receiver. The wide receivers get into patterns at a 15-yard depth in the seam between the backers and the deep defensive backs. The tight end gets deep to drive off the safeties and make certain that there is a seam for the wide receivers. The running backs get a depth of five yards into the secondary and get in the seams between the line-backers. This should work if the defense is a three deep zone.

If it is recognized as a two deep zone, the wide receivers go wide and deep. With the tight end deep in the middle and the wide receivers deep on the sidelines, the quarterback can look at the two defensive backs and determine which of the three receivers is most likely to be open.

If the defense is a man-to-man, the tight end runs a sharp post to get away from the strong safety, the wide receivers comeback patterns help them to get free (but if the safety takes away the inside, the end runs an "out"), and the running backs run to the flats. Their speed should help to free them from the slower linebackers.

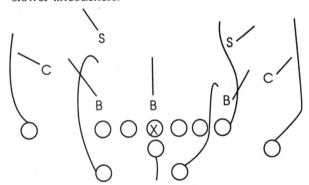

Basic pattern with halfback primary vs. three deep

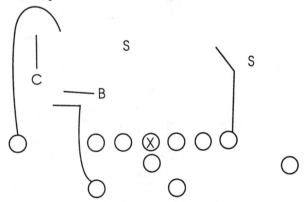

Adjustment vs. two deep safeties

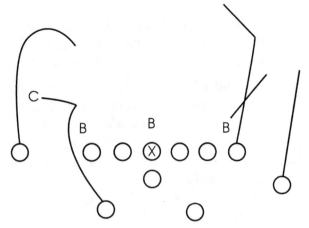

Adjustment against man-to-man

Here is an "all curl" pattern that many teams use as a horizontal stretch. On the two-receiver side, it is probable that only one of the receivers will be double-covered. After the quarterback sees who the linebacker is covering, he can be reasonably certain that the other receiver can break free.

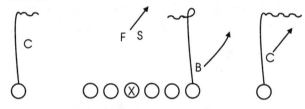

Raider all-curl pattern

Here is a pro-style pattern that should work against a zone or a man defense. The inside curl pattern crosses the outside curl pattern. Against a zone, both receivers can look for the seams; against a man defense the crossing gives the effect of a pick.

Chargers crossing curl

Here is the "option passing series." From the basic "pro set," the flanker starts downfield. Assuming that he encounters a zone defense, he will expect to run a sideline pattern at 12 yards. If he finds that the defense is in a man-to-man coverage, he can either fake his cut to the outside then break deep (an "out and up" pattern) or if he thinks he can outrun his defender he runs the "fade" pattern. The tight end hooks inside or outside, wherever he sees the better opening, and the near running back runs a swing pattern. The passer should try to hit the flanker first.

The tight end is the second choice. The back is there as a safety valve, to have someone to "dump" the ball to if everyone else is covered.

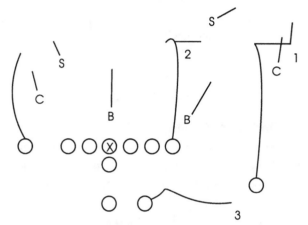

Raider option series

Sometimes the pattern will be run with the running back going in motion wider than the flanker. The flanker is still the first choice as a receiver, but now he runs the "hook in or hook out" pattern that the tight end ran in the previous illustration. The running back who was in motion is now the second option. If the defense plays deep on him, he stops and turns toward the quarterback and waits for the pass. If he is covered tight, he starts running upfield. If he can beat the defender, he runs a "fade" pattern. If not, he hooks. The tight end is now the No. 3 option. He blocks and then runs a delayed pattern over the middle. He is now the "dump" man.

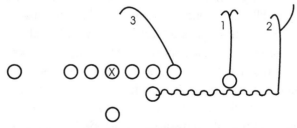

Option series with back in motion to flanker side

To run this series to the split end side, motion a back to the split end side. The pattern is similar to the previous one.

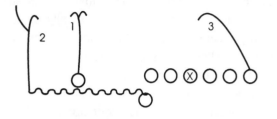

Raider option series to split end side

Each defensive alignment has obvious advantages and disadvantages. A team playing a tight bump and run loses some of the support for the run from the cornerbacks, but they take away most of the short pass patterns. Most teams playing bump and run keep two safeties deep, although some pro teams use only a single safety.

Against such defenses, the following is a pattern that Terry Donahue at UCLA used. He would send the wide receivers deep to occupy the corners and safeties, then work his other three receivers against the three linebackers.

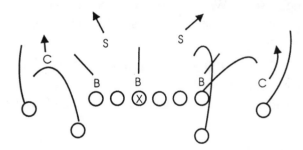

UCLA's pattern against two safeties

UCLA also would give more freedom to receivers to get open in a specific area. The quarterback would then just look left to right or right to left to find the first open man, and then fire.

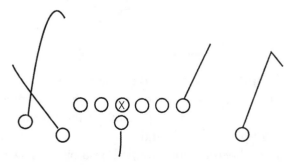

A UCLA pattern that works the seams

Any team that uses a sophisticated passing attack should have adjustments that are made as the receivers see the short zones develop. The deep routes do not need adjustment because they are still threats and stretch the defense vertically. Inside routes may gear down in the short zones so that they are under the linebackers' coverage. Outside routes may not need adjustment unless the corner forces the run and opens up the zone. Then shallower routes or even fade patterns might open.

The run and shoot offense was developed by "Tiger" Ellison, a former high school head coach and assistant to Woody Hayes at Ohio State. It was refined and popularized by "Mouse" Davis when he was head coach at Portland State and later with the Denver Gold of the now defunct United States Football League. He also is responsible for its use in the NFL where he became an offensive coordinator. Originally it offered five series, each with its own reads. It had reads in its running attack and reads in its passing plays.

Here is the tight double slot formation with the left half in motion. This is called the "Gangster pass right" series. When this play is called in the huddle, no one on the offense knows which of the options will develop.

Option 1. If the man covering the left end was three or more yards inside the end, the quarterback could throw the "automatic" pass. The X end would run an "arrow" pattern.

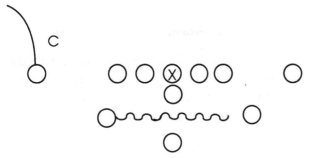

Automatic pass to X end

Option 2. Where would the fourth defensive man from the center play after the left half went in motion? Was he close to the slotback (blitz position), head up on the split end (hardnose position), or halfway between and dropped off a bit (walkaway

position)? If the No. 4 defender was in a "blitz" position, the right end would run a look-in pattern. The quarterback would run down the line and throw on his third step.

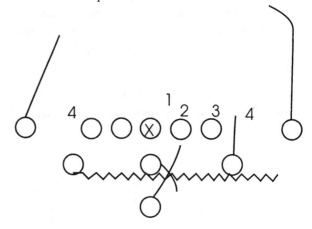

Right end runs look-in pattern

Option 3. Against the "walkaway" four man, the right end starts downfield, makes a 30-degree break and curls. The slot hooks near the inside linebacker so that he can "cherry pick" him, and the motion man swings wide. The rule is, "he left-I right; he right-I left; he up-I back; he back-I up." In other words, if the walkaway No. 4 man comes up or goes wide, the pass is thrown to the end running a curl. If the walkaway man drops off or comes to the middle, the quarterback hits the halfback in motion.

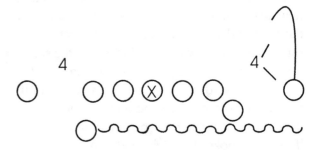

Right end runs curl, halfback goes in motion

The right halfback might also be the pass receiver. His rule is that if the near linebacker blitzes, he releases upfield as a "hot" receiver and catches the ball over his inside shoulder. If the backer follows the motion man, the right slotback releases and catches the ball over his outside shoulder. If he plays in his normal position, the slot "picks" him by running a hook pattern between the linebacker and the curling end.

If a team consistently runs a "hardnose" cornerback on the split end, a special pass is called. It is not part of the basic series of reads.

Another adjustment that often has to be made is to control a defender who follows the motion man across the field. In this situation, the quarterback could throw back to the left end, who has single coverage. Another alternative is to call the following special: the ball is snapped early to enable the right slotback to "pick" the "unwelcome stranger" as he covers man-for-man, works to the flat zone, or drops to the hook zone.

zone. The quarterback and the right wingback first look at the inside linebacker. If he blitzes the wingback, the wingback runs a "hot" pattern and releases into the area vacated by the inside backer. If the inside blocker doesn't blitz but the outside backer does, the "hot pattern" is run into the wider area. If neither blitzes, the key becomes the strong safety. The motioning back runs deep, the right wingback runs short. Whichever way the strong safety runs, the quarterback throws to the receiver in the other area. Meanwhile, the right split end is running long to take the cornerback away from the area of the pass.

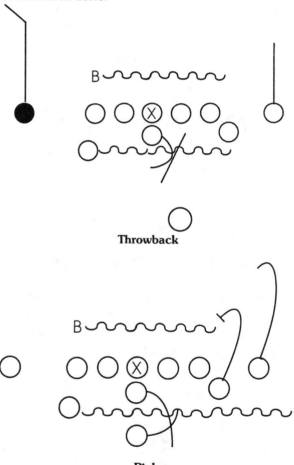

Throwback

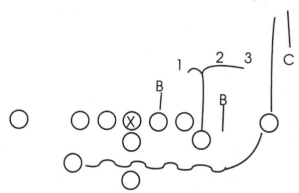

"Run and shoot" vs. zone defense

Should the defender come across with the motion man, it is most likely a "man-to-man" defense, so the quarterback has the ball snapped earlier than normal. The motioning back then cuts upfield and "picks" the man covering the right wingback. They cross. Whoever is free gets the pass.

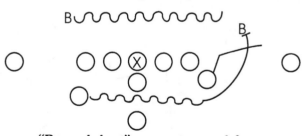

"Run and shoot" vs. man-to-man defense

Pick
HANDLING THE "UNWELCOME STRANGER"

This "run and shoot" offense was designed for a high school team, so you see that reading defenses can be done at any level of football. In fact, "reading" must be done if the passing attack is to be worked to its maximum potential.

One of Mouse Davis' series follows. The left wingback motions toward the right. If no defender follows him, it is assumed that the defense is in a

This reading and interpreting of the defense is essential to any modern passing attack. It must be quick, it must be accurate, and it must be done with at least a half-ton of maniacs charging after the quarterback. Still, we expect quarterbacks to stay calm while being attacked by a 280-pound defensive end. The quarterbacks really do earn their money.

Attacking Man-to-Man Defenders

The simplest strategy is to just outrun the defender who is playing man-to-man. Two possible problems arise, however. If you are playing against a top pro team, you are being bumped for five yards and then you are going to have to outrun the cornerbacks who run a 4.4-second 40-yard dash. If you are playing a team that plays a looser man-to-man, the defender has a head start of three to 10 yards on you. Consequently, most man-to-man routes require that the receiver use techniques to break away from the defender. The simplest such moves are the hooks and the outs.

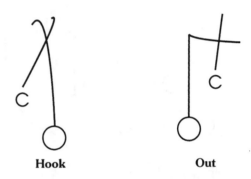

Hook   **Out**

To free himself, the receiver can lean into the defender to get him off-balance and then make his break. If the defender stays close to the receiver, a double breaking route such as a "hook and go," an "out and up," or an "in and out" (Z out) can be called — if the quarterback has time for these slower patterns.

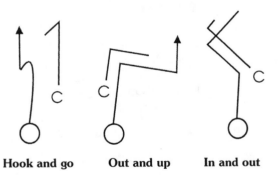

Hook and go   **Out and up**   **In and out**

Another common route against bump and run coverage is the "fade" route. In this route, the receiver runs to the corner of the end zone, "fading" away from the passer. The ball must be thrown over the defender while the receiver uses his body to keep the receiver away from the spot where the ball is to

be caught. A short pass is an easy interception, so the passer must hit it exactly — or overthrow it.

Pick plays, where one man screens another's defender, is a common pattern, especially on the goal line, where most teams play "man" coverage.

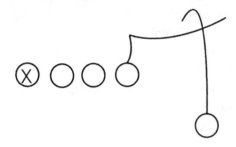

Two-man pick

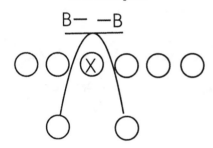

Crossing backs pick

Counters for the Passing Attack

Just as running teams must have counters, so must passing teams. Teams that drop their linebackers quickly to stop the pass may be countered with the fullback or quarterback draws.

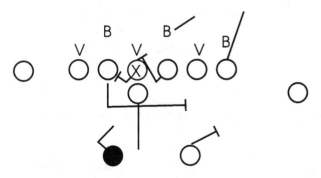

Fullback draw with a trap

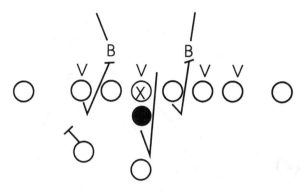

Quarterback draw

Against teams that rush several players, screen passes may work. While the receivers run deep and the quarterback drops nine or more steps, the linemen set up a screen for the receiver.

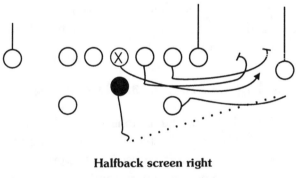

Halfback screen right

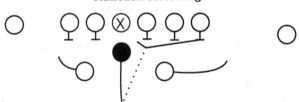

Tight end middle screen

The shovel pass was developed by Jack Curtice and popularized when Lee Grosscup played for him at Utah. Here, one side of the line drops back in a retreating pass protection while the other side blocks aggressively as if for a run. The receiver runs to the gap created by the different blocking schemes and takes a short pass, often an underhanded or basketball chest pass, and then runs into the secondary where he laterals to a teammate when the defender tries to tackle him. The player to whom he laterals often scores.

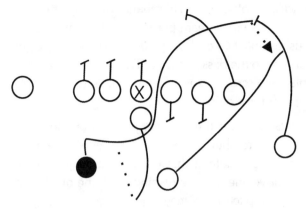

Jack Curtice's shovel pass

The Two-Minute Offense

The two-minute offense is the name given to the change in attack patterns that might occur when a team is behind and must score in a short amount of time. This approach to the game is most likely to happen during the last two minutes of either half, but particularly at the end of a game.

To stop the clock, the offensive team must either get the ball out of bounds or make a first down. Of course an incomplete pass also stops the clock, but doesn't advance the ball. Once in a while it is more important to stop the clock and save precious seconds than it is to take the time to call a play, even if such a play were successful. In such situations, the quarterback hurries the team into formation and throws the ball out of bounds or into the ground near an eligible receiver.

Usually in a "two-minute" situation, the team has an automatic play or series of plays. After an incomplete pass, the quarterback might call two or three plays to be run in sequence or until the clock stops and the next huddle occurs.

The types of plays that fit into the two-minute attack are usually "out" patterns to the wide receivers or swing passes to the backs in which the receiver can get out of bounds after the reception. Hooks or curls to the immediate receivers, flood patterns or delayed patterns to the backs that gain a first down also might be a part of the plan.

The defense being played is also a factor. If a team is playing a "prevent" or "victory" defense which is set to stop the long pass with four deep backs, the offense has little chance of completing the bomb. Usually a team playing this type of defense rushes only two or three players and commits eight or nine to the pass coverage. This may make a draw play or a screen, especially a middle screen, a likely option for a gain.

Sometimes the defense plays extra wide and attempts to shut off the "out" patterns, so a pass down the middle might work for a large gain. If the defensive linemen are rushing hard, the quick trap or quick pitch plays may work for good yardage.

The type of play called depends on the amount of time left and the number of timeouts remaining. The quarterback, rather than the coach, controls much of the two-minute offense. If he doesn't have time to huddle, he should use hand signals to communicate with the wide receivers. These may be essential if there is excessive crowd noise. In order to conserve time, the quarterback should eliminate or shorten the huddle. He can even direct the attack when moving from the huddle to the line of scrimmage. Every second counts.

The Goal Line Passing Attack

Near the goal line, the defense usually plays a man-to-man defense. Because of this the "pick" type plays, such as crossing patterns to the tight ends or between a tight end and flanker, often work. A delayed pattern also might work. In a delayed pattern, a receiver first blocks (making the defender think that the play will be a run) and then releases after the defender has committed to the run. Play action passes often work near the goal line because the defenders are prepared to stop the run.

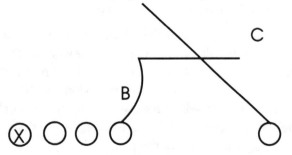

Pick pattern vs. goal line defense

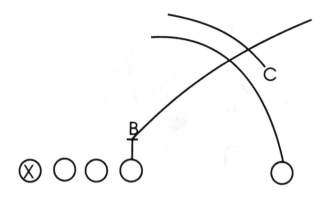

Delay pattern vs. goal line defense

Another pattern that often works is the bootleg run or pass. Defenses usually don't assign a man to watch the quarterback, so he is often free. Some teams use him as a pass receiver on occasion for that reason. He may pitch out to a running back, who stops and throws to the opposite side of the field to the uncovered quarterback.

Passing — More than Throwing

Don Shula, of the Dolphins, has described "passing" as a mental achievement, while "throwing" is strictly physical. However, it takes a great deal of time to teach proper throwing and catching techniques. Players must learn how to run routes, how to protect the passer, and how to read the defenses. The pros have the time to develop this type of game. Some colleges take the time. As Tiger Ellison has shown us, high schools can make the time too.

The passing attack has some disadvantages. Cold and wet weather can make it much tougher to pass because of the wet ball — although this is less true in the pros, where the ball is changed after every play. High school teams that don't platoon their offensive and defensive squads might not want to pass too often because passing games take longer and the players get more tired.

Still, it cannot be denied that a good passing attack can move the ball and can score more often. Tiger Ellison said that before he developed his "run and shoot" offense, his team scored about every 20 plays. With the "run and shoot" installed, it scored about every 10 plays.

9

Theories of Defense

Most successful coaches believe that defense is the key to winning at any level of play. "You win with defense" is a common axiom in the coaching profession. So while the young coach is spending more time "drawing O's" for the offensive plays, the wisened old coach is usually playing with the defensive X's.

With equal material, a team should be able to stop the 11 offensive players with 17 men. If the defense ran a gap-8 alignment to stop the run and had defenders in all six short zones and in all of the deep three passing zones, the offense would be hard-pressed to move the ball. Unhappily for defensive coordinators, the rules committee still allows just 11 men on each side of the ball. So the challenge is how to get the maximum running and passing defense with only 11 men.

The offense has many advantages over the defense. It knows whether the play will be a run or a pass. It knows the point of attack, and it knows the snap count. In the old days, the defenders' major advantage was that they were able to use their hands and arms much more than the offensive players. Today, the offensive blockers are allowed to extend their hands in blocking. This greatly reduces what little advantage the defenders had.

Another change that hurts the pro defense is not being able to bump pass defenders after they have passed beyond five yards of the line of scrimmage. (High school and college defenders are still allowed

to "bump" offensive players as long as they are potential blockers.)

With the rules, especially the professional rules, favoring the offense, it is much more difficult to field an effective defense. Still, it is the flaming desire of the defensive coordinators and the defensive team members to hold their opponents scoreless.

Defensive linemen must stop the run in their areas of responsibility and then pursue the ball carrier if the play is in another area. They must be ready to rush the passer aggressively, but still react to the draw play or the screen pass. The linebackers must stop the run, yet they must also be able to react to their zones if a pass develops. Defensive backs must stop all the long and short pass patterns while still helping to make tackles on running plays.

For a defensive team to stop an offensive team, it must be in an effective alignment, use the proper keys to get the defenders to the right spot, and have techniques that enable those duties to be accomplished.

Defensive Alignments

Early defensive teams generally used the Tight-6 line, with the fullback and center as linebackers, and the halfbacks and quarterback as defensive backs in a three-deep alignment. They played man-to-man pass defense with the defensive halfbacks on the offensive ends and the quarterback as a safety.

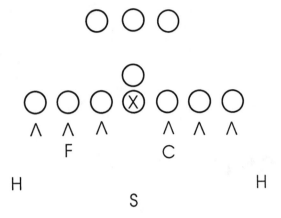

Tight-6 alignment

Soon the 5-3 and 7-diamond alignments were devised against the pass or the run and to confuse the blocking assignments. The defenders either crouched low and charged through the offensive linemen to their areas of responsibility or stood up and used their hands to ward off the blockers.

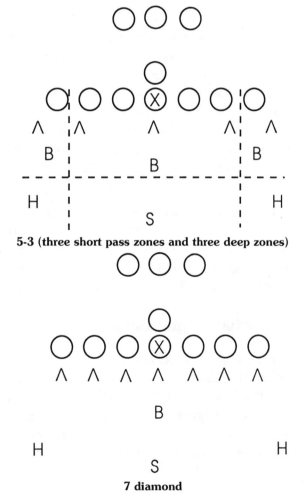

5-3 (three short pass zones and three deep zones)

7 diamond

As offenses attacked more effectively, defenses were forced to become more effective in alignment and in technique. General Robert Neyland at Tennessee developed the Wide Tackle 6, which reduced the offense's ability to run wide, but it also increased the vulnerability to running plays between the guards. This weak area had to be strengthened by having outstanding athletes with effective techniques at the guard spots. Sam Boghosian, longtime Raider assistant, and Dave Levy, longtime Charger and Lion assistant, played these positions side by side at UCLA on the 1954 championship team. What they lacked in size they made up for in technique and toughness.

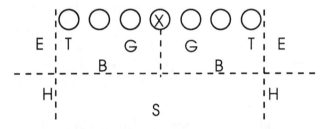

Wide Tackle 6
(ends and backers dropped into four short zones,
while defensive backs covered the three deep zones)

As pursuit to the ball became more of a necessity, linebackers were moved closer to the middle so that they could pursue to either side of the field more effectively. The ends were then dropped back to become outside linebackers.

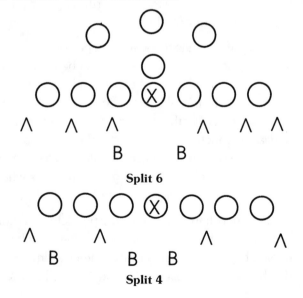

Split 6

Split 4

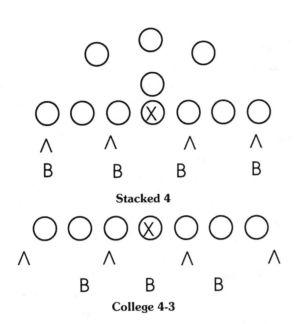

Stacked 4

College 4-3

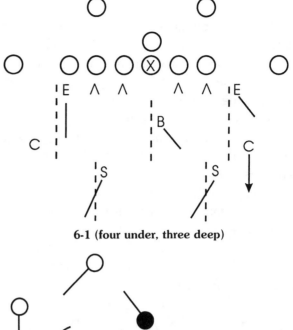

6-1 (four under, three deep)

As the passing game with wide receivers developed in the pros and as the split-T option attack took over with the colleges, coaches began to work with four defensive backs.

Steve Owens of the New York Giants is credited with being the first to use the "umbrella" defense with four defensive backs. In his 6-1 umbrella, the ends and linebacker could drop to the three hook areas while the cornerbacks could cover the flats (a five-under, two-deep zone), or one back could rotate to the flat with the others playing three deep (a four-under, three-deep zone). With a run to one side, the defensive backs could rotate up and still be in a three-deep secondary.

Following is the seven-man front with four defensive backs:

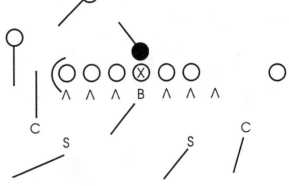

6-1 rotating to a wide run or run-pass option

Using four defensive backs makes it easier to vary the coverage. It changes the zones that each defender covers and also makes it easier to play man-to-man pass defense. It also makes it easier to adjust the defense to the offensive strength. If a team comes out in a winged formation, an umbrella defense only has to rotate, with a cornerback becoming a defensive end. An eight-man front team would have to adjust linemen and/or backers.

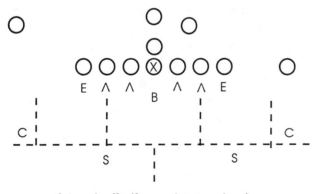

6-1 umbrella (five under, two deep)

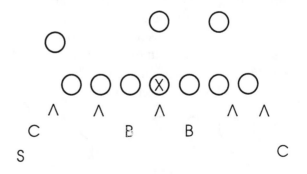

Okie 5-2 with rotated secondary adjusted to a wing T

With the soundness of the four deep backs proven, Earle "Greasy" Neale of the Philadelphia Eagles developed a new alignment, the "Eagle." He used a middle guard who was tough enough to plug up the inside, yet could pursue. His tackles took the guard-tackle gap, often crashing down to stop the trap play. (The tackle who was on the pulling guard might stop the play from behind, while the tackle who was being trapped would be playing the trap block aggressively. The ends could crash down to stop the off tackle play. The linebackers played on the ends, so they had a good tip as to whether the play was a run at them or a pass or run to the opposite side. (If the end released it was a pass or a run the other way.)

Eagle defense

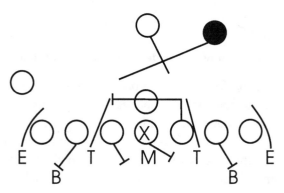

Eagle vs. the inside trap

This became the forerunner of the modern pro 4-3 defense. The thinking was that if you wanted the tackles to crash to the guards, why not put them there initially? If the ends were assigned to get to the off-tackle area, why not put them there first? And if the middle guard was to pursue the play, why not move him back to a linebacker spot?

Pro 4-3

Meanwhile, in the late 1940s and the early 1950s, as the split-T attacks became more potent and more common in college, it was found that the normal eight-man front was ineffective in stopping it. So Bud Wilkinson at Oklahoma, the foremost exponent of the split-T attack, developed the defense to stop it. The "Okie 5-2" is still the most common defense in high school and college, and is the father of the pro 3-4 defense.

In the original "Okie" defense, the nose guard had to be able to control both sides of the offensive center and stop the quarterback sneak. The tackles had to control the outside of the offensive tackle for the dive play. The linebackers keyed the guards and mirrored their movements to react to the pass, the inside dive, or the trap. The ends had to stop the "off tackle" play and the quarterback on the option play. The cornerbacks played closer to the line than they did in Steve Owens' "umbrella." They would rotate up if the flow of the backs came toward them. Their job would be to take the widest back — the man to whom the quarterback might pitch. The other backs had now rotated into a three-deep alignment.

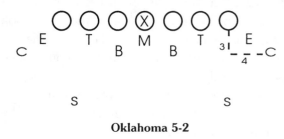

Oklahoma 5-2

Linebackers react to the keys of the offensive guards by "mirroring" the guards. That is, if the guard comes toward the backer, the backer goes toward the guard. If the guard drops back in pass protection, the backer drops to his passing zone. If the guard blocks to his right or left, the backer comes up to fill that area. If the guard pulls behind the line of scrimmage, the backer also moves in that direction, without crossing the scrimmage line.

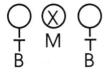

Guards block straight (a dive or wide play)

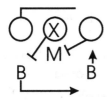

One guard blocks down, one pulls (a trap play)

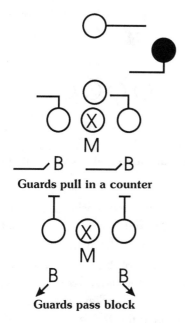

Guards pull in a counter

Guards pass block

The Chicago Bear "46" defense, which helped the Bears win the 1986 Super Bowl, was a different alignment than is usually found. Every one of the 11 defenders stunted or blitzed at some time.

With two linebackers near the tight end, one was always available to rush without giving up any pass coverage to that side. Closer to the center, you can see that the middle guard and tackle show an "Eagle" alignment, but while a true "Eagle" has no inside linebacker, the Bears had Mike Singletary as an "Okie" linebacker. This gave them a great deal of strength to the tight end side. On the other side they put Richard Dent at a weakside defensive end. The offense always had to be concerned with him, and often had to use two men to block him.

Bear 46 defense

Unusual alignments are often designed to take advantage of particular strengths of the defensive personnel. The 1980 Raiders did this to enhance Ted Hendricks' multiple talents.

The defensive linemen aligned in a standard four-man front (on the offensive guards and tackles). The safeties and strongside linebacker were also in normal positions. However, because they played so much man-to-man pass coverage with the cornerbacks, they could move the weakside and middle backers closer to the strong side of the offense. The weakside backer, who would normally play outside of the defensive end, played nearer the guard. Hendricks, rather than being over the center, played near the offensive tackle. From here, he was able to stunt to any area on his half of the alignment. This alignment gave a defensive overload both to the strong side and to the weak side of the offense.

Techniques of Line Play

Some coaches want to constantly attack the offense with their defense by having the defensive linemen charge through an offensive lineman or through a gap in the line. Stunting teams do this with their linemen and linebackers. A "slant" charge is used to go from a man to a gap or from a gap into a man. It changes the attacking point one-half man. A "loop" is used to go from one man to another or to a gap. It moves the attacking point at least one man away from where the defender lined up.

Following are some examples of stunts using line slants and loops with blitzing backers.

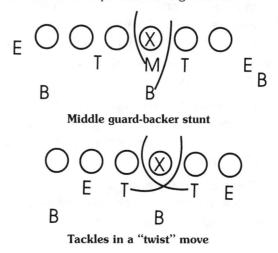

Middle guard-backer stunt

Tackles in a "twist" move

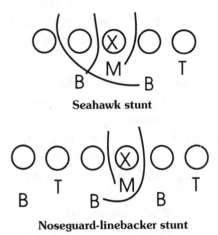

Seahawk stunt

Noseguard-linebacker stunt

A team may align in one defense and then have everyone slant or loop to one side or the other. The players might be instructed to slant to the strong side of the formation or to the wide side of the field.

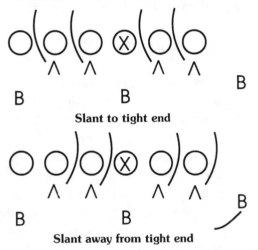

Slant to tight end

Slant away from tight end

Penetrating defenses have their advantages. If the defenders guess right, they will be at the point of attack and can drop the runner for a loss. Also, if a pass develops, the defensive linemen are already in their pass rush and gain a few steps over where they would have been if they were "reading" the offensive linemen.

The disadvantages are that if the play goes away from the penetrating defensive lineman, he is not in a good position to pursue the play, so it might break for a long gain.

Many teams only penetrate across the line of scrimmage on stunts, which they call very infrequently. They are primarily concerned that the of-

fense doesn't get the easy score. They use techniques in which the defender reads one or more linemen and then reacts to the ball without (generally) crossing the line of scrimmage. It is hoped that, if all the defenders react correctly, the offensive team cannot make more than two yards per running play, and winds up punting on fourth-and-four.

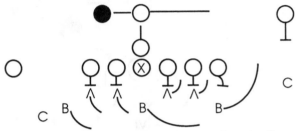

A pro 4-3 defense reading and reacting to the flow

The simplest "read" for a defensive lineman is to read the offensive blocker's head. If he puts his head on your right side, it is obvious that he is trying to block you away from the play, which must be going to your right. So by using a forearm rip or a hand "shiver," the defender should be able to free himself from the blocker, move "across his face," and then make the tackle.

With these techniques, it is essential that the defender not go behind the blocker or he will not be able to pursue quickly.

The following photographs illustrate these techniques (the defensive player is in white):

Hand shiver

Defensive Line Theory

Some coaches want the defender to control the man in front of him. If he can do this, he can control the gaps on each side of him. This is what was expected of the guards in the previously mentioned Wide Tackle 6 defensive alignment. With the skill and the size of today's offensive linemen, it is often difficult to totally control a man and both gaps. Consequently, many coaches have changed their defensive theory to that of "gap control." In a gap control defense, the defender may still play on an offensive lineman, but he has primary responsibility for only one of the gaps.

Some coaches just call for a defense, such as Okie, Eagle, Split 4, 5-3 and so on. The defenders know where to line up for each defense. To upset the offense, the team might "overshift" or "undershift" its line. When doing this, the linebackers generally shift the other way so that the defense is still balanced.

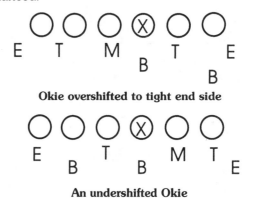

Okie overshifted to tight end side

An undershifted Okie

Some years ago, Bear Bryant at Alabama popularized the "numbers" defense. This allowed for a great deal of variation in calling defenses. By calling a number, the player knew where to line up and what technique to play.

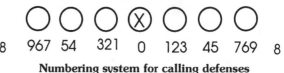

Numbering system for calling defenses

The 0, 2, 4 and 6 techniques were head-up reading techniques by the nose guard, tackle, and end. The 1 and 7 techniques were inside gap control techniques used by the defensive tackle and end, and the 3 and 9 techniques were outside gap control

Forearm rip

A more complicated read is that which the nose guard (nose tackle in the pros) must make. He must be able to read the one-on-one block, the trap block, and the pass block, and he must also be able to handle the double-team block.

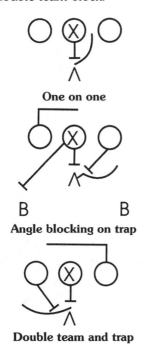

One on one

Angle blocking on trap

Double team and trap

techniques used by the tackle and end. The 8 technique is that of a wider defensive end.

By calling two appropriate numbers, the linebacker could align the linemen on his side of the ball in many different spots, and then go to the appropriate spot. For example, if the linebacker on the tight end side called a 59, his side of the line would be an "Okie 5-2," and if the weakside linebacker called a 03, his side of the line would be an "Eagle."

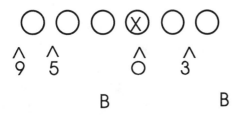

59 and 03 calls

Linebacker Play

As mentioned at the start of this chapter, a good defense would have at least 17 men on the field — eight linemen and nine pass defenders. Because we are only allowed 11 men, some players must do double duty. The linebackers are the primary double duty players. They must stop the running play, and they must defend against the pass. Many plays are designed to force the linebacker into mistakes. The play action pass, for example, makes the linebacker play run while a receiver sneaks into the linebacker's pass zone responsibility. The draw play coaxes the linebacker to drop back, then a run comes at him.

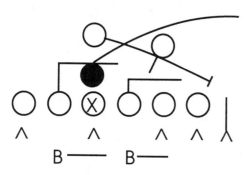

Play action pass

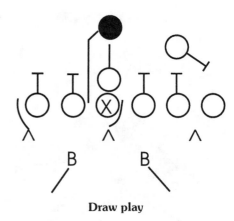

Draw play

Backers can use many keys to react to a run or pass. An outside backer playing on an end might key his end. If the end releases, the backer drops. But he needs another key to be sure the area he is vacating will not be attacked by a running play — especially a counter action or a reverse. Inside backers may key the uncovered lineman. As with the Okie 5-2, the backer can mirror the guards, and if the guards drop back in pass protection on every pass and there are no play action passes, the linebacker should be able to handle both run and pass responsibilities.

Linebackers also can cover two areas of responsibility with controlled stunting. If the running keys are valid, one linebacker might "scrape" into a gap and react as a slanting lineman. The other backer then "shuffles" to back up the vacated area.

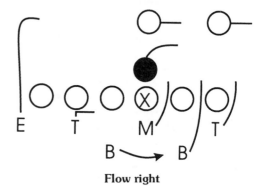

Flow right

With the defensive linemen shooting the other gaps, the defense is like a gap-8 goal line defense to the side of the backfield flow, but with only five men. For the linebackers to react correctly, however, their keys must be nearly foolproof. Here are examples of "keys" (looking at only one player) and "reads" (looking at two or more players).

If the offense does not cross its backs, a key from the near back is easiest. In the traditional split-T attack a straight key is possible, but the counter comes from the fullback, so the off linebacker must first key his halfback to stop the dive threat and then check the fullback for the counter. This is a "read."

Here is an example of an Okie defense stunting to an Eagle. The scraping linebacker leaves the guard and takes the area inside the offensive end. The shuffling linebacker changes his key from the near halfback to the fullback after the first step.

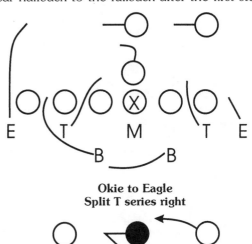

Okie to Eagle
Split T series right

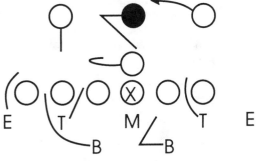

Split T counter
Shuffle backer takes fullback

Against a team using a series in which the backs cross, the backer should key the offside back.

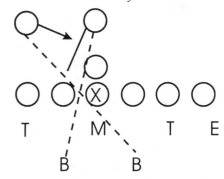

CROSS KEYING
Cross buck with backers scraping and shuffling

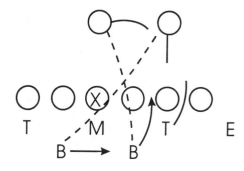

Split T series

If teams pull their guards, the backers will have to "read" through the guards to the backs. Depending on whether the backs cross or not, the backer's read could be near guard to near back or near guard to far back. If the guard pulls, he becomes the main key. If the guard does not pull, the back is the key.

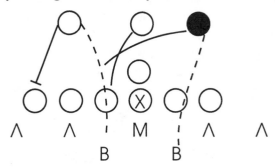

STRAIGHT READ THROUGH THE GUARD
Inside belly series

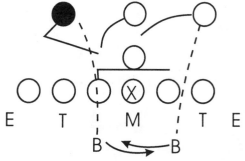

Belly counter with guard pulling

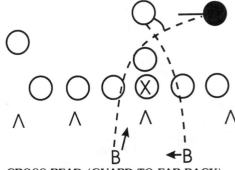

CROSS READ (GUARD TO FAR BACK)
Cross buck from wing T

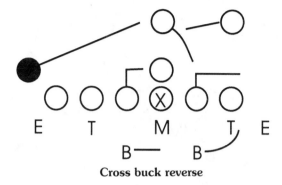

Cross buck reverse

Techniques for Defensive Backs

The defensive back's technique depends on whether he is playing a man-to-man or a zone. Generally the back takes a few steps back as he takes his key. A defensive halfback might key the offside end or end and tackle. If both go downfield (in a college or high school game) it is a run or a pass behind the line. (In high school and college, linemen can go downfield on passes completed behind the line of scrimmage. Of course in a pro game the tackle going downfield can only indicate a run.)

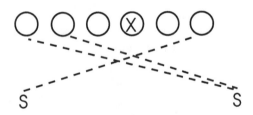

Keying the offside tackle and end

The back might also key any uncovered linemen, such as the guards in an Okie alignment, but many teams have pulled their uncovered linemen behind the line of scrimmage to take away this key.

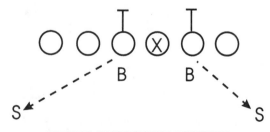

KEYING UNCOVERED LINEMEN
Guards drop back for pass blocking
(backs play for pass)

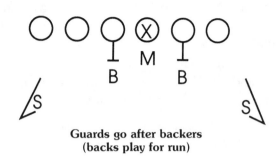

Guards go after backers
(backs play for run)

Zone teams drop to their zones if a pass shows. They also might rotate their zones if the passer moves to a new position.

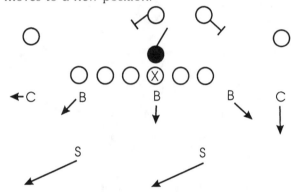

Backs and backers dropping to their zones
(four under, three deep)

Backs and backers can react to a rollout pass by changing their responsibilities. (Note that because the player in the strong side flat comes up to force the play and the others have rotated, there is no one in the flat zone away from the flow.)

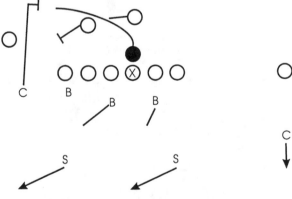

Rollout with corner forcing the pass

With teams passing more, especially in certain situations, defensive coaches have begun to put in more defensive backs than the standard four. The five-back (nickel defense) and the six-back (dime defense) have defensive backs coming in to substitute for linebackers on "passing downs." The advantage of such moves is that the backs have better speed and pass defense skills, and are less likely to be "burned" in one-on-one, man-to-man coverage against running backs. The disadvantage is that they tend to be weaker against the run than the linebackers would have been.

Theory of Secondary Alignment

It takes three men to cover the deep secondary zones, therefore many teams use the three-deep secondary, which has been around since the earliest days of the game. Others will rotate or otherwise disguise their intentions as to whom will be in each zone. In the following diagram, the four-deep backs started in an umbrella alignment. This made it easy to rotate to the flow of the backs.

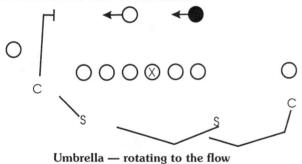

Umbrella — rotating to the flow

With more teams using two wide receivers, it became impossible to rotate up to stop the run because it would leave the wide receiver unattended. Consequently many teams started to "invert" their safeties. The safeties then became responsible for the run support while the corners were primarily responsible for the pass.

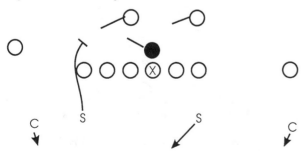

Inverted four deep with safeties giving run support

With the umbrella defense or the invert, zone defensive teams generally played with three deep backs in the zones. Some college and high school coaches decided that they could teach better if they had the same three people in the deep zones all the time. However, they liked the seven-man front of the Okie defense. So with seven up front and three deep, they had an extra man. He was called the "rover" back. (Frank Broyles at Arkansas termed him "the monster," a name that became almost universal for teams using the rover.)

The rover or monster could be put in the middle of the defense, but usually he went to the wide side of the field or to the strength of the offensive set. In determining the strength of the offense, his rules were to go to the side of a flanker or slot back or away from a split end. This rover back usually had responsibility for wide runs and for the wide flat pass zone.

In man-to-man defense, the defenders can play up close and "bump and run" with the receiver. This is a favorite ploy of the Raiders. Al Davis gets the credit for the way they play pass defense. Years ago, Al had the idea of playing football pass defense like basketball players play man-to-man defense. So while most teams playing a "man" defense give the pass receiver a good "cushion" of air, the Raiders play it tightly.

Although there is usually a "free" safety, he cannot cover the whole deep secondary, so the cornerbacks must do most of the job themselves. If the receiver is faster than the defender, he can easily get open on a streak pattern. The Raiders try to guard against this by signing very fast football players to be their cornerbacks. Teams running the bump and run have the theoretical advantage of being able to take away all of the patterns that the receiver might run. The major disadvantage is that the man covering a wide receiver can't be much help in stopping the running play.

Many teams playing man-to-man defense have their defensive backs start five to 10 yards from the receiver. This has the advantage of being able to take away the long pass with a slower defender and possibly getting some run support from the cornerback. It has the disadvantage of being open to underneath patterns and to double-cutting patterns such as the out-and-up or hook-and-go.

As you can see, many alignments and techniques are available. Some teams use one basic alignment most of the time and stunt from that set. Other teams use multiple defensive sets. The important point is really the effectiveness of the individuals playing the defense. How well do they read their keys? How well do they escape ("shed") their blockers? How well do they pursue to the ball carrier? How well do they play pass defense? Of extreme importance is the type of defense called to counter each offensive situation. Do they have the proper pass defense when the offense is most likely to pass? Have they properly selected a pursuing or a penetrating defense when they expect the offense to run?

Factors of Field Position

Field position, including both the yard line and hash mark, can affect the type of coverage. The yard line can affect the depth that the receivers can run, as follows:

- Closer to offensive team's goal line restricts the vertical distance of the pattern
- Closer to the defensive team's goal line restricts the chances of completing the long pass because of the time factor and chance of a safety if the passer is sacked.

Formation and backfield set tell how the perimeter of the defense is being manipulated. The wider the wideouts, the wider or deeper the defensive backs must set. If the backs are set wide, there is a greater threat of a swing pass or another type of pass pattern to a back.

Flow of the backs can signal the most likely area that the offense can attack.

Split or divided flow, with the passer remaining between the tackles, enables the offense to attack any part of the field via the pass.

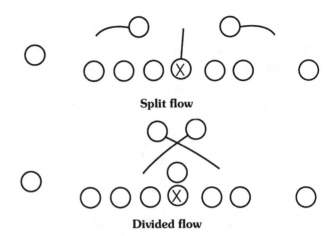

Split flow

Divided flow

Full flow play action, with the passer staying between the tackles, also enables the offense to attack the whole field with the pass.

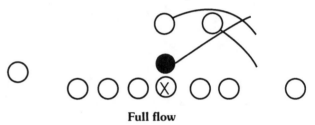

Full flow

Split flow, with the passer in a bootleg action, is more likely to result in a pass to the side of the ball.

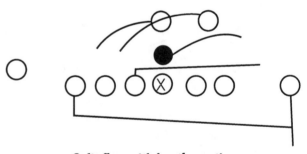

Split flow with bootleg action

Full flow with rollout is more likely to attack the flow side of the play.

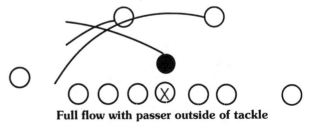

Full flow with passer outside of tackle

The quarterback set-up point should relate to the depth of the patterns, as follows:

- *Three-step drop.* Expect a short pattern in the five-yard area or a timed pattern.
- *Five-step drop (about a seven-yard set up).* Expect intermediate routes in the 14 to 18 yard area or delayed patterns such as an end dragging or a back out of the backfield.
- *Seven-step drop (about a nine-yard set up).* Expect deep vertical routes such as streak, post, or corner.

Pass patterns are designed to stretch the defense in different ways. The defensive backs must be prepared for each of them, but the week-to-week strategy might indicate that only one or two of these theories is primary for the opponent.

Vertical stretch is the ability of the passing team to extend the defense to its maximum depth from the line of scrimmage.

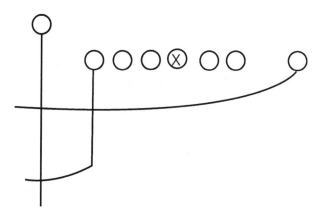

Vertical stretch

Horizontal stretch is the ability of the offense to stretch the defense from sideline to sideline.

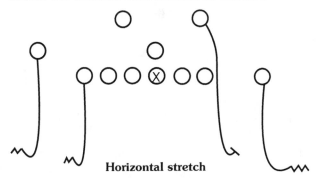

Horizontal stretch

Combination theory is the ability to affect the defensive coverage, particularly the undercoverage of the backers, on the inside and outside either in the horizontal plane, the vertical plane, or both.

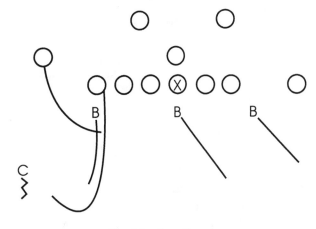

Combination theory

Front and back theory develops a horizontal stretch in two vertical planes.

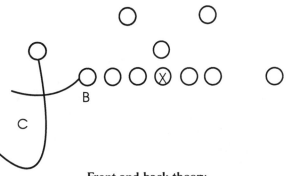

Front and back theory

Flood theory is a horizontal stretch on three vertical planes.

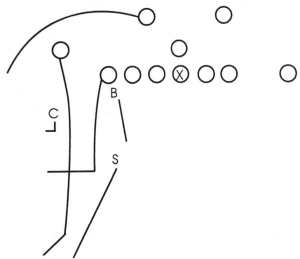

Flood pass

Taking Away Specific Areas

The most common type of zone coverage is the four-under, three-deep responsibility. Against a team that throws short, the coach might often want to play five-under with two deep zones. Both might be open to the intermediate area passes of 14 to 18 yards. To take away this intermediate area, the coach might play five-under man coverage with two deep zones. This should take away all passes under 18 yards but could be vulnerable to long passes splitting the seams of the deep two safeties. With the undercoverage men watching men rather than the ball, this five-under man defense is vulnerable to the run.

Coaches must recognize that there is a defense for whatever the offense wants to do, but every defense has its weaknesses. Because of this, the coach might want to change covers at certain times but not be predictable in so doing. For example, if he plays a five-under man, two-deep zone on every third-and-long situation, his team may be open to a quarterback draw or bootleg or even a sweep into an area being cleared by receivers.

Special Situations

The *"prevent" or "victory" defense* is often used during the last few minutes of a half when the offense is expected to pass a good deal because it is behind. Teams that use such a defense usually rush fewer players and use more defenders in the pass coverage. They will always try to stop the long pass by playing deeper and perhaps adding a safetyman behind the regular safeties. A team playing this defense is usually vulnerable to short passes and passes in the 18- to 25-yard area downfield.

Many teams use their regular defenses during a "two-minute" attack, believing if it was good enough to stop the opponents for the first 58 minutes of the game, it should still work in the closing moments.

Goal line defense is an essential aspect of many games. Most teams prefer to run in this area, because of the reduced passing area, so teams mass to stop the run. To do this, they usually play man-to-man pass defense. The defenders on the wide-outs (wide receivers) will possibly be able to help on a wide run. The linebackers assigned to the running backs will be available whether their men are involved in a run or a pass.

Some teams play a zone defense occasionally against a team that uses a lot of drop-back passing near the goal line. Usually they commit five men to the short zones. Stopping the run is usually done by penetrating at least six defenders. Usually two will be in the center-guard (A) gaps, two in either the guard-tackle (B) gaps or tackle-end (C) gaps, and two attacking from outside the ends.

Gap 8 goal line defense

6-5 goal line defense

10

The Kicking Game

With the emphasis on "special teams," the kicking game has become more important in the eyes of the fans. Coaches, especially the "field position" coaches, have long known the importance of the kicking game and have emphasized it in practice and in their games. A great number of the most successful coaches place the kicking game second in importance only to defense, with the offensive game being third in importance.

Many coaches believe that if a team makes two more mistakes than its opponents in the kicking game, it almost undoubtedly will lose that game. A blocked punt, a long kick return, a muffed catch, or a missed extra point can be disastrous to a team's chance of winning. Many of the so-called "breaks" in a football game occur during the kicking phase of the game. They are not really breaks at all because the "lucky" team has practiced all season to make those breaks occur.

The kicking game incorporates offensive and defensive aspects. The punt and kickoff are defensive plays, but the kick returns, the field goal and extra points, the fake kicks, the punt and extra point blocks, and even the seldom seen quick-kick are thought of as offensive weapons.

The Kickoff

Most teams prefer to receive the kickoff if they win the coin flip. Strong defensive and kicking teams often choose to kick the ball. Their hope is that they can hold their opponents inside the opponent's 30-yard line and make them punt. They can then take over somewhere around their own 40-yard line.

The basic kickoff play puts the kicker in the middle of the field, with five tacklers on either side of him. Many coaches, however, use other alignments to increase the effectiveness of the play.

Some teams kick the ball from a hash mark rather than the middle of the field to reduce the opponent's options for a return. Their thinking is that it is more difficult for a team to return the ball to the other side of the field. Every step that the ball carrier takes to the far sideline gives every member of the kicking team one more step into the receiver's territory, reducing the chance of an effective return. If the receivers return to the side of the kick, the defenders each have less territory to defend.

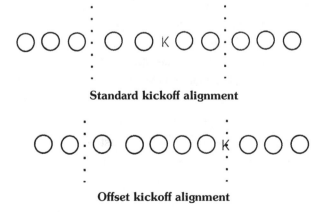

Standard kickoff alignment

Offset kickoff alignment

Some coaches start a couple of rushers farther back than the kicker so that they can get a longer and faster rush toward the receivers. Usually one of these men will be a "wedge breaker" whose assignment is to dent the four- or five-man wedge of blockers which most teams use for their returns. Some coaches use two kickers, aligning one to kick deep to one side of the field with the other kicker ready to kick to the opposite field or to kick an onside kick.

In the following diagram, kicker "1" is used to kick deep to the right side of the field, and kicker "2" is used to kick shallower to the left or to kick the onside kicks:

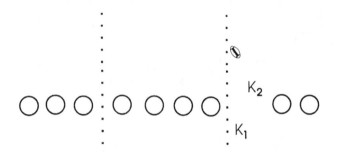

Two-kicker kickoff

Many kickers today can kick the ball into the end zone consistently. Obviously, this is the ultimate in kickoff strategy. The problem for the coach is when he doesn't have a great long ball kicker. One solution is to "squib kick" the ball.

To squib kick the ball, the kicker generally lays the ball on its side rather than teeing it up. He generally kicks it off center, so that it takes those uncontrolled bounces that only a football can take. Watching the receivers attempt to catch a squib kick is something like watching Wile E. Coyote trying to catch the Roadrunner.

The onside kick is often used near the end of the game when the team that has just scored is still behind. However, it is used by some daring and intelligent coaches when the return team drops back too quickly. Some coaches threaten the onside kick on every kickoff. They may start with all of their players close to the kicker. The kicker can kick straight ahead 10 to 15 yards and the kicking team has 11 players near the ball. They can then either

perform their onside kick or take the normal kickoff positions. If the receiving team comes up close to stop the onside kick the kicking team can kick to an area of the field left vacant by the receivers.

A few coaches use the onside kickoff at least 70 percent of the time. Their thinking is that they have between a 30 and 50 percent chance of recovering the ball. Even if they don't recover it, the opponent has the ball only 10 to 20 yards closer to the goal than if it had made a normal return. The onside kickoff alignment can be the same as the regular kickoff or, in obvious onside kick situations, all of the cover men can be placed near where the ball will be kicked. Usually the ball is set on one hash mark and kicked to the wide side of the field.

The assignments of the cover men include those who block the receivers, those who attempt to recover the ball after it has gone 10 yards, and a "fielder" who will be near the sidelines to stop the kicked ball from going out of bounds.

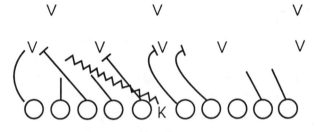

Onside kick from normal alignment

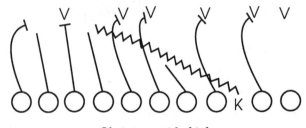

Obvious onside kick

Kickoff Coverage

Covering the kickoff is another important consideration. Every kick coverage has two men responsible for the outside — the ends. One or two men also act as safeties. The other seven or eight men attack the ball carrier in one or two waves, keeping appropriate distances between themselves so that the ball carrier cannot easily go around them or run through a gap in the wave. Most teams also have a couple of "mad dogs" who sacrifice their bodies as they attempt to break the wedge of blockers who convoy the ball carrier until he finds a gap in the defense and runs for daylight.

The kickoff team may also use players designated as linebackers or as safeties. Some teams use one safety, usually the kicker, while others use two. Some play one or two men slightly behind the phalanx of "mad dogs" and also employ one or two safeties. It is essential that the defenders stay in their assigned lanes as they run down the field. If they all run directly to the ball, they open a hole in the defense that the running back might exploit for a long run. The lanes are generally about five yards apart, but reduce to three or even two yards apart as the attackers get close to the ball carrier.

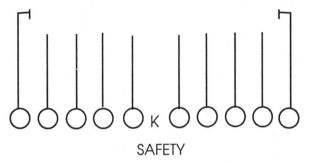

Straight kickoff coverage

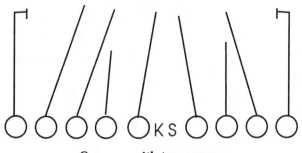

Coverage with two waves

Because some teams assign men to block on the return, many coaches cross their rushers as they run downfield. (Members of the kicking team are usually assigned numbers.) This is particularly true of the ends, because many teams use a trap on the end as part of their blocking scheme. Crossing the ends and one or two other men can foul up the blocking assignments of the return team.

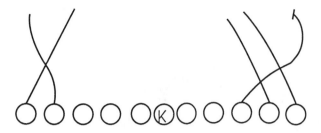

Coverage with crossing rushers

The Kickoff Return

Generally the kickoff can be considered a success for the kicking team if its holds the return team inside its own 25-yard line. It is a definite success for the returners if they get the ball to their own 35. Kickoff return strategies involve either a wedge block, cross blocking, double teaming, trapping, or the setting up of a wall of blockers to one side of the field. These skills may be used in combination.

Examples are as follows:

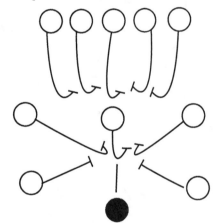

Double wedge return

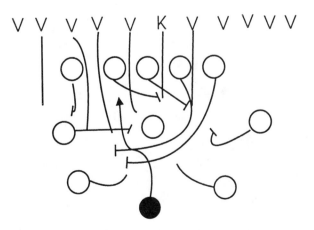

Cross block return

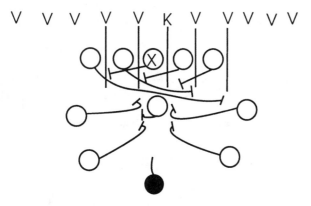

Cross block and wedge

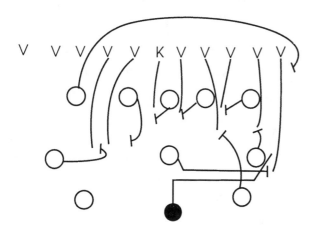

Trap on the end

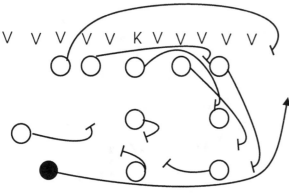

Reverse with a wall

The kickoff return play gives coaches the opportunity for special trick plays, such as the reverse, fake reverse, or a long lateral pass after the play starts one way that moves the ball back to the other side of the field.

Then there is the notorious "bubble play," in which the receiving team huddles around the ball before the kicking team members have a chance to get downfield. At the signal, all the receivers break their huddle faking that they have the ball. The tackling team now has to sort out the real ball carrier and tackle him. It may not be the most effective play in football, but it sure is fun to practice. It was more effective when it was invented 80 years ago. The first "bubble play" coach had a leather oval, which looked like a football, sewn on each jersey. You can imagine the confusion among the tacklers!

The Punt

Many coaches believe that the punt is their most effective offensive play. How many other plays average 35 to 40 yards? In designing the punt play, coaches must be concerned with the protection of the punter and with the coverage of the kick. The best protection would be very tight to reduce the punt rush, and the best coverage would place the kicking team members far apart to reduce the protection of the punter. So, a happy medium must be achieved. In high school and college, the kicking team members can release to cover the kick at any time. At the pro level, only the widest two players can release immediately. The others have to wait until the ball has been kicked.

The long-used "tight punt" formation gives good protection but is poor on coverage. It is often used today when a team is punting from its own end zone and must avoid a blocked kick. Here, the punter is generally 10 yards behind the center.

In the traditional spread punt, the kicker lines up 13 to 15 yards behind the center. The halfbacks are in the center-guard gaps and the fullback lines up five to seven yards deep to protect the punter. This gives the effect of a nine-man line. Some teams have actually used eight-, nine-, or 10-man lines.

Another type of formation is the semi-spread or the "tackles back" formation. In this alignment, the team has the advantage of seven men releasing quickly to cover, yet has three big linemen as protectors for the punter. In any of these formations, the coach can elect to put one or two men extra wide.

An effective punting team generally takes six-tenths of a second or less to get the snap to the punter, then no more than 1.2 seconds for the punter to get the kick off. If the overall kick takes 1.8 seconds or less, it probably will not be blocked. If it takes 2.1 seconds or more, a blocked punt is likely.

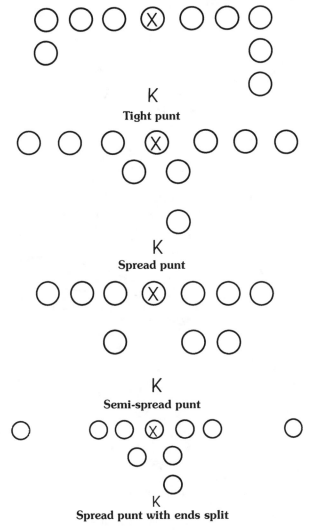

Tight punt

Spread punt

Semi-spread punt

Spread punt with ends split

Punt coverage usually starts with one or two men getting to the ball immediately. A second wave, generally the center, guards and tackles, are five or 10 yards behind the first men. They must stay in their proper coverage lanes about five yards apart. There are two people designated to be "ends" or contain men who can stop any wide plays or reverses. There will also be a safety man or two.

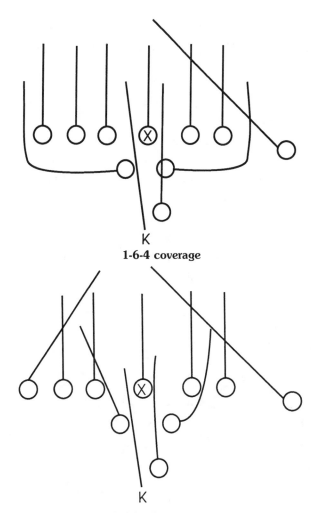

1-6-4 coverage

2-5-2-1-1 coverage

Because the object of the punt is to gain as many yards as possible, it generally is not best to kick into the end zone. The pros now keep statistics on how effective their punters are in starting their opponents inside their 20-yard line. To kill the ball inside the "20," kickers either kick out of bounds or use a "squib" punt in which the ball is kicked to about the "10" while the covering team attempts to let the ball bounce toward the goal line but not cross it.

The Punt Return

Most teams elect to return punts rather than block them because it is difficult to block a punt and the risk of roughing the punter is high.

When returning the punt, a team generally tries to hold up the tacklers on the punting team. With the pros able to release only the two widest men on the snap of the ball, most teams use two men to hold up each of them. In high school and college, all potential tacklers should be delayed. It takes about two seconds for a kicker to get off his punt, and most good punters hang the ball up for about four seconds and kick about 35 to 40 yards, so the punt coverage team has about six seconds to cover 35 to 40 yards. Most special team players run a 40-yard dash in under five seconds, so returns cannot succeed unless the coverage people are held up for at least two seconds.

Most receiving teams form a wall of players on one side of the field. They usually choose the wide side, or a return left against a right-footed kicker. (Generally the ball drifts to the right of a right-footed kicker and to the left of a left-footed kicker.)

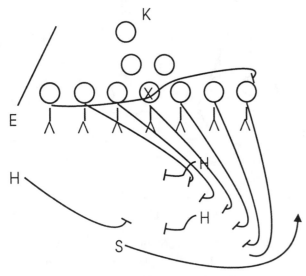

A sideline return with a single safety

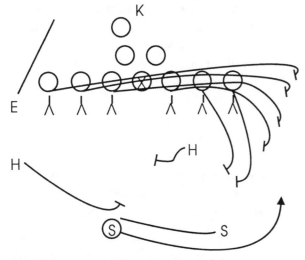

A sideline return with a reverse or a fake reverse

In the criss-cross return, safety No. 1 knows he will get the ball. If he catches the punt, he fakes the reverse. If safety No. 2 catches the punt, he hands off to safety No. 1. If the punt coverage men take wide lanes, the ball can be returned up the middle.

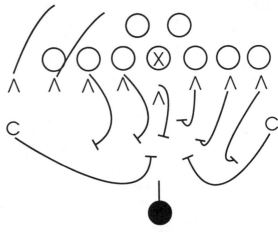

Middle return

Another type of return starts up the middle, then one of the defenders is blocked out (trapped) and the play breaks outside.

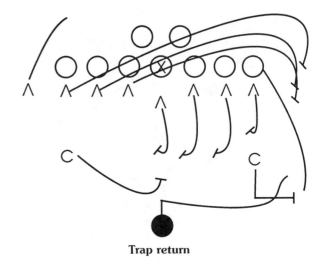

Trap return

The punt can be considered a success for the punting team if it nets 35 yards. It is a success for the returners if the punt nets less than 25 yards.

Punt Blocking

Often the scouting report plays a large part in determining whether or not to attempt to block the punt. A center who makes slow snaps to the punter or who is often inaccurate may issue an invitation to block his team's punt. A kicker who takes too long to get off a punt or who takes more than two steps before kicking is a prime target for a block.

Of course, game situations may call for a block attempt, such as when a team is behind late in the game or when the opponent is backed up close to its end zone. (Scouts often time the punter in pregame practice and in the game to determine if he is a good candidate for a punt block.)

The ball is usually kicked from about three yards in front of where the kicker started, so most punt blockers aim for a spot four to five yards in front of the kicker's starting point. This is eight or nine yards behind the center, so punt blockers have about 1.8 seconds to run eight to 12 yards, depending if they are in the middle or the end of the defensive line.

Following is an example of a heavy rush in which six blockers are at the line (excluding the offensive center who cannot be counted on to make the long snap and then block effectively). If any of the blockers chooses the wrong man to block, a blocked punt may result. Many coaches put a defender on the center to charge him. This may rattle him and increase the possibility of him making a poor snap.

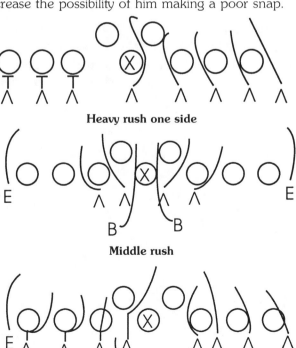

Heavy rush one side

Middle rush

A 10-man rush

Every team should rush at least one man in case of a bad snap. Some teams try to block every punt. Here is an example of a punt block that tries to free three people with the other eight in a return:

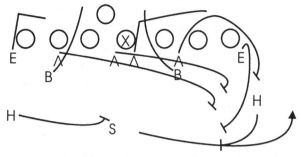

Double tandem rush and return

The Quick Kick

The "field position" advocates are strong advocates of the quick kick. They might use it on any down. "Possession" coaches seldom use a quick kick, and if they do, they are likely to use it only on third down and long yardage. Most coaches today are "possession" coaches, so the quick kick is seldom seen in modern day football.

Properly executed, a quick kick can gain 60 or more yards, while a regular punt is more likely to gain only about 35. There is also little chance of a runback with a quick kick, and as many advocates of the quick kick have observed, there is a very high likelihood of the team returning a quick kick clipping one of the members of the kicking team, so this adds another 15 yards to the kick.

Field Goals and Extra Points

The abilities of modern kickers have increased the chances of successful field goals and extra points. Less than 30 years ago, fewer than 100 field goals were kicked each year in major college football. Today there are hundreds each year.

Experience has taught coaches that it is best to tee up the ball about seven yards behind the center. If the rushers are tall, eight yards is safer. The blockers can form a solid block and force the defense around the kicking formation. If the kick is made within 1.2 seconds after the ball is snapped, it probably will be successful.

On field goal attempts that fall short, the defending team has an opportunity to return the kick, so the kicking team must be alert to covering the ball after it is kicked. Every team has at least one fake field goal as well as a special play that can be signalled if there is a foul up or "muff" on the snap or the hold. The holder, for example, can yell "Go!" to signal the ends to release for a pass. The holder must be able to make the play, which is why quarterbacks often are used to hold for kicks.

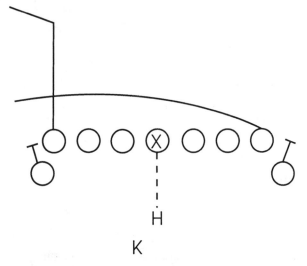

Emergency play
bad snap, holder yells "go," ends release for pass

Defending the Field Goal

In high school and college, the defense must nearly always be ready for a fake field goal or extra point because the offensive team can score two points for a run or pass after a touchdown, while only one point can be scored on a kick. In the professional game, only one point is possible, so the conversion attempt is nearly always a kick. College rules now award a team that stops a PAT (point after touchdown) two points if it advances the ball over its goal line. Consequently, when a defensive team blocks a PAT kick or intercepts a pass, it has an opportunity to score. Most teams try to block the field goal or extra point by either attempting to collapse the middle of the offensive line or by overloading at the end of the line. The scouting report is very useful in determining the most obvious weakness in the offensive blockers.

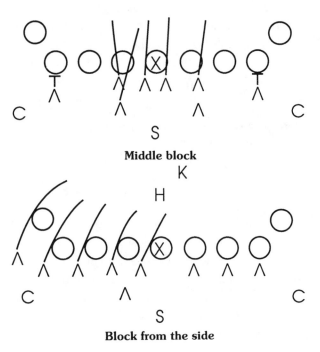

Middle block

Block from the side

Making the Breaks

As you can see, kicking situations offer many opportunities for a big play. A blocked punt is at least a 50-yard gain for the blocking team — 35 yards that would have been gained on the punt and the 15 yards behind the line where the kick was blocked. A blocked field goal returned for a score by the defense is seen as a 10- or 11-point play — the three points that the kicking team didn't score and the six or seven that the kick blocking team did score. Such a play is a great momentum builder for the blockers.

11

Movement and Contact

Football is a game of movement and contact. Your players must be able to move quickly in any direction. After moving, they must be able to make contact effectively. These are the most basic fundamentals of football.

Movement

A football player must be able to move forward, backward, sideways, on all fours, and in many awkward positions. He must therefore be agile, quick, and at times fast. (There is a real difference between quickness, which can be greatly improved through learning, and all-out speed, which is largely genetic.) He must be able to move so that he will be ready to make contact. That movement must be trained by the coach.

Running forward is the basic form of movement. In the old days, coaches often told their players to just "fall and then put your feet in front of you." Today there is a great deal of information and research on how to increase a runner's efficiency.

The mechanics of running require that a player does the following:

- *Runs on his toes.* The final power of the push-off comes from the muscles that extend from the ankle. By running on the toes a player's landing is cushioned, thereby reducing the shock of his landing.

- *Lifts his thigh to reach forward for the stride.* This helps to lengthen the stride. Lifting the thigh quickly forces the hip extensors in the other leg to push backward faster. This is critical in running faster.
- *Pushes back powerfully with his hip extensors, the gluteal muscles and hamstrings.* This is the primary component of speed.
- *Keeps his torso and head slightly forward.*
- *Keeps the arms flexed at the elbows at approximately 90 degrees.* The arms should move forward and back, not across the body.

In running, it is important for the coach to understand the importance of the cross extensor reflex. When the right leg moves forward, the left arm moves forward. By putting extra effort in the swing of the arm, the action of the leg can be increased. This is particularly true when the arm is driven back and aids in forcing the opposite leg forward.

A major weak link in sprinting ability is the slowness of the quadriceps (front of thigh) in pulling the thigh forward fast. The faster the thigh comes forward, the harder the hamstrings in the other leg can push backward. (Some coaches have used the Russian sprint training technique of running downhill or having the athlete towed behind a car. While this might increase quadriceps reaction times in some players, it is a very dangerous technique that can injure muscles, so it is not recommended.)

The power leg should be "popped backward" (extended quickly) to get maximum thrust. The driving leg should straighten. At the end of the pushing phase of the stride, the knee should "punch" forward, not upward. While a longer stride aids in developing speed, it is essential that the feet get off the ground quickly.

The runner should stay low to get started, but should straighten up in order to gain speed. The eyes control the head and the head controls the rest of the body. Keep the eyes forward. This brings up the head.

Up and down (vertical) movement reduces a person's speed. The runner must strive to be "horizontal" without having the head bobbing up and down. The eyes are a key factor in keeping the head and torso horizontal. If the head moves too far back, the body is forced more vertically because the push-off from the toes is upward.

The back should be slightly arched. The shoulder blades should be held in and the butt should be under the torso. The palms of the hands should face inward, not downward. The thumb should lightly touch the forefinger. The elbows should be bent at 90 degrees. As the arms swing up and down, the hands should move from chest to pocket — that is, from nipple height to the back of the hips. At the end of the backward arm swing the wrist should uncock. It should feel as if the runner has a hammer in his hand and snaps the hammer at the end of the swing. This extra effort is communicated to the opposite leg that is reaching forward and forces a quicker and farther extension of that leg and a lengthening of the stride.

Speed comes from what happens in the downward and backward phases of the stride. While basic all-out speed is largely inherited, the strength and form necessary for developing one's maximum speed can be taught. (Grateful acknowledgment to Jim Bush, the track coach at USC, former track coach at UCLA and running coach for the Los Angeles Raiders and the L.A. Dodgers, for contributing to this section.)

Running backward (backpedaling) is essential for defensive backs and linebackers, and is useful for offensive linemen in pass protection. It also can be used as an exercise for aiding the healing of pulled hamstrings. In running backward, the muscles in the front of the thigh and leg supply the power. The upper body must lean slightly forward. The chin should be held down. And the arms should be held similarly to the way they would be held if running forward.

The runner must reach backward with the toe in order to extend the stride as far as possible. It is impossible to have a backward stride as long as a forward stride, so one's backward steps must be very quick.

The following can be used as drills:

- Running backward for 10 or 20 yards
- Backpedaling five to 10 yards and then breaking the direction the coach signals
- Backpedaling against a receiver and then breaking with the receiver when he cuts.

Backpedaling is used in both a zone or a man-to-man defense.

Another type of backward running involves the legs running forward but the head and eyes facing backward. This is used by some zone defense teams, but it is a good agility drill for every player. The basic drill for this type of running involves changing directions every three steps.

The movement for a "three-step-and-turn" drill would be as follows:

Start to the left with a left lead step (the line of the foot should be in the exact line of the run); the next step is a crossover step with the right leg, and then another left leg step. As the left toe is planted, the toe pivots in the direction of the next direction of the run. The next step is a right step, then a left crossover, then a right step. The right toe then pivots and the left leg opens for the next step.

The pivot is essential in making this drill effective. It is a very long pivot. If the player is making 90-degree cuts, the pivot must be 270 degrees. If the player is going straight back, the pivot must be 360

A

B

C

D

Proper foot action for three-steps-and-turn-drill, with 270-degree pivot

degrees. The extensive pivot is necessary because the player continues to face the coach (or the passer in a game) as he runs backward.

The players start the drill moving at a 45-degree angle to the sideline. After the first pivot it is a 90-degree angle to the first path, and so on. As the players get more proficient at the drill they can do it on a straight line backward.

Moving sideways is another important football fundamental. Players must learn to move laterally while keeping their bodies squared to the line of scrimmage. The first type of sideways running teaches the player to move sideways facing the line of scrimmage, but not crossing the feet. The player assumes a hitting position (knees bent, torso leaning forward, head up, feet 1½ to 2 feet apart). The player moves the feet as quickly as possible and then moves on the coach's signal left or right.

The coach also can signal the player to move backward or forward in this drill. The backward movement simulates retreat pass blocking and the forward movement simulates blocking footwork and power running technique.

The second type of sideways running is the universally used "carioca" drill. This drill teaches the player to be able to perform a crossover step while keeping the torso facing the line of scrimmage. It also works to loosen the hips and to increase agility. While running directly to the side (such as on a yard line), the player crosses the following foot in front of the body, then steps with the leading foot, then steps with the following foot behind the body. The trailing foot steps ahead of the leading foot on one step, then steps behind the leading foot on the next step. The drill should be done going right and then left.

Moving on all fours is another basic drill for agility and speed. Because football players are sometimes knocked down, they must be able to either move quickly from that position or be able to get back up and move. Sometimes the player must be able to move on all fours in a game. Teams that use scramble blocking have their blockers on all fours during the block. Teams that move their defensive linemen before the snap will need this drill.

The crab position is approximately the same as a four-point defensive stance. The feet should be slightly wider than shoulder width. The feet are pointing toward the hands. The head is up. The back is approximately parallel to the ground.

In the crabbing drill, the coach signals which direction the players move while in the crab position. They can move forward, backward, right, or left. When moving, it is essential that the basic crab position be maintained. The hands or feet should not move more than six to eight inches (for a big man it might be as wide as 12 inches) away from the original position. The hands and feet shouldn't ever come closer together than they were in the original position. If the hands or legs are close together at any point in the movement, the player's base is reduced and he can be pushed over. Consequently, when doing the crabbing drill, foot quickness is much more important than overall speed.

Another all-fours skill is the ability to roll, come to the crab position and then jump to the hitting position. A drill for this is to have the players start in the crab position. On the coach's signal the players roll in one direction, then jump to a hitting position. The coach signals the players to get down to the crab position, then signals again to roll in another direction. This is often done with a seven-man sled.

Training for speed is done with quality work. Long runs do not help in the development of speed. Long runs help to develop more of the slow-twitch muscle fibers, while speed work or weight lifting help to develop the fast-twitch fibers. Football is not really an endurance activity, so the slow-twitch muscles are not as important as the fast-twitch muscles.

(There are three types of muscle fibers: slow twitch (red), which store hemoglobin and are essential in endurance activities; fast twitch (white), which are used for strength and speed work; and intermediate fibers, which can be trained to become either slow- or fast-twitch fibers, depending on the type of exercises done. (To illustrate the importance of these types of fibers to different types of athletes, the percentage of quick-twitch fibers in sprinters is 63 percent, in weightlifters 60 percent, in cyclists 41 percent, and in marathoners 17 percent.)

Quick-twitch fibers are developed by weightlifting, plyometrics, and sprinting. The weight training exercises used for speed should be specific. The abdominal muscles, the calves, and the thighs are of primary importance. Shoulder flexors and extensors are also important.

One's ability to be strong or fast depends on several factors, as follows:

- The number of muscle fibers in a muscle that are able to contract at one time. No one can make all of their muscle fibers contract simultaneously.
- The number of quick-twitch fibers in the muscle. The athlete is born with a certain percentage of these, but he can develop them from the intermediate fibers that he inherited.
- The strength of the individual muscle fibers. Strength-building exercises can increase the cross sectional diameter of the muscle fibers, thereby making them stronger.
- The mechanics of the muscle attachment to the bone. The inherited length of the bones and the placement of the tendon into the bone is very important in developing strength. For example if two people have forearms that are 12 inches long and one has a biceps tendon that attaches one-half inch from the joint and the other has a tendon that inserts an inch from the bone, other things being equal, the person with the attachment farther out on the bone will be stronger. For running, if one athlete has a longer heel bone, with the calf muscle therefore attaching farther from the ankle, he will have an advantage over a person with a shorter heel bone.

Plyometrics are a relatively recent addition to the techniques useful in developing speed and power. They increase the number of muscle fibers contracting at one time. The theory of plyometrics is that when the muscles are forced into powerful eccentric (lengthening) contractions, more muscle fibers are being called into the contraction. If the muscle is immediately forced into a concentric (shortening) contraction, many of those muscles will respond.

If an athlete jumps from a box between one and four feet high, many of his calf muscle fibers must be used to catch him. If he can immediately jump upward, many of those muscle fibers contract and help him to jump higher than he could ordinarily jump if he had started from a standing position.

An athlete should be well-conditioned before starting in a plyometric program. Also, the plyometric program should be done with relatively few repetitions during a week and only a few days a week. Remember, it is quality, not quantity, that is essential for speed work. (See the chapter on weight training for more on this subject.)

A highly successful sprint and conditioning program has been developed by Jim Bush, the head track coach at the University of Southern California. He has a player run 100 yards at about 85 to 90 percent of his maximum speed. The player then jogs back to the starting position. This must all be accomplished within two minutes. As the two-minute period ends, the player runs another 100 yards at 85 to 90 percent efficiency. The cycle is repeated 10 times, so it is a 20-minute drill. It emphasizes running fast under control and conditioning.

Coach Bush emphasizes that all-out speed is not generally essential for football players. What is important is how fast they can run while still being under control. This allows them to cut, spin, and maintain balance, something a player cannot do if he is running all-out. For this reason, Coach Bush believes that football coaches put too much emphasis on the 40-yard dash time and not enough emphasis on controlled running. A football game is not a track meet.

Contact

Probably the first skill that coaches should teach their players is the proper position for contact — the hitting position. The concepts to teach in helping a player learn the hitting position are as follows:

- The legs supply the power. They drive the body through the opponent.
- The back should be slightly arched. The head should be up.

- No matter how high the contact is made, whether at the knees or the chest of an opponent, the head must be higher than the shoulders, the shoulders higher than the hips, the hips higher than the knees, and the knees higher than the ankles. This enables the hitter to hit up and through the opponent.

When a player hits up and through an opponent, he puts more of the opponent's weight on himself. This makes the opponent "weigh less" and makes the hitter "weigh more." This is because the hitter has more weight on his cleats and the person being hit has less weight on his.

An essential factor to get across to players is that as they hit, they must be off-balance. If they are balanced, the person they are hitting will knock them backward. They must be more off-balance, in a forward manner, than the opponent to knock the opponent back.

A rough equation can be used to show the importance of this to a player, especially a smaller player: (The actual equations necessary to calculate the linear and angular forces involved in hitting are far too complicated for this book.)

The weight of the player multiplied by the forward speed of the player equals the momentum of the player (the moment of force). Or:

$$WT \times SP = FORCE$$

The weight of the player might change during the hit if the hitter is hitting upward — making himself heavier and his opponent lighter. The forward speed of the player means the speed toward the goal line. If a ball carrier is running parallel to the line of scrimmage and is hit by a player running toward his goal line, the ball carrier has no forward speed because he is not going toward his goal line. If he is moving at a 45-degree angle toward his goal line, such as he might be on a slant play or during a sweep, he would have half of his actual speed credited toward his forward speed. If both players are moving at 45-degree angles, each would have half of his actual speed applied toward the equation.

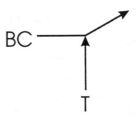

Ball carrier parallel to line, tackler straight at goal

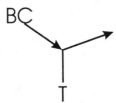

Ball carrier at 45-degree angle to goal

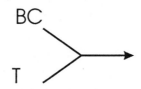

Both players at 45-degree angles

Both players heading toward their goals

Sometimes the ball carrier hits lower than the tackler. When this happens he has the advantage and probably will push the tackler backward. However, if the tackler is very big and the ball carrier very small, the weight advantage in the equation might be such that the tackler wins. But if both weigh about the same and the back is moving faster and lower, the back would have a higher "moment of force" in the equation and would win the battle.

Teaching the hitting position can be done with the players in their warm-up alignments. Coaches should check to make sure the players':

- feet are under their shoulders or slightly wider
- toes are straight ahead, with feet parallel with the sidelines
- knees are bent
- torso is slightly forward
- head is up

When teaching the hitting position for tackling, have the players' arms out to the side or close to the body, but the elbows bent at a 90-degree angle, depending on which tackling technique you are going to teach. If you are teaching offensive line, you can have the players take their hitting position with their arms out in front of them, such as in the set-up for pass blocking.

Because this is a basic fundamental, it should be reviewed every day during the warm-up or agility periods of the practice.

Proper form for diving

When this is accomplished, the player should learn to "dive and drive." In this drill the player dives out as in the diving drill, but after he extends his legs in the diving action he drives his legs, taking as many steps as possible, before landing on his chest. He should be off-balance through this entire dive and drive action. As he becomes more proficient he will be able to take more steps before hitting the ground. The coach should make certain that he stays low throughout the drill. Obviously the higher his head is from the ground the more steps he can take. But this defeats the purpose of the drill. The head should never be more than $2\frac{1}{2}$ to 3 feet above the ground.

This drill is essential to every aspect of contact — the blocker scrambling in a low block, the tackler driving through his opponent, and the runner driving for extra yards. Runners should do the drill with a ball in one arm, covering it with two arms just before contact with the ground.

Tackling is the basic defensive fundamental. Although defensive linemen often tackle by simply reaching out and grabbing the ball carrier, they should learn the fundamentals of form tackling.

In the ideal tackle, the tackler has his head up, back arched, legs driving the back through the ball-carrier, arms wrapping hard around the ball carrier, eyes open, and is driving the ball carrier backward.

High form tackling teaches the defender to hit with the legs, keep the back arched, keep the eyes open, and wrap the arms. In practicing this technique, the ball carrier moves into the standing tackler who is in the form tackling position (back arched, feet wide, and arms out to the side).

Hitting position for an offensive lineman

Teaching getting off-balance is important because every block and tackle starts and/or ends with the aggressor being off-balance forward. This skill can be done in a diving drill. The players line up in a three- or four-point stance. On the coach's signal they all dive out on the grass. It is best if they do it one at a time so that the coach can check to see that the drive is somewhat upward — head up, head above shoulders, shoulders above hips, hips above knees, knees above feet.

Two arm techniques can be used. The first is the wrap-around technique. Here the tackler keeps his arms wide and swings them parallel to the ground as he makes contact. If the ball carrier dodges the tackler there is a good chance that the arms will still make contact with the runner and bring the tackler into the ball carrier, even if his body extension has missed the target point on the runner.

The second technique has the tackler with his arms at his side but bent 90 degrees at the elbows. The tackler drives the arms up and under the arms of the runner. This upward action completes the body extension of the tackler, giving more upward force. Also, if the arms are driven under the armpits of the runner a fumble is more likely.

When the ball carrier is six to 12 inches from the tackler, the tackler explodes his legs, aims his nose about four inches from the side of the ball carrier, makes contact, extends up and through the ball carrier, and makes his arm contact, either wrapping up the ball carrier or driving him upward. He should also "grab cloth" because it gives the tackler more chance to control and hold the ball carrier.

If using the wrap-around technique, his arms must be kept parallel to the ground. (Players tend to drop their arms lower than shoulder level. This humps the back, which places more strain on the lower back muscles and reduces the upward drive of the tackle.) He then carries the ball carrier five or six steps. His arms must be wrapped hard or he drops the offensive man.

The coach should check to make sure of the following:

- The tackler's back is arched, not humped
- The eyes stay open through the tackle (the eyes should "explode" open as his legs "explode" upward)
- The arms are parallel with the ground, if using the wrap-around technique and he "grabs cloth"
- The legs maintain a wide base throughout the tackle

Wrap-around tackle

Lifting the ball carrier

Upward arm drive

This skill should be taught moving forward into the tackle, alternating hitting with the right shoulder and then the left shoulder. It should then be taught moving diagonally into the ball carrier with the right shoulder and then the left shoulder, keeping the head in front of the ball carrier. It can also be taught full speed with the ball carrier three yards from the tackler.

This skill is seldom seen in a game, but it should be taught because it emphasizes all of the basic fundamentals of tackling. When it is seen in a game it is generally in the kicking game or it is a linebacker stepping into a hole with only a ball carrier coming at him.

The low form tackle is more like what happens in a game. The fundamentals remain the same as in the high form tackle, but the tackler is off-balance and lower as he makes contact. His base is wide. His head is up with his back arched. He explodes through the ball carrier as he drives his legs. He finishes with his body on top of the ball carrier's and his arms still wrapped around the ball carrier.

It is essential that a tackler learns to get off-balance as he explodes. This is true whether he is hitting directly into the ball carrier or attacking from the side. Because injuries often occur when drilling this technique, some coaches have the tackle performed onto a high jump pit. This virtually eliminates the chance of an injury to either player from hitting the ground.

Stripping the ball is seen more and more at the professional level. It is still not used enough at the lower levels. Remember that if a ball is stripped from the offense and recovered by the defense it is worth at least the distance of a punt. So a stripped ball fumble would be worth at least 35 yards — three-and-a-half first downs.

One way to strip the ball is to lift outward on the ball carrier's elbow with one hand, then punch the ball past the elbow with the palm of the other hand. This can be worked on during tackling drills with the second or third tackler going for the ball.

Lifting ball carrier's elbow

A common method used by the pros is to grab the ball or the ball carrying arm and pull it downward. This releases the ball. This technique is especially effective against players who do not carry the ball properly — carrying it at arms length rather than in the crook of the elbow.

Pulling downward on arm

Drills

Form tackling. This drill should be done with the ball carrier being tackled into the foam pits used by high jumpers and pole vaulters. Because tackling a ball carrier onto the ground often results in injuries to one of the players (broken arms and sprains are not uncommon) the risk of injury is greatly reduced.

Full speed tackling. Many drills can be used for full speed tackling. The most common are as follows:

- Both players on their backs with their heads touching or nearly touching. On the coach's command the players jump up and the defender tackles the ball carrier.
- Both players crouched but facing away from each other. On the coach's command they spin and make contact.
- The tackler on his back between bags two yards apart. The ball carrier is three yards away. They both move on the coach's command.
- One-on-one with a blocker is done between bags spaced two yards apart. The blocker attempts to block the tackler, the ball carrier reads the head of the blocker and attempts to make the tackle.

12

Offensive Line Fundamentals

Offensive line fundamentals can be taught in many ways. The stance and the types of blocks employed should be determined by a team's offensive theory. Coaches using a quick-hitting offense might choose to use a four-point stance and scramble blocking (on all fours). Run-and-shoot passing teams probably will use a balanced three-point stance or even a two-point stance.

Stance

The three-point stance is used by most teams. The traditional three-point stance begins with the right toes even with the left instep. The feet are shoulder width or slightly wider and are perpendicular to the line of scrimmage.

From this basic foot position, the player bends the knees, squats, then aligns the outside of his right hand just inside the line of his right foot. The hand is placed about 18 inches ahead of the inside edge of the toes. The fingers can be extended, with the weight on the pads of the fingers, or can be somewhat flexed so that the weight is carried on the second knuckle and the middle bone of the fingers. The back should be nearly horizontal, with the hips slightly higher than the shoulders, and the head should be up.

Individual differences must be accounted for in placing the width of the feet and the placement of the hand. Shorter players should have their hands closer to their feet. Very big players generally have

Three-point stance

their hands farther from their toes. It is the length of the torso that determines just where the hand will be most effectively placed. The other arm will be held below the shoulders with approximately a 90-degree angle of the arm and shoulder and a 90-degree angle at the elbow.

Adjustments to this basic stance can be made according to the coach's offensive theory. A team that "fires out" hard might place the hand farther forward or put more weight on the hand. A team that pulls, cross blocks, traps, or drops back in pass protection usually has a more balanced stance without excessive weight on the hand.

Another adjustment might be the placement of the feet. A team that pulls and angle blocks a great deal might be more effective if the feet are not staggered, with both feet equidistant from the line of scrimmage. Whatever foot position you choose, remember that it is easier to pull toward the foot that is farther back. So a right guard who generally pulls right would be in a better stance having his right foot back. However, if he pulled primarily across the center he might be better off with the left foot back. If he pulls both ways he might be more effective having both feet nearly even.

The four-point stance (both hands on the ground) is preferred by some coaches. This enables the players to have more weight forward with less discomfort on the hands. Four-point stance teams are usually quickness teams that need to explode into the defenders quickly to make a hole for the ball carrier.

It should be noted that it is not how far forward the hands are from the feet that enables the player to get off the ball fast. What is important is how far the shoulders are over the hands. The farther forward the shoulders, the more weight is being carried on the hands and the quicker the player can move forward. Of course, he can't pull or angle block as effectively nor can he drop back in cup protection as quickly. Some coaches allow their linemen in a four-point stance to "cheat" by pulling their shoulders farther away from the line of scrimmage if they are pulling or pass protecting. Moving the shoulders back takes more weight off the hands. However, alert defenders might be able to pick up this key.

As mentioned previously, your players' stances should be determined by what you want them to do. Hayden Fry, the Iowa coach, has put his tight end in a standing (two-point) stance. His thinking was that the tight end could see the defensive backs and linebackers better and therefore was a more effective receiver by standing rather than using the traditional three-point stance. So in Fry's theory of offense, the little that might be lost in blocking effectiveness is more than made up for by the increased ability as a receiver. And, in fact, Coach Fry said that his ends really didn't lose much effectiveness as blockers.

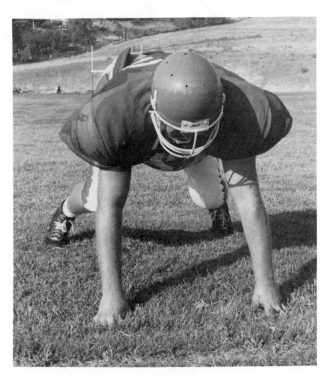

Four-point stance

The Center Snap

The center is the most important lineman on most offensive lines. He should be a leader, and for many teams is the best blocker. His stance utilizes the same principles as the other offensive linemen. If he is to angle block and cup protect he should be more balanced. If he is going forward most of the time, he should have more weight forward. The center may have only one hand down, the one that's on the ball, or may have one hand on the ball and the other on the ground for support. The "four-point" center stance is more useful when the center is blocking straight ahead on quick plays.

Starting from a four-point stance, the center lifts one hand — usually the right hand for right-handed players. The coach places the ball exactly where that hand had been. The player then places his hand on the ball. This is the position he takes as soon as the huddle has broken and he has led the team to the line of scrimmage.

Snapping the ball is an extremely important fundamental. The play can't get started if the ball is not snapped properly. The method of snapping the ball should be determined by how the coach wants the quarterback to take it. Most teams have the snapper turn the ball as it moves from the ground to the quarterback's hands.

In coaching the snap, start with the ball in the quarterback's hands just exactly as he wants to take it — usually with the laces across the fingers of his passing hand. From this "perfect" position, the snapper reaches up and takes the ball from the quarterback and puts it on the ground. Note where the laces are. This is where they should be before the snap. Most right-handed centers find that they must start with the laces 1/8 to 1/4 of a turn counter-clockwise.

Only the center can be "in" the line of scrimmage. The line of scrimmage is actually a zone bounded by two planes. Each plane extends from each end of the ball, parallel with the goal lines, and as wide as the sidelines. The plane extends from the ground to the sky. Consequently any player, other than the center, who puts his head or his arm into that zone is offside (encroaching) if the ball is snapped while he is in that zone. In high school football, merely putting any part of the body into that zone, even if the ball isn't snapped, is a penalty. This penalty is called "encroachment" and is a five-yard penalty.

When the center comes to the line of scrimmage and assumes his pre-snap stance, he should adjust the ball so that it is just the way he wants it for the snap. The referee generally places the ball with the laces straight up. The center should adjust the ball by placing all five fingers on the near end of the ball and twisting it until the laces are where he wants them. By adjusting the ball this way, he will not ever be penalized for attempting to draw the opponents offside with a false snap. This type of penalty is more likely to be called if the player puts his hand on top of the ball and then moves it.

When the laces are properly positioned, the snapper should put his hand on the ball and slowly tip it to whatever angle he desires for the snap. After this angle is achieved, he should not move the ball lest a penalty be called for attempting to draw his opponents offside.

Adjusting the ball

The T-formation snap should be as fast as the center can make it. Strong latissimus dorsi and triceps muscles are necessary for a hard snap. The snapper should drive the ball hard up into his crotch where the quarterback's hands will be waiting. The snapper should be stepping into his block as he snaps the ball. It is not "snap, then block" but rather "block while snapping."

Because the snapper is moving as he snaps the ball, the quarterback must move his hands forward with the snapper until he knows for certain that he has the ball. Many fumbles occur because either the snapper slows his arm movement as the ball approaches the quarterback's hands, or the quarterback pulls his hands away before he has control of the snap.

Snapping the ball

The long snap used in single-wing type offenses and in shotgun attacks is much more difficult to master. In this snap, the positioning of the laces in the pre-snap adjustment should be for the comfort of the snapper, not the quarterback. Usually the right-handed snapper turns the laces at least a quarter-turn clockwise (to his right). He takes a grip as if he is going to pass the ball.

The snapper can use a one- or a two-handed snap. In a one-hand snap he merely passes the ball between his legs. If using a two-hand snap he puts his non-power hand (the left hand for right-handed snappers) on top of the ball. It is there simply to guide the ball. Using two hands usually helps enable a straight pass because the shoulders are forced to stay even. If only one hand is on the ball, the right shoulder might drop and the ball might drift left.

At the lower levels of football, the snapper should look at his target. It is generally best to aim the snap at the thighs rather than at chest height. During the excitement of the game, the snapper is highly likely to make his mistakes as high snaps. A snap aimed at the thighs that is three feet too high is not a problem, but a snap aimed at the shoulders that is three feet too high may result in a large loss on the play.

At the higher levels of play, the snapper may practice the blind snap in which he looks at his blocking target rather than at the target of his snap. It is even more important to aim the ball low when snapping blind because the chance of missing the target is much greater.

The Start

The start is the first action from the stance as the player moves toward his blocking assignment. Many coaches work on "stance and start" at every practice. Because the offense knows the snap count, it should be able to get a slight jump on the defense. In fact, a well-coached team can have its bodies six or more inches out of the stance before the defenders begin to react to the movement of the ball or the offensive linemen.

Coaches can illustrate how big a jump their offensive linemen can get on the defense by taking a coin and giving it to a lineman. The lineman holds his hand wide open with the coin in his palm. The coach puts his hand about 12 inches above the player's hand and tells the player to close his hand to protect the coin as soon as he sees the coach's hand start moving downward toward the coin. Unless the coach has the quickness of a turtle, he always wins. This should prove to offensive lineman the importance of their starts.

Because offensive players move on sound (snap count) and defenders move on movement, starts should be practiced with the snap count. Offensive linemen should "get off" on the ball. They do this by anticipating the snap count — if that is possible with the cadence that the team is using.

Cadence and the Snap Count

The snap count should be geared to getting the offensive players starting at the same instant. A secondary consideration is to fool the defense. Teams that vary their snap counts from play to play might fool the defense in one of two ways. If they generally go on the second count, they can sometimes go on the first count and catch the defenders not quite ready to play. Or they can go on the third count, hoping that the defenders jump offside on the second count, because they expected the ball to be snapped earlier.

The number of syllables in a snap count is important for the offense. While some teams use only a single syllable, such as "go," "hike," or "hut," other teams use a two-syllable count, such as "hu-two" (hut two), and other teams use a three-syllable count such as "a-hu-two" (a hut two) or "re-dee-go" (ready go). Dr. Fred Miller, now athletic director at San Diego State University, did his master's thesis on snap counts. He found that the three-count snap count got the offensive linemen firing off quicker on the ball. Apparently the previous two syllables alerted them to the snap count more effectively.

Rhythmic and non-rhythmic cadences are also a consideration when determining your approach to the snap count. In a rhythmic cadence the counts are equally spaced, such as "go-go-go." In a non-rhythmic cadence the pauses between the counts vary. So a non-rhythmic count might be "go———go—go———go." Non-rhythmic cadences might force the defense to jump offside. Some quarterbacks do this very well by varying the tones of their voices. If the snap count is on 3, but he calls the second count louder than normal, the defense might jump.

Should you vary the snap count? A number of years ago the No. 1 team in the nation went on the first snap count every play of the season. The coach felt that he didn't want his players making a mistake, so he never varied the count. Some coaches use a long count and nearly always go on the last sound, but might occasionally go on an earlier sound hoping to get the jump on the defense, which is used to having the ball snapped on the last sound.

An example would be a cadence in which the quarterback says, "Set...down...hike...ready go." At least 90 percent of the plays start on the "ready go" count. It would be understood that if no snap were called in the huddle, "ready go" would be the snap count, so no offensive player should ever move before hearing "ready go." Therefore, an offensive offside or motion penalty never should be called, eliminating a major potential offensive mistake. However, the ball might be snapped earlier, perhaps giving the offense a small advantage over the defense that had become used to going on the "ready go" command. If the play is called on an earlier count than "ready go," the worst that should happen to the offense is that an unalert player would be late in starting — but that would not cause a penalty.

A major part of coaching is eliminating mistakes. If you can eliminate all offside and motion penalties by the offense, you have made a major stride in offensive success, because it is very difficult to overcome any offensive penalty.

In using such a multiple-syllable cadence, in this case a four-word cadence, the coach might tie certain offensive responsibilities to each word. For example, the line might break the huddle and align in a two-point stance. On "set," the offense takes its down stance positions. On "down," the offense shifts. On "hike," it goes into motion if that is part of the play. On "ready go," the ball is snapped. If there is no shift or motion, the quarterback might have the ball snapped on "set," "down," or "hike." If there is a shift but no motion, the ball could be snapped on "hike" or "ready go."

Starting in a two-point stance gives the offensive team an advantage. The defensive linemen must be in their down stances (three- or four-point stances) because they know the ball can be snapped with the offense in a two-point stance. The longer the defenders are in their down stances the more cramped their muscles become and the less likely they will be able to react quickly to the movement of the offense.

Shifting from a basic set to a different set, such as a tight-T to a wing-T or tight ends to split ends, requires the defense to make an adjustment that increases its chances of "blowing" an assignment.

Blocking

Blocking is the basic offensive fundamental. And because most of the blocking is done by the offensive line, most of its time should be spent working on this. Several types of one-on-one blocks are available, as are several types of double-team blocks, and a wedge block. There are two basic blocking techniques: the higher-targeted drive block and the lower scramble block. These techniques are used whether the blocker is blocking straight ahead, at an angle, in a double-team or combo block, or executing a running trap or lead block.

The Drive Block

The drive block is the most basic block in football. The objective of the drive block is to get the opponent moved away from the line of scrimmage, and hopefully to be knocked off his feet. The contact can be made with the heels of the hands or with the shoulder. Some coaches teach the use of the hands for most situations but use the shoulder contact in short yardage situations. Others use the shoulder block all the time.

The hand contact technique makes it more likely that the defender can be stood up and possibly pushed onto his back and "decleated." It also might enable the blocker to maintain contact with the defender for a longer period of time. It therefore might be more desirable for teams that allow their backs to "option run" — looking for any hole that develops. This is more common for I-formation teams.

The first step is with the foot farther from the line of scrimmage. The palms of the hands, with the fingers pointing upward and the wrists close together, drive under the shoulder pads. This is called "the fit." Depending on the interpretation of the rules at your level, the player might be taught to "grab cloth" so that he can better control the defender.

The eyes must be under the defender's chest and looking up at his neck. The elbows should be inside the shoulders and pointed toward the ground. The legs supply the power of the block. When the blocker feels that he has the leverage on the defender and is lower than him, he explodes his legs and arms, knocking the defender upward and backward. This should "decleat" the defender and knock him off his feet. The blocker continues to follow through with his block and finishes the block by landing on the defender. The unofficial record for "decleaters" in one game is 35, by a USC lineman.

Coaching points for the hand technique include the following:

- Aim under the shoulder pads.
- Hit on the sternum with the heels of the hands, fingers pointed up.
- Keep the elbows pointed down and inside the shoulder pads.
- Drive the hands up and through the defender's chest.
- Widen the feet while taking short choppy steps.
- Keep the feet pointed straight ahead.
- Finish the block by continuing to drive, lifting the defender with the arms and legs.
- Drive over the defender, knocking him on his back and then landing on him.
- Stop only on the whistle.

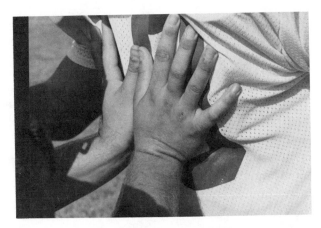

HAND CONTACT TECHNIQUE
Hand fit

Contact

Explosion

Finish of "decleater"

The shoulder contact technique, however, might be better in protecting the hole with the blocker's head. This may be preferable for teams that hit quick and have a designated hole to attack, such as a wishbone or veer team. It also is more effective against hard-charging defenders in short-yardage situations. In this block, the blocker steps with the foot on the same side of his body as the shoulder with which he will block. This is called the "near" foot. Some coaches want a hard charge directly into the defender, while others want the blocker to dip, by dropping the "far" knee, which enables him to hit more on an upward path.

The eyes should aim at the near number of the defender — the number on which the blocker's shoulder will contact. It is important that the eyes aim at the body and then have the head slide to the side. If the eyes aim at the side of the defender's body, the point where they actually end, the blocker may miss his target completely.

As the contact is made, the blocker should widen his elbow so that his blocking surface is widened. He then lifts and moves his opponent. The lift is made easier by having him "look to the sky" as soon as he has made contact. When the blocker actually looks at the sky, he can't help but drop his butt. This will give him a lifting action on the defender. He should also "pinch with his ear" to aid him in maintaining contact with the defender. Without the constant attention to applying pressure into the opponent, the opponent might slip off the block. Another aid in reducing the defender's ability to slip the block is to bring the far hand across the blocker's chest and into side of the defender.

The feet should remain parallel with the direction of the block, and they should widen to $2\frac{1}{2}$ to 3 feet. The wider base makes it easier to maintain contact with the defender.

Keeping the blocker's feet perpendicular to the line of the block is essential for two reasons. First, the action of the hip and knee are more effective if in a straight line. Second, if the feet turn out, a very common mistake, the blocker is pushing with the inside edge of his shoe and the few cleats near that inside edge. He has much more traction if all of his cleats are in contact with the ground. This is possible only if his feet are pointing forward. Many coaches emphasize that the feet be turned inward to compensate for players' natural tendency to "toe out."

The feet should take short, choppy steps. If the player took long steps he would have only one foot in contact with the ground for a long period of time and could be easily thrown off the defender.

Coaching points for the shoulder block including the following:

- Aim at the near number.
- Explode into the defender starting with the near foot.
- Extend your blocking surface on contact by widening the forearm.
- Look to the sky.
- Widen the base and keep the feet straight.
- Take short, choppy steps while finishing the block.
- Stop only after you have heard the whistle.

The Scramble Block

The scramble technique is a quicker and lower method of getting to the defender, but the blocker doesn't get the effect of lifting his opponent. The point of aim of the eyes is the lower part of the opponent's thigh.

When scramble blocking, the blocker explodes on the defender using the same technique as described in the "dive and drive" drill. The near shoulder should make contact with the opponent and the opposite hand should be on or near the ground. The player then scrambles as he maintains contact.

Scramble block

The defender might not be contacted effectively because he is slanting away from the block. Because of this, the scramble blocker must always be prepared to use his leg to make the block. If the blocker's head and shoulders have missed the target he must bring his inside leg up to contact the defender. The thigh should be parallel with the ground and should contact the opponent's thigh.

Using the thigh

After the thigh makes contact with the opponent, it drops back toward the ground. The foot returns to the ground. If properly done, the blocker has his near knee between the legs of his opponent and is driving on all fours — "crabbing."

Basic Blocking Techniques

The person being blocked is not always directly ahead of the blocker. Therefore, football terms have been devised to tell the blocker who or how to block. There may be some small variations in techniques, but basically the drive block and the scramble block are used in any of the following situations. Usually it is up to the lineman to determine which technique he will use. Of course it is up to the coach to see that the lineman has ample opportunity to practice whichever of these situations he will use in a game.

The hook block is used when the defender is slightly outside of the blocker. The objective is to stop the penetration of the defender and, if possible, to move him down the line back toward the center rather than driving him into the defensive backfield.

To make this block, the player can either step out with his outside foot (a position step) and then make one of the above-mentioned drive blocks, or can scramble with a reverse shoulder block.

The angle block is used when the defender is set farther away from the blocker, either to the inside or the outside. He might be in the gap or on the next offensive player in or out. Often an angle block made on a man outside is called a "reach" block. A block made on the man inside is a "cut-off" block.

The first step should be with the foot nearest the defender. The second step crosses the first. The block can then be high or low, but in either case the blocker attempts to get his head in front of the defender to stop penetration.

If using the higher drive block, the blocker can use his hands or a shoulder technique. The defender probably will not see the blocker, because he has been concentrating on the blocker closer to him.

Against a man in the gap who is charging hard, the scrambling "reverse shoulder block" might be the better technique. In this block, the player steps directly parallel with the line of scrimmage and makes contact with the shoulder which had been his far shoulder — the shoulder away from the target defender. From this point it is a scramble block. The point of aim is dependent on the speed of the charge of the defender. If the defender is quick, the blocker must move straight down the line in order to cut off the defender's penetration. If the defender is slower, the angle of approach can be more toward the line of scrimmage.

Reverse shoulder

Using the thigh

The cutoff block is similar to the reach block, but it is made from the "outside in" rather than from the "inside out."

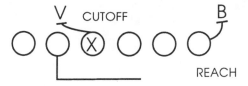

Cutoff and reach blocks

Blocking a linebacker who is aligned in front of the player is more difficult than blocking a lineman. This is because the blocker does not know where his target will be (possibly stunting) and the backer has more room to see the block and maneuver around it. If a blocker is playing a linebacker who is keying him, he might be able to fire out directly at the linebacker and the backer charges into the blocker. This is called the "he come, I come" key. But if the blocker charges hard straight ahead and the backer is stunting or keying a back and moving toward the play action, the blocker will miss his target.

Many plays are designed to block the linebacker with a man farther out on the line of scrimmage in the direction of the play, (a seal block), or by pulling a man through the hole (a lead block).

After contact is about to be made above the waist, the blocker can use either the higher drive block or the lower scramble technique. Whichever is used, contact must be maintained. It is not important to move the backer; keeping him away from the ball carrier is enough. An effective ball carrier can help the blocker by setting up the defender, faking one way to make the block easier, then cutting back.

The downfield block is similar to blocking a backer, but is even more difficult unless it is well-timed. If the blocker maneuvers just ahead of the ball carrier, the runner can set up the block with a fake, wait for the block, then cut off of it. Because the blocker can no longer initiate his block with low contact, it is generally easier to use the hands on the defender, just as in the high drive block.

The downfield block must start high, above the waist, but can drop low after contact, or if the defender puts his hands on the blocker and wards him off. When blocking high, the blocker merely makes and maintains contact with the defender. Often the defender will fall down because the blocker is moving forward fast while the defender might be moving forward slowly or even moving backward. When using this higher blocking technique, one blocker might be able to make several blocks on one play.

When forced low by the defender's hands, the blocker should bring his thigh up, as in the scramble block. He is then blocking with his side and his thigh.

Using the side and thigh

A newer approach to the downfield block utilizes the hands into the chest of the defender. As the blocker gets right next to the defender he yells "Hey!" to get the defender to turn toward him. He then hits the defender in the chest with his hands in the proper "fit" position. This block also can be used on punt and kickoff return blocking.

The double-team block is basic to power football. It should always create a hole. The two major methods of double teaming are the driving block and the post and pivot.

The driving block has both blockers shoulder blocking into the defender. The inside blocker has his head inside the defender and the outside blocker has his head on the outside. This block generally drives the defender into the path of pursuing linebackers, but it might open a hole for a "scraping" backer.

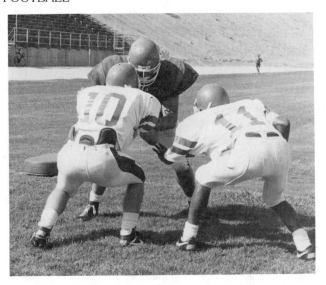

Post and pivot

Double teaming a man in the gap is done by having the two players who are double teaming take their first steps with their inside feet and step together. This should seal their bodies together; they then drive the defender straight back.

Double-team block, with tight seal of hips

The post and pivot block has the inside man on the double team hitting up and into the defender. This should stand up the opponent. The driving blocker then blocks the defender down the line of scrimmage. This type of block reduces the chance of a scraping or stunting linebacker of coming into the hole, but it doesn't cut off the deeper pursuit.

Man in gap to be double teamed

Stepping together to make the seal

The key point in making any double-team block is that the two blockers "seal" their shoulders and hips so that the defender cannot split their block. The defender tries to defeat the double team by either splitting it or dropping to the ground and keeping himself in the hole. The blockers must therefore get under the defender and seal themselves together in order to make the block effective.

Some coaches prefer to teach the double team as merely the start of the block. When the blockers start the defender backward, the inside player releases and picks up the defenders in pursuit.

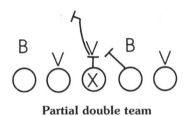

Partial double team

The trap block has the blocker, usually a guard, passing behind at least one of his fellow linemen. He should get as close as possible to the blocker at the inside of the hole. He then finds the defender outside of the hole and takes an "inside angle out," blocking with the shoulder closest to his own backfield. If the defender is charging aggressively it is an easy block, but if the defender plays correctly he will be close to the line of scrimmage and reduce the size of the hole, so it becomes a difficult block.

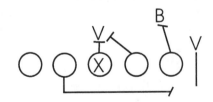

Trap by off guard

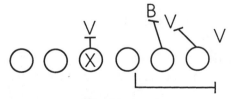

Onside trap

The load block is similar to the trap, but the play will be going wide so the blocker protects the running back by keeping his head between the potential tackler and the ball carrier. The load block generally is low and similar to the scramble technique. This type of block is used by both backs and linemen.

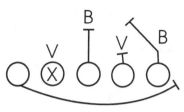

Load block

When the blocker makes contact he should drive his inside forearm into the crotch of the defender and then turn his body upfield so that he can protect the sideline with his head.

The lead block has the blocker, usually a pulling lineman or fullback, lead the ball carrier through the hole. If no one is in the hole, he should look inside to pick up a pursuing backer. A shoulder or drive block should be used.

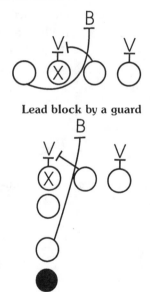

Lead block by a guard

Lead block by a fullback

The wedge block is a power block, usually used in short-yardage situations. Three or more players block an area. The middle man in the wedge, usually the center, should get under the defender so that he doesn't fall down and trip the wedge.

Here, the players outside of the center block into the next offensive man inside of them. The guards block into the armpits of the center and the tackles block into the armpits of the guards. If backs are involved, they block into their linemen.

The wedge was a staple of the single-wing full-back buck, but it can be effective for T-formation teams in quarterback sneaks or fullback bucks. It is effective against a defender who plays high and uses a hit and react technique, but is not as much against a hard-charging penetrating lineman.

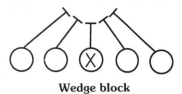

Wedge block

Combination (combo) blocks are exchanges of responsibilities between adjacent players who block someone other than the man nearest them. These combinations give the linemen better angles for their blocks, so the blocks should be more effective than if they blocked the closest defender.

A cross block has the outside man going first and blocking the man to his inside, either a lineman or a backer. The inside man then blocks the next lineman out. His technique is similar to that of a trap block. This block is often used when the linebacker is the inside man of the two defenders near the hole.

Cross block on two defensive linemen

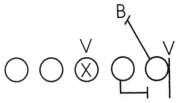

Cross block on a backer and a lineman

A fold block can be used when the objective is to hit the defensive lineman first and the linebacker second. The second blocker moves behind the first blocker and then goes after the linebacker.

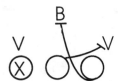

Fold with linebacker on the inside

Fold with linebacker on the outside

A scoop block is used when the outside lineman bumps his man and then goes after the linebacker, who was inside him. The inside offensive lineman blocks out on the lineman who was bumped.

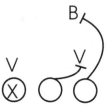

Scoop block between a guard and tackle

Pass Protection

Cup or retreat blocking is done by quickly "setting up." In the set-up, the blocker pops his body into the blocking position while taking a position step to be able to get an inside position on the pass rusher. If the team is using "zone" rules, the blocker sets up ready to take on whomever comes into his area. If the team is using "man" blocking, he takes the man on him, period. The following techniques can be used for the set-up for "man" blocking.

If the rusher is head up, the position step would be to the inside with the inside leg. If the rusher is on the outside shoulder he is already where the blocker wants him, so he doesn't need a position step. If the defender is wide to the outside, the blocker steps with the outside foot and quickly slides to a position where his outside foot splits the defender (outside foot in line with the rusher's crotch).

The depth of the set-up depends on the alignment of the potential pass rusher. Many coaches prefer the set-up to be on the line of scrimmage. Some coaches prefer that the blocker set up a foot or more back from the scrimmage line. By setting up on the line, the rusher doesn't have as much area in which to generate speed or to fake.

Also, by setting up close to the line of scrimmage, the blocker makes the rusher fight for every foot that he gains into the offensive backfield. Also, if the quarterback is dropping only three or five steps, he has more clear area in front of him. If he is dropping seven or nine steps, the set-up on the line of scrimmage would not be as important. Another factor in favor of the quick set-up on the line of scrimmage is that the smaller offensive men are at more of an advantage starting close to the defender rather than dropping back and letting the larger rusher have a run at them.

If the blocker has to move laterally a step or two to get to his assignment, he might have to get some depth in order to be able to meet the rusher. A basic rule for most teams using man blocking in cup pass protection is "big on big and small on small." This means that the offensive linemen block the defensive linemen and the offensive backs are responsible for the linebackers.

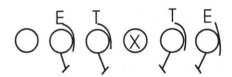

Big on big vs. a four-man front

Big on big vs. a five-man front

The position of the body in the set-up will be "hips down, head up." The feet should be shoulder width apart and slightly staggered, with the inside foot forward. They should be taking continuous quick steps. The weight should be on the balls of the feet. The knees should be flexed and slightly ahead of the toes. The torso should be slightly forward. (Some coaches prefer the torso to be nearly straight up so that the weight is more balanced. This is more likely to be effective if you have bigger but slower blockers.) The shoulders should remain square to the line of scrimmage. The head should be up with

the eyes looking at the top of the numbers or the lower part of the neck of the pass rusher.

Depending on the rules and the experience of the players, the arms may be "locked out" straight or may be kept close to the body. If they are locked out they will contact the rusher and maintain contact with him. (While illegal, it is very common for players using this technique to grab the opponent's jersey in order to maintain contact.) With the blocker's arms straight, the rusher has a better chance of grabbing the arms and going over or under them in his attack.

At the college and professional levels it is more common to keep the arms in closer to the body and punch at the rusher's numbers with one or both arms. It is similar to the last six inches of a bench press. The elbows must start and return to the side of the rib cage. They should not be wider than the shoulders. The blocker punches, with his hands open and facing the rusher, then recoils before the rusher has a chance to grab his arms. Some coaches teach bringing the arms only six inches back, other coaches teach bringing them farther back so that they are less of a target for the pass rusher to club or grab.

If the rusher is trying to grab the blocker, the blocker should counter by hitting the rusher's arm. The blocker must always be prepared to counter whatever moves the rusher is using to attack him.

As the rusher attacks, the blocker must remain between the rusher and the quarterback. He must also continue to keep his shoulders square to the line of scrimmage. If his shoulders are not parallel with the line of scrimmage, the rusher can more easily go behind the blocker's back and get to the passer.

Most of the blocker's hitting action should be up into the rusher. If the blocker hits out too far, he will be off-balance and can be grabbed and pulled by the rusher. The feet must move continuously and never cross. Their width should be shoulder width. If the blocker must move laterally, his steps should be short and quick. As he moves laterally, the width of his stance will widen six to eight inches and then recover to the shoulder-width starting point.

Coaching Points

- A quick set-up is absolutely essential to effective pass protection.
- The feet are shoulder-width and always moving.
- The feet are pointed straight ahead.
- Position should be gained inside the rusher. Always protect the inside.
- The knees are flexed and slightly forward of the toes.
- The head is up, with eyes looking at the top of the numbers.
- The shoulders are parallel with the line of scrimmage.
- Punch the arms up and into the numbers of the rusher.
- Let the opponent come to you.
- Honor inside fakes, but ignore outside fakes.
- Keep the rusher's hands off of you.
- Pop up, not out, at the rusher.
- Give ground slowly.
- Remain up and balanced. Only if beaten should the blocker try to cut the rusher with a low block.
- After the pass is thrown, cover in case the ball is intercepted.

Countering the Pass Rusher

Against the club and swim, the blocker recoils the arm being clubbed and then, as the rusher starts his swim, the blocker hits the rusher under the arm pit or chest with the other arm as the swim move continues. The blocker continues to move his feet in the direction of the defensive move and then hits the rusher with his near arm and continues with his regular pass protection technique.

Against the club and rip, the blocker uses a similar technique. He recoils the arm being clubbed, moves his feet in the direction of the defensive charge, then hits the rusher on the outside of the ripping arm under the pad, or, if the rip has been completed, under the arm pit as with the counter against the swim technique.

Against the spin, the blocker uses whatever counter is necessary to thwart the rusher's first move, then as the rusher spins he hits him in the back with the arm nearest the direction of the spin. He recovers his feet quickly and forces the rusher to go parallel with the line of scrimmage. The rusher must not be allowed to gain ground toward the passer while he is spinning.

Drills

Drills should fit directly into a coach's theory of offense and the fundamentals used. Some recommendations follow:

- *Stance and start.* These should be checked daily. If linemen are always going forward, that is the way they should go in drills. If they pull a great deal, then their start should be varied between straight ahead, right, and left pulls.
- *Stance and set-up.* If cup protection pass blocking is used, quick set-ups should be practiced daily.
- Blocks should be taught in slow motion, especially during spring practice or the preseason. Players should be given the opportunity to "feel" the proper stance, the step with the proper foot, the "fit" into the defender, and the drive of the legs.
- Boards and chutes are often helpful in teaching blocking. The boards (1 x 12's, six feet long) are used to teach the blocker to keep his feet wide. If his feet come in too close together, he will step on the board and slip. Chutes are designed to keep the blocker's body low during the hit and drive phases of the block. Coaches can build or buy chutes.
- Drills should be aligned for all of the defensive alignments a team might face, teaching the blocks or blocking combinations that will be used against them.

13

Offensive Backfield Fundamentals

Offensive backfield fundamentals include the following:

- Make and take the handoff
- Prevent fumbles
- Run with power
- Run with finesse
- Block
- Catch passes

How much time you devote to any of these phases should be determined by the duties of the player in the game. The fullback probably will spend more time on blocking and power running than the tailback, but the tailback might work more on finesse running and preventing fumbling.

The center-quarterback exchange in the T-formation starts with the quarterback placing his passing hand tight into the crotch of the center with the back of his hand providing upward pressure. The other hand faces forward with the palm and fingers vertical, pointing at the ground. The hands should be a minimum of a 90-degree angle to each other. Less than 90 degrees might result in the lower hand being hit by the ball on the exchange. The wrists should touch. It is especially important in younger players to have the wrists touching so that the ball is not driven up between the wrists, resulting in a fumbled snap.

Wrists together

Thumbs together

Another method of taking the snap has the top hand up, as described earlier, but the other hand is to the side with the thumbs touching.

Whichever method of taking the snap is used, the quarterback must stand as tall as possible so that he can see as much of the defense as possible. He must also give upward pressure with his top hand against the center's crotch so the snapper can feel where he should place the ball. As the ball is snapped the quarterback must be certain to ride the center with his hands as the center charges forward. To do this, the quarterback must have aligned very tight to the center.

The first step of the quarterback depends on the type of play called. Many option teams have the quarterback's first step forward and into the line of scrimmage. Other teams have the quarterback opening up to the play or reverse pivoting and turning away from where the ball will eventually be run.

Ideally, teams should have at least three centers and three quarterbacks, and each quarterback should be accustomed to taking snaps from each of the centers. How often have you seen a new center or quarterback enter the game and fumble the first snap? The chances of this occurring can be reduced if players continually take snaps, with the quarterback and center each taking their first steps.

If the center or quarterback are injured during a game, the substitute should take some snaps with the starter before entering the game, to reduce the chances of a fumble when under the pressure of the game.

The stance of a running back should be determined by the type of formation, the type of offense (what he is expected to do), and the individual abilities of the back (quickness, speed and so on) The stance can be a two-, three-, or four-point stance. Whichever stance is used, the head must be up and the eyes forward. The back should not look to see where he is going. One of the easiest cues for a defender to spot is the glancing of a back toward his point of attack.

The two-point stance is used by teams that want their backs to be able to move laterally fast or to be able to see the defense more effectively. The stance can be nearly upright, as the quarterback and tailback might take. This enables them to see the defense well, but doesn't allow for speed in any direction. The two-point stance might also be a semi-crouch that allows the player to move forward faster than in the upright stance and be able to move sideways quickly. The weight should be concentrated on the balls of the feet. One way to do this is to have the player curl his toes slightly. This places the weight forward.

One of the dangers with the two-point stance is that the player might get too eager and lean or step before the ball is snapped. This results in a five-yard "backfield in motion" penalty. Some coaches have their players take a two-point stance for the lateral quickness, but lightly touch one hand to the ground to prevent them from leaning before the snap.

The three-point stance is the most commonly used. The amount of weight on the hand depends on how fast the ball carrier must move forward. If speed to the inside is most important, the inside foot should be back. This would be preferred in a wishbone attack. If speed to the outside is most important, the outside foot should be back. If lateral speed in both directions is important, the feet might be parallel or nearly parallel. Most teams use this stance. Whichever stance is used should be used throughout the season. Changing stances during a game depending on the assignment would tip off the defense.

The four-point stance is sometimes used. It is most likely to be used by fullbacks on triple-option teams. It helps to get more weight forward and hitting the inside holes more quickly.

Timing the play is particularly important in certain offenses. The split-T dive, the triple option offenses such as the wishbone and the veer, and the belly series must be timed so that the fakes and the handoff are made at precisely the right instant. To "time the backfield," the coach might adjust the stance of the player (two- or three-point, amount of weight forward, and the placement of the feet) and he might adjust the placement of the player by "cheating" him. The cheat can move the player forward or back, right or left, depending on what he is expected to do on the play.

Some coaches cheat the back differently on each type of play. This can tip off the defense as to the type of play if they are alerted to it by scouting reports and practice. Other coaches make a one-time cheat that is used on every play.

For example, if a halfback is slower than desired in getting to the dive hole and moving laterally across the middle, the coach might put him in a more balanced three-point stance with the inside leg back and move him closer to the line of scrimmage and closer to the center than would be normal. If a back is too quick getting to the dive hole, he might be moved back and/or have more weight on his feet than on his hand in his stance.

The start for the running backs is the first step or two that the back takes after the snap. For a running back the first step should be a lead step (moving the foot closest to the hole first) or a cross-over step (the foot farthest from the hole moving first). Some coaches prefer that a running back take his first step as a crossover, others prefer that the first step be a lead step. Some coaches time the back to see which step is more effective for him. In a sweep or a quick-pitch action, the type of step isn't really very important — whichever step gets the back there quickest is the step to use.

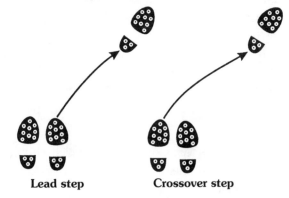

Lead step   **Crossover step**

Some plays require precise timing, so the type of step is of extreme importance. The timing of some plays requires a lead step, others require a crossover. For example, if the coach wanted his tailback to take two steps in one direction and then counter the

other way, the first step should be a crossover. If the play is starting right, the first step would be with the left foot, then with the right foot, then the back would cut to the hole after planting his right foot. If the coach wants the back to cut after the third step, the first step would be a lead step (right foot), then a crossover (left foot), then a right step and cut.

The quarterback's first step depends on the type of play being run. Some coaches like the quarterback to always use an "open" pivot, opening toward the hole, while others prefer a reverse pivot, turning away from the hole and then moving toward it. The open pivot gets the quarterback to the handoff point quicker on wider plays. The reverse pivot hides the ball better from the defense.

In a typical wishbone offense, the fullback is into the hole so quickly that the quarterback should always open to the hole. He must be reading the charge of the defensive tackle as he reaches back to find the fullback. On the other hand, on a crossbuck, the quarterback might be more deceptive by reverse pivoting (turning away from the hole) and then faking or giving to the fullback and halfback as they cross behind him.

On a speed option play or the split-T dive series, the quarterback might step forward toward the line of scrimmage on his first step. On a freeze option he generally steps backward as he makes a fake to the fullback before starting on his option path. On a wishbone triple option series he steps back as he puts the ball into the fullback's gut and rides him, then he takes it out and attacks forward into the line of scrimmage as he attacks the defensive end on the option play.

If the play is a pass he may step backward on his first step and backpedal to his passing spot. This enables him to see more of the defense as it adjusts to his passing action. However, it is faster if he takes a step back with his passing side foot, then a crossover with his other foot, then runs back to his passing spot to set up. In this crossover and run technique he is looking downfield at the defense but he won't be able to see the adjustments on his backside very well.

As with other fundamentals, the coach must determine exactly what he wants from the backs on each play and then select the stance and start that enables the back to best accomplish his job. There is no "best" stance. The stance chosen must be geared to offensive theory and to the individual strengths or weaknesses of the player.

Making the handoff is also determined by the type of offense a team is running. Most teams have the quarterback hand off with one hand. Wishbone, belly, and veer teams usually start with a two-hand plant of the ball into the first back running through the line. The quarterback reads the appropriate lineman and decides whether to take the ball back or to leave it with that ball carrier.

Whether one or two hands are used, the target should be the stomach of the ball carrier. The quarterback should keep his hand on the ball long enough to make sure the handoff is not fumbled.

Taking the handoff is most commonly done with the running back lifting his inside arm up to shoulder level. The angle of the arm and shoulder and the angle at the elbow should each be 90 degrees. The thumb of the upper hand points down. This helps to keep the elbow up.

Proper handoff

The arm and elbow should be kept in front of or inside of the shoulder for two reasons. First, if the elbow is outside of the line of the shoulder it can hit the quarterback. Second, if it is too wide the ball carrier cannot clamp down on the ball as easily.

The runner's lower hand should be facing upward and should be just past the mid-line of the body. It should be held several inches below the navel so that the target area for the quarterback is large.

The runner's eyes should be on the area toward which he is running. He should feel the ball as the quarterback puts it into his belly and rides with him. He should then clamp on to the ball with both hands as he heads into the line. It is important to have the ball in both hands because tacklers often rip at the arms and force fumbles.

Making a pitch on an option play can be done with one or two hands. Some coaches teach the quarterback to look at the defender whom he is optioning. If the pitch is dictated, he pushes the ball away with one hand, knowing that the running back will be in the exact position to receive it. Other coaches have the quarterback look at the running back and pitch with one hand. Other coaches prefer that the quarterback look at the running back and make a two-handed pitch like a chest pass in basketball. This is the most accurate method, but it exposes the quarterback to a hit from the side.

On a sweep play, the pitch is generally a two-handed toss to the running back. If the play is a quick pitch, it is usually an underhand spiral pass. (A right-handed quarterback making a quick pitch to his right reverse pivots and passes the ball with his right hand. If the quick pitch is to the left he open pivots and makes the lateral underhand spiral pass immediately.

Whichever type of pitch is used it should be aimed slightly ahead of the running back and at chest height.

Catching the Pitch

The running back must catch the ball with two hands. He should look it into his hands and then put it away into the proper ball carrying position before thinking of dodging tacklers. If the pitch is errant the running back should fall on the ball rather than try to pick it up and run with it. A number of pursuing defenders will be trying to pounce on any loose ball, so he must get to it quickly and save it for his team.

Carrying the ball in the open field is done with one arm. The forward end of the ball can be controlled by placing the index finger over the end, by straddling the end of the ball with the index and middle fingers, or by cupping the ball with the hand.

Pressure should be felt in three areas: the fingers cupping the end of the ball, the ball on the inside of the elbow, and the elbow against the rib cage.

Carrying the ball

Many times college and professional players carry the ball in one hand. This invites fumbling. Remember that an offensive ball carrier who fumbles and loses the ball has just cost his team a minimum of 35 yards — the yardage they would have gained on a punt. A fumbled ball is not merely an unlucky "break" or a turnover, it is a major loss of yardage.

Many coaches prefer that the ball always be carried in the right arm, hoping that this minimizes mistakes — especially those made when changing the ball from one arm to the other. Most coaches prefer the ball to be held in the arm away from the tacklers. So on a sweep left, the ball is held in the left arm. Very few coaches advocate changing the ball from hand to hand while running.

When the ball carrier is about to be hit, he should cover the ball with both hands to reduce his chance of fumbling. Defensive coaches often teach their players to rip at the ball as they are gang tackling the ball carrier. Some coaches believe that rather than placing both arms over the ball, the ball need only be brought across the body with one arm. This should reduce the defender's ability to rip at it.

Faking

The quarterback can fake by putting the ball or a hand into a ball carrier and then taking it back. This is done on cross bucks, belly action, and other plays in which the ball might be faked or given to the first back and then faked or given to the second back.

After making a fake with the ball or the hand, the quarterback can fake with his eyes. He can watch the man he faked to rather than the ball carrier. This is particularly important on play-action passes. The quarterback can also fake by pretending that it is a play-action pass. In this case he can move deeper into the backfield in a waggle or bootleg action with his hand on his hip, pretending that he has the ball.

If the quarterback's fakes hold only one defender from pursuit, he has done a good job. If he holds a linebacker in on a play-action pass or keeps a defensive back deep when faking a pass on a run play, he greatly improves his teams chances for success. Most coaches do not work enough on quarterback faking.

Running back fakes are of two kinds. The first is when the runner is not carrying the ball but has received a fake handoff from the quarterback. He should cover the imaginary ball with two hands and plow into the line, hoping to freeze the linebacker or be tackled.

The second kind of fake occurs in the open field. It will be a change in direction or a change of speed. The most effective fake is to get the defender moving one way and then to cut behind his back. It helps a great deal if the runner can get the potential tackler to cross his legs. If he can, it is a perfect time to make the cut.

Change of pace is a change of speed, either faster or slower. As has been noted, generally a running back runs under control until he is in the open field. If running under control, the back can speed up just before the tackler prepares to make contact. This might leave the tackler out of position. Changing pace to a slower pace or stopping can also throw off the tackler. The problem with this once-popular move is that the pursuing defense of today might catch the back who slows up too much.

A speed fake is most effective when the runner is faster than the defensive back. It should be executed about six yards in front of the defender. The back should fake one way, then accelerate the other.

The open field fake is often accompanied by another action to ward off the tackler. The straight arm or stiff arm, the flipper, a lowered shoulder, or a spin can each aid in getting past the tackler or in making a few extra yards. The stiff arm is an open-handed punch at the opponent's helmet or shoulder pads that is designed to either keep the opponent away from the ball carrier or to push the tackler down to the ground. It can be used with either a crossover step or a spin. If the ball carrier is using a left straight arm and is cutting to his right, he brings his left leg through fast and high as he makes his cut and drives away from the tackler. If he is using the left straight arm and wants to cut left, he spins away by pivoting on his left leg and bringing the right arm and leg away from the tackler — spinning and then continuing downfield.

Stiff arm with spin

The flipper or the shoulder are power moves used to get extra yardage through the tackler. The flipper is a forearm rip into the tackler that is designed to punish him and possibly loosen his arms from the tackle he is attempting to make. The shoulder is used when the ball carrier lowers his body and drives for extra yardage. They are more effective if made while cutting behind the tackler. In the open field it is best if the runner can get head-up with the defender. This enables him to cut right or left.

Blocking

Backs block with the same techniques as the linemen (see Chapter 12). The differences are that the backs get a run at their targets so they can deliver more of a blow, but their targets are harder to hit because the defenders have more time and room to maneuver and fake. Also, the defenders are usually bigger than the offensive backs who are blocking.

Larger backs generally use the techniques described in the previous chapter for the drive block. A smaller back usually aims lower and uses the scramble technique. In cup pass protection he often has to take on a much bigger man who has a run at him; this takes a great deal of courage.

The types of running play blocks most often used are the lead block through the hole (such as an isolation block) and the log block in which the back blocks a wide defender on a sweep by placing

Stiff arm with crossover step

his head between the tackler and the runner. He might also use a trap type of block on an off-tackle play or aid a lineman on a double team.

The blocks of the backs are made easier if the coach has designed the plays to freeze the defender and if the ball carrier fakes to set up the block.

Pass blocking by a back is similar to that of the linemen mentioned in the previous chapter. The difference is that the defensive lineman or linebacker has a running start and generally outweighs the offensive back. Because of this it is essential that the running back sets up properly between the defender and the ball. He must be ready to pop into the rusher should the rusher attempt to run over him. If the rusher adjusts his path to go around him, the blocker can use his quickness to further redirect the rusher's route.

As with the offensive linemen, the back should have his feet parallel, his knees bent, his back straight, his head and eyes up, and his hands in front of his jersey with his elbows down.

Setting Up the Block

The runner should use and help his blockers. Experienced runners who can outrun their blockers usually slow down and run under control so that the blocker can do his job. The most effective place from which to set up a block is two to three yards behind the blocker. A simple step right forces the tackler to honor the fake and move in that direction. The blocker takes the defender in either direction — in this illustration it would be to the right. The back then cuts left.

Power Running

Whether running through the line or driving into a tackler for extra yardage, the ball carrier must change his running style. He should widen his legs — some power runners have their feet more than 24 inches apart. This helps keep the ball carrier from being easily knocked off-balance when hit from the side.

He also must run lower with more body weight forward and be ready to explode into the tackler. Some runners run so low and with so much power that if they are not hit at the line of scrimmage they fall anyway — after gaining about five yards. This is the kind of running needed in short-yardage situations.

Running with balance is also important. The effective runner should be able to absorb hits, spin, and cut while maintaining his balance. This is another reason that running full speed is not always essential in football. The runner who is hit while running full speed does not have balance, he has momentum. The runner who is under control is better able to set up blocks, fake, and cut. So there is a place for both controlled running and for all-out speed. The effective runner knows when to use each.

The coach can help a player learn balance. A good drill is having the back "run the gauntlet," in which he is hit by players with hand dummies, has other dummies thrown at his feet, and has players ripping at his arms. Remember, if you want to improve a player's fundamentals you must develop drills to accomplish what you want to have him learn.

Drills

1. *Center, quarterback, running back.* The center snaps the ball. The quarterback takes the steps necessary for that play, such as an I-formation pitchout or a veer dive.

2. *Handoff drill, back to back.* Ball carriers line up in two lines facing each other. The player in the first line has a ball. He runs at a player in the other line and stays to his right. He hands off with his left hand. The receiving player has his inside (left) arm up. The receiving player then hands to the player in the next line. This continues until the coach stops the drill. It is then repeated with the first player running to the left of the player running toward him. The handoff is now made with the right hand and the receiving player will again have his near arm (right) up.

3. *Load blocking on dummy.* Offensive back drives at dummy and blocks, keeping his head on the side opposite the line of scrimmage. (See shoulder block technique in the previous chapter.)

4. *Trap blocking on dummy.* Back runs at dummy and slides his head to the line of scrimmage side. (See shoulder block technique.)

5. *Stiff arm and crossover drill.* Hit dummy with left stiff arm, cross over left leg. Repeat with right stiff arm and right cross over.

6. *Stiff arm and spin.* Hit dummy with left stiff arm, spin to left. Repeat with right stiff arm and spin right.

7. *Three steps and cut drill.* The back takes three steps one direction and cuts, then three steps the other way and cuts. The speed and the angle of cut can be increased as the back gets more proficient at the technique.

14

Passing and Catching

Nearly all teams use the pass as an integral part of their offenses. As the pass has become more important, the fundamentals of the passer and the receiver have become more specific and detailed. Consequently, there is much more to practice today than there was a few years ago. As with other fundamentals, skills as common as passing and catching must be practiced correctly every day, even at the professional level.

Passing

Taking the snap is the start of any play. For a T-formation quarterback, the passer's hand should be protected from an errant snap. This is done by placing it high in the center's crotch. The fingers should be relaxed, spread, and extended so that the snap does not hit a finger and sprain it. The other hand should be touching the upper hand and should be held at a greater than 90-degree angle to the upper hand. This angle reduces the chance of the fingers of the lower hand being jammed by the snap.

The quarterback must adjust his stance to the height of the center's crotch. The quarterback's knees must be flexed so that he can get his hands into the crotch without bending much at the waist. The snapper should never be asked to adjust to the height of the quarterback. The quarterback rides the center as he charges out for a block or steps back in cup pass protection. The snap must be handled or the play is stopped before it begins. After being certain that he has the snap, he brings the ball to his chest with both hands. His first step is determined by the type of play action to be used: drop back, sprint-out, roll-out, bootleg, waggle, play action and so on.

The drop back can be either a backpedal or a crossover and run. In the backpedal, the quarterback pushes off as he rides the center. He can step with either foot, but most prefer stepping first with the passing side foot. He pushes off hard with his toes and moves back quickly as he watches his defensive keys. This type of action is more difficult to learn and slower in getting to the set-up area, but it affords good vision of the entire defense. It is especially important to use the backpedal drop when a blitz is expected.

Players who use the crossover step gain speed getting to the set-up area and can learn the technique more easily, but they sacrifice good vision of the backside defenders because his back will be toward them. In the crossover drop, the passer steps with the passing-side foot, crosses over with the other leg, and runs back to the passing spot. Both types of drops should be learned by quarterbacks whose teams use a sophisticated pass offense.

The set-up spot, the spot from where the pass is thrown, may be one, three, five, seven, or nine yards back, depending on the depth of the pattern. The one-step drop is used on such plays as a quick slant. The three-step drop is used on hitches and other patterns that break at about five yards. The five-step drop is used on longer patterns, such as those breaking at eight to 10 yards. The seven- and nine-step drops are used for long curls and deep patterns. The coach must select the proper distance back to give the passer a chance to make the proper reads and to give the receivers time to make their cuts or get to the proper area.

Quick feet are essential to the elite passer. As he drops to his spot, stops his backward movement, and steps up into the pocket, his feet should be moving quickly. This enables him to quickly face the open receiver. After he has made the quick move toward his target, he steps with the non-passing leg directly at the target and throws the ball.

A common error in most hitting and throwing actions is for the player to "step in the bucket." This means that he is not stepping directly at the target and that his hips are open to the target. Such an error causes a loss of power and accuracy.

The grip should be nearly correct as the ball arrives in his hand from the snap. However, as the passer drops to his spot he should make the final adjustments of his grip. The size of the passer's hands make some difference in exactly how he grips the ball. The smaller-handed player has to grip the ball a bit farther back to be able to control it and to get the maximum amount of power on the ball without it slipping out of his hands.

The most commonly accepted grip has the ring finger and little finger, and sometimes the middle finger, on the laces. The index finger will be one to two inches from the end of the ball and on the seam. The thumb will be 2 to 3½ inches away from the tip of the ball. The ball is gripped by the pads on the ends of the fingers and thumb. The palm should not have pressure on the ball, and passers with larger hands might have no contact between the ball and the palm of the hand.

The non-passing hand should be lightly touching the far end of the ball. This helps in keeping the grip and in preventing fumbling. If the passer is hit before releasing the ball, having two hands on it can greatly reduce the chance of the ball popping out of the passing hand. The ball should be carried in both hands at chest height while the passer is dropping back and held until the passing action starts.

Setup for pass

Stride forward

The throwing action begins as do all other hitting and throwing actions. There is a step and a weight shift, a turning of the hips, and a rotation of the shoulders. This is followed by the forward movement of the upper arm, then the elbow extension, then the wrist rotation. All throwing and hitting moves start from the feet and end with the wrist. The stride forward should be long enough for an effective weight shift forward — 2½ to 3 feet is average. The length of the stride depends on the passer's height and the distance of the throw. Long passes generally require a longer stride. The toes of the lead foot should point directly at the target. As the stride starts forward, the throwing arm starts back. The hand should be drawn back close to the head.

Ball starts forward

The ball should stay close to the ear for most passes. For long throws the passer may bring the ball farther back to gain more power. Keeping the ball close to the head rather than allowing it to drop far behind the shoulders, as a baseball pitcher would do, enables a quicker release.

The football pass is more like a catcher's throw than a pitcher's throw. After the step, the passer shifts his weight to the forward foot. As this happens the hips open toward the target, then the shoulders rotate into the pass. The muscles of the upper chest stretch as the shoulders rotate. This gives upper chest muscles more potential power, because the stretch reflex increases their readiness to contract. From this position, the arm starts forward. The chest muscles bring the upper arm forward. The forearm lags behind the elbow. This stretches the triceps so they can generate more power. Next the triceps contract and the ball starts forward. The speed of the forearm is important in keeping the nose of the ball up. This makes it easier to catch. The index finger is the last part of the hand to touch the ball.

Follow-through

If the ball is released too late, it noses down and falls short of its target. Occasionally this happens with experienced players who are nervous; they hold the ball too long because of increased muscle tension. The follow-through has the palm of the hand turning down and the fingers pointing at the target. After the arm has followed through straight, with the palm of the hand down, the arm can cross the body as it completes the follow-through.

Passing while running, as in a sprint-out or roll-out, requires that the passer get his shoulders parallel to the line of scrimmage. The ball should be held in both hands. Many coaches attempt to get their passers stepping into the pass so that they can use the same action as in a drop-back pass. A passer running right and making a cut on his right foot can pass on his first step (as the left foot lands), the third step, or the fifth step. If he is running left and cutting on his left foot he can pass on his second or fourth step — the steps with the left foot.

Passing while scrambling might not allow the passer to step correctly or even use the proper arm action. It is important, however, to get the shoulders perpendicular to the line of flight of the ball. Without the proper step, the power generated is not as great. For this reason, the passer should develop strong abdominal, chest, and triceps muscles.

The target varies with the type of pass. It isn't enough to just throw the ball to another player. The pass must be aimed so that it reduces the chance of an interception. For that reason, shorter passes are generally thrown low. Out patterns are generally thrown low and to the outside. Fade patterns should go over the outside shoulder of the receiver.

Receiving

The *effective receiver* must know how to get to the proper area, make the catch, prevent the fumble, then run with the ball.

Catching the ball starts with the eyes. The eyes should focus on the ball, even the spin of the ball, so that the player does not lose concentration. It is common for players, even at the pro level, to take their eyes off the ball at the last second and look for running room. To be safe, players should watch the ball until it has been tucked under the arm.

The position of the fingers depends on where the ball will be caught. The surest catching position is with the thumbs and forefingers touching or nearly touching. This is the position that should be used if at all possible. Even if the player is running deep he has a better chance to catch the ball if he turns back toward the passer and takes this hand position.

Catching with thumbs in

Catching with thumbs out

If the ball is low, such as below the waist, the hands can be held with the thumbs out and the little fingers in. If the pass is overthrown, this "little fingers in" position also is used. Catch the end of the ball. (Some coaches coach to "catch the near stripe.") If the ball is coming fast it often splits the hands and the receiver finishes the catch gripping the middle of the ball. If the receiver tries to catch the ball at or near the middle, it is likely to go through his hands.

The receiver should *cushion the ball* as it comes toward the body. He should reach out for the ball so that he can "give" with it, and keep watching the ball.

The receiver should then *tuck the ball away* into one arm and cup his hand over the end of the ball, continuing to watch it. (Often "overcoaching" a point, such as watching the ball until it is tucked away, pays off with reduced mistakes. By teaching the player to watch it past the point where he really needs to, he will be safe even if he takes his eyes off it a bit early.) After the ball is tucked away, the receiver becomes a runner.

Getting off the line of scrimmage is often difficult because the defenders are trying to hit the potential receivers and delay them, thus changing the timing on the play. A wide receiver being hit by a bump and run defender should not allow the defender to push him along the line of scrimmage in either direction. He should work to get directly behind the defender through a fake or a deflection technique.

The simplest fake is the "head bob." This is merely a movement of the head in one direction as the receiver takes his first step straight ahead or in the opposite direction.

A variation of the "head bob" is the head and shoulder fake. In this action, the receiver steps one way as he moves toward the defender, then he cuts quickly the other way and gets behind the defender. Sometimes a double fake is needed. If the single fake has worked well, the defender will learn to counter it, so the receiver can fake one way, fake the other way, then get behind the defender.

Deflection techniques are used by the receiver when he wants to knock the defender's hands off him. One method is to rip the closest arm up and through the defender's arms. If the receiver is cutting right it will be the left arm that is ripped up. Another technique is the "swim" in which the receiver brings his inside arm up and over the defender's arms knocking them downward. These techniques can be used in combination such as a head fake one way then a rip up as the receiver makes his cut. Another technique, used often by tight ends, is the fake block. The receiver comes out low and makes contact but slides off the defender and continues downfield.

Getting open must be done within the theory of the offense. Some coaches have the receivers run disciplined routes so that the passer knows where they will be as he makes his reads. The design of the pattern should get at least one receiver open. Other coaches want the player to get open any way he can. By working together, the passer should be able to anticipate how the receiver gets open against different types of coverages. In hook and curl passes, the receiver is generally just asked to get between or in front of the defenders in the underneath zones.

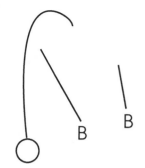

Curl pattern between backers

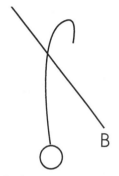

Curl pattern under backers

Running the route depends on the offensive theory. The traditional way is to run to a point, such as five or 10 yards, come under control and make a cut. The cut can be 90 degrees, sharper than 90 degrees (on a sideline pattern), or less sharp (post, corner and so on). The player may make a fake before cutting. Of course against a team playing a true zone defense, the fake should not be effective.

In an angular pattern, the player plants the foot away from the cut and then makes the hard cut and accelerates. If he is cutting right, he plants the left foot. On the more angular cuts, 90 degrees or more, the player must be very much under control, even stopped, as he makes his cut. The objective is to put distance between the receiver and the defender by getting the defender moving back, then stopping and cutting away.

A second method is to run faster at the defender but run in a slightly S-shaped pattern — a "weave." The receiver tries to get the defender moving back fast and get close to him. The cut is more of a curve. The hope is that the receiver gets distance between himself and the defender through speed.

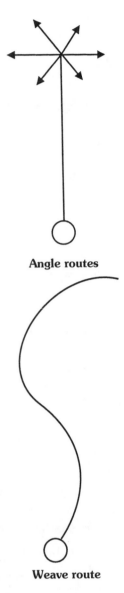

Angle routes

Weave route

Getting loose in man-to-man coverage is best done by: changing directions, (such as a hook and comeback, in and out, hook and go, out and up); getting the defenders legs crossed and then cutting the other direction; getting close then leaning into the defender and breaking the other way.

Drills for Passing

1. Start on both knees. Check the grip, and make sure the ball is kept near the ear and the follow-through is straight at the target, with the palm of the hand facing down.

2. Do the same drill on one knee, first with the right knee down, then with the left knee down.

3. Drop back to the proper depth (one, three, five, seven, or nine steps) and throw at a target.

4. Run in a circle to the right with another passer and throw to him. Keep the shoulders square.

5. Run in a circle to the left with one other receiver.

Drills for Receiving

1. Play catch, with ever-increasing velocity on the passes. Throw high, low, right, left. Check hand position.

2. Have receivers run toward the passer and catch passes thrown high, low, right and left.

3. With the receiver running in place and looking over the right shoulder, the passer throws softly five to 10 passes high and to the right; low and to the right; low and to the left (the receiver must turn back toward the passer); and high and to the right (the receiver must turn away from the passer, see the ball over his left shoulder, and make the catch).

Repeat the same drills with the receiver looking over his left shoulder: 10 passes high left, 10 low left, 10 low right, 10 high right.

15

Defensive Line Fundamentals

Many coaches believe that defense is the most important part of football, and defensive play starts with the linemen. They have the first opportunity to stop the run and the pass. As with the offensive line, stance, charge, and reaction are important.

However, while the offensive blocker knows where the play is going and how he will block for it, the defensive lineman must neutralize the blocker, react to keys the offense gives him, then pursue the ball and make the tackle. In the past, the defenders' primary advantage was that they could use their arms. This advantage has been reduced because the blockers can now use their hands in their blocks.

The stance for a defensive lineman generally has more weight forward than with the offensive lineman. This is because a good offensive lineman will have moved about six inches before the defensive lineman can begin to react to the movement. The offensive lineman therefore has more weight forward than he had while he was in his stance. By having more weight forward, the defender is better able to equalize the momentum of the offensive player.

The defensive stance can be a three- or a four-point stance. If the player's stance has a great deal of weight forward, the four- point stance might be more comfortable. Players who do a great deal of slanting and looping (defensive lateral movements) might use stances that do not have as much weight forward as would the players who are hitting directly

into the blockers. So the type of stance is often adjusted, depending on the defensive theory of the team or the assignment for that particular play.

If forward momentum is important, such as in a pass rush, the feet should be staggered. If lateral movement is important, such as in a looping charge, the feet should be parallel. The back should be straight. The hips can be higher than the shoulders. The shoulders should be even. The head should be up. The eyes should be focused on the man ahead.

Four-point defensive stance

The alignment is generally head up, inside or outside shoulder, or in the gap. If the lineman's responsibility is the gap, he may play very close to the line of scrimmage. If he has to control a man and is being defeated, such as the nose guard in an odd man front or the defensive guards in a wide tackle six, he may back off the line to give himself more time to read and adjust to the block.

Pre-snap cues might help the defender make an educated guess as to where the ball will go. He can use his intelligence and observational ability to give him hints as to where the play will attack. Prior to the snap he can glance at the position of the backs. Have they "cheated" into a different position from which the scouting reports have noted that a special play will be run? Is a back wider, possibly signalling a quick pitch? Is the back cheated up, maybe signalling a dive or trap? He can also look at the eyes of the backs. Often backs look at the area which they will attack, either as a ball carrier or blocker.

The blocker in front of him may be peeking laterally, possibly signalling a cross block or pull. He also might be leaning in the direction of the pull. He might have more weight forward than normal. This may be signalled by a change in color of his knuckles, more red or white. Less weight on the hands may signal a pull or a pass block.

The charge begins on the movement of the ball (the snap) or the movement of the offensive player. Both should occur at the same time. The target of the charge can either be a man or a gap. If charging into a man, the blocker must be beaten by neutralizing him. If charging into a gap, the defender must beat the blocker by avoiding him. The charge must be low. Remember that the low man nearly always wins in football. The defensive lineman must hit hard enough with his legs to be able to stop the offensive blocker's charge. He must also get under the offensive blocker and lift him.

His initial charge is with leg power, with the back arched slightly, and the head up. Defenders are allowed to use their hands and arms more than are the offensive blockers. This makes it easier for the defender to ward off the block and get under the blocker.

Block protection is a term that denotes the type of hand or arm action used to ward off and control the blocker. There are several types of block protection. The terminology for block protection varies, with several types of names for each technique. The choice of technique depends on the player's build and his assignment. A shorter player is probably able

to get under a taller player with a hand shiver. Any player can use the forearm rip or the other techniques that follow.

The hand shiver (jam or forearm shiver, in older terminology) is the most common use of the hands. In the hand shiver, the defender hits up and into the offensive blocker. He drives his hands into the blocker's chest or the lower part of the shoulder pads. The "fit" is the same as if he was using his hands for blocking — the heels of the hands under the shoulder pads, fingers pointed up and the wrists close together. The arms should "lock out," keeping the blocker at arm's length. His elbows should be under his shoulders as they start their lift. If his elbows are wide, the blocker's legs can overpower the arms (triceps) of the defender and the blocker has a better chance to get into his body. If the defender makes his arm movement with his elbows down, even if he can't lock out his arms, he still has his forearms between himself and the blocker.

Hand shiver

The arm lift is a one-handed shiver used primarily when the defender is protecting a gap different from where he lined up, such as controlling the outside gap from an inside shoulder alignment. The player steps with the foot farthest from the direction he is moving (the "far" leg), and hits upward with the "far" hand lifting under the pads as in the two-hand shiver. The near hand is then free to play the outside of the blocker. So, if moving to the right he would step laterally with the left foot, hit with the left hand, then keep the outside leverage with the right arm and hand.

The forearm rip (forearm lift or forearm flipper) is a second type of shiver. Here, the defender makes a hard charge with his shoulder into the blocker, while lifting his arm up and through the defender. The arm should have a 90-degree angle at the shoulder and elbow. The power comes from the shoulder muscles (deltoids). As the forearm hits under the pads of the blocker, the defender's back arches more, the hips drop, and the legs assist in the lift. By this time the blocker must be defeated.

Blockers can now use their hands, so it is more difficult to get close enough to the blocker's body to rip into it. However, the forearm rip can get the blocker's hands off the defender's body and the defender still has one arm free. This technique can therefore be used in a gap control defense or when slanting or looping.

After the blocker is defeated, the defender carries out his assignment. Most teams use a "gap responsibility," meaning that the defender neutralizes his man and then protects a gap. After it is certain that his gap is not the hole which the offense is attacking, he can pursue the ball.

Forearm block

The forearm block (arm bar) is used to control one side of an offensive lineman. It is generally used when controlling the gap to the side that he is aligned. It can be used to help open a hole for a stunting linebacker to rush a pass or kick. If controlling a gap for a pass or run, he should align so that he can hit with the arm farthest from the gap. In this move, the defender drives his forearm into the area between the blocker's shoulder and neck. If controlling the outside gap, he steps with his outside leg and uses his outside forearm. If controlling the inside gap, he steps with his inside leg and uses his inside arm. If using this move to open a hole for a stunting linebacker, especially a kick blocker, he can hit with the arm farthest from the blocker and drive the blocker away from the hole by turning the blocker's head and body away from the hole.

The butt and control (or blast and grab) is used against blockers who aim high. The defender drives his face into the blocker's chest with his hands hitting near the low part of the blocker's numbers. He grabs the opponent's jersey and hand shivers him as he neutralizes his charge and fights the pressure. This technique provides a great deal of power. He then fights the pressure and disengages.

Varying the Charge

The defensive lineman might not always want to hit the man in front of him. He may angle into a gap or might hit an adjacent man rather than the one against whom he was lined up.

Forearm rip

The slant charge is a direct charge at an angle from an alignment on a man to an adjacent gap (a penetrating charge) or into the next offensive man (a controlling charge). If it is into the gap, the more common slant, he should align on the line of scrimmage. He steps diagonally with the far foot (the left foot if going right) and then with the near foot. He protects himself from the nearest blocker with his far hand as he charges into the gap. He aims at the near hip of the adjacent offensive lineman.

Some coaches use a slant into an adjacent man. This may be done from a gap alignment or from a position about a foot off the line of scrimmage and on a man. The charge is the same except that the target of the charge is the near shoulder of the adjacent man. He shivers the man, usually with a hand shiver, and reacts to the pressure.

The loop charge is made around the adjacent man. It might be from an inside position on a man, around his head and into a gap that he penetrates. It can also be made from the adjacent man to the next man on the line of scrimmage, in or out. If looping, the defender needs more distance from the line of scrimmage — as much as a yard, depending on the width of the line splits and the abilities of the blockers.

The charge is started with the far foot stepping laterally, then the near foot. The far hand must offer block protection. If the target is the gap, the defender penetrates. If it is the adjacent man, he hits and reacts to the pressure.

The goal line charge starts with a stance that has the feet close to the line of scrimmage and a great deal of weight on the hands. Upon the snap, the defender dives through his man or through his gap at about knee height. He then brings his legs up quickly and continues penetrating into the backfield.

Reading the first step of the blocker can assist the defender in knowing how to react as he is making his initial charge. Many coaches teach their blockers to step with the foot on the same side as the shoulder with which they will hit. This can give the defender a jump on his reaction. He can start his lateral movement before seeing which way the blocker's head moves.

If the blocker pulls, the defender can follow the pull. However, if a team uses the "influence trap," he must be aware that a trapper might be coming from behind. This is more likely to occur if his man pulls outside and a guard from the opposite side of the center traps him.

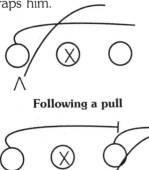

Following a pull

Influence trap

If his man blocks the next man in or out, he should hit him to slow the blocker's charge. He can expect a similar block on him or a trap. If he is blocked by an adjacent man, he must fight the pressure. However, he must also expect a trap. The scouting report can give him an idea as to what type of blocking scheme he must counter. Most traps come from the center out, but some teams now trap from the outside in.

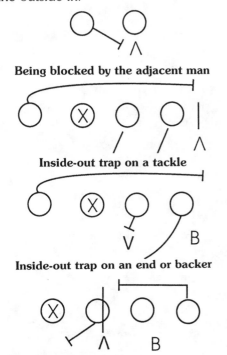

Being blocked by the adjacent man

Inside-out trap on a tackle

Inside-out trap on an end or backer

Outside-in trap

Playing the angle block can be expected if the offensive man lined up on the defender blocks the next man to either side of him. If the man on him blocks to the defensive right, he can expect a blocker coming from his left, a cross block coming at him from the right, a trap block from the right, or a lead block from a back. The defender must fight the pressure of the blocker and not be driven off the line of scrimmage.

The first move he should make is into the blocker in front of him keeping him off his assignment. This does two things: it helps the defender regain his balance as he recognizes who will be attacking him, and it slows the blocker lined up in front of him and reduces his ability to block another defender. After seeing or feeling the man who is attacking him, he should hit him with a forearm rip with the arm nearest the blocker. He should then work to control him and fight the pressure with his far hand and legs. If all else fails, he should drop to all fours to create a pileup at the line of scrimmage.

Overcoming Various Blocks

If the blocker on the defender blocks down on the next man and the defender feels no pressure, he probably is being set up for a trap block. He should then narrow the gap between himself and the blocker who is blocking down the line. He should not move across the scrimmage line but should set for the trap, preparing to play it with his outside arm, with a forearm flipper, or his hands. Some coaches teach their players to drop to the inside knee when they feel no pressure. This puts the defender lower than the trap blocker and can reduce the trapper's effectiveness.

Seeing the near back's first step might also give a hint of the type of play being run. Is he coming right at the defender as a blocker or a ball carrier? Is he moving across the center, indicating that the play will not come quickly at the defender? On a pass play, the defender should check on the first step of the near back. If he steps out, it probably will be a pass block. However, if the fullback stays in one spot or a halfback steps inward, it is likely to be a draw play.

Protecting the gap responsibility is essential for teams that play gap control defenses. If playing gap control, the defender hits into the blocker with his head and shoulders and then slides his head to the side of the gap that he is controlling. While doing this, he hits upward with the hands in a hand shiver, stops the offensive charge, then separates from the blocker. The feet keep moving while the legs provide upward and forward pressure on the blocker.

Fighting the pressure is the next job of the defender. If the defense is playing a "hit and react" technique, the defender "reads the head" of the blocker. This means that he is aware that the blocker is trying to take him one way, opposite the blocker's head, and will try to fight through his head. The defender should never go around the blocker, but always cross the face of the blocker going to where the ball carrier probably will run. As he reacts to the pressure of the block, the defender must never cross his legs as he moves toward the ball. His feet must be wide so that he has lateral balance. His legs should move quickly, taking short, choppy steps.

If the blocker drops back in pass protection, this signals the defender to attack the blocker, attempt to turn his shoulders, then take the proper pass rush lane. In this reaction, the defender should use his hands, not his forearms, because it gives him more ability to maneuver and whip the blocker.

Fighting the double team block can be done a few ways. The defender can take on one blocker. He can drop to the ground to reduce the effectiveness of the block. He can split the block. Or, if defeated, he can spin out of it. If the outside blocker is an overpowering player, he may just attack through the inside man or through the gap.

If the blockers have not been able to get under him, the defender might be able to drop to the ground and trip the blockers. This reduces the effectiveness of the double team because they have not been able to continue to drive the defender.

In splitting the double team, the defender can drive his body into the inside man while pushing with his hands against the outside man. He attempts to "split the seam" of the block by not allowing the blockers to seal their bodies together.

Splitting the double-team block

If defeated by the double team block, he can spin out. If the block is high, such as into his chest, he can use the high spin-out. In doing this, he throws his inside arm toward his back and steps back with his inside foot. This exposes his outside shoulder to the block of the outside man. As he turns, the outside blocker is pushing on the back of the defender's outside shoulder, which helps him in his spin. As he completes the spin, he gets low and attempts to come back into the hole.

High spin-out

If the double team is low, such as a scramble block at knee level, he might be able to spin over the outside blocker. In doing this, he throws his outside arm up and over the back of the outside blocker. The blocker pushes on the back of his outside shoulder and helps him spin over the blocker's back. In order to do this, the defender must have met the block low. He cannot use this spin unless he is as low as the blocker.

Spin against single blocker

These spins also can be used against single blockers who have made effective shoulder blocks from straight on or have had an angle on the defender and are blocking down on him. Remember, the spin should be a last resort because the defender has his back to the ball for an instant. Also, if the defender spins as his first reaction, the blocker may "false block" him, hitting him on one side (the side away from the direction he wants him to move) and letting the defender spin himself out of the hole.

Some double team blocks are delayed, with the initial drive block by a lineman joined by a running back or a man in motion as the second part of the block. The block is played the same way as when two linemen are blocking, but the fact that the second man is a bit late and was not in the blocker's triangle makes it a surprise.

Defeating the scoop block is done by hitting the blocker who is hitting him with his head outside or is faking a hook block and then releasing outside. On a true hook block, the shoulders of the blocker are low. They are higher on the scoop block because he is trying to slip the block and attack the backer.

The reaction should be outward through the head of the first blocker. As the first blocker slips by him, he must be alert to the blocker coming from the other side. He should head upfield, making penetration, as he gets his body ahead of the second blocker. He can use the near hand or both hands into the chest of the second blocker to redirect him.

Playing the lead block is difficult because the blocking back is not in the defender's immediate field of vision. However, the back is generally smaller than the lineman so there should be a mismatch at the collision point. If the back blocks high, the defensive lineman should jolt him by getting under his pads, lift him and knock him backward.

Generally, the back should block low. In this case, the defender must protect his legs so they don't get knocked out from under him. He hits the blocker's shoulder pads and knocks him to the ground and into the hole, while being ready to make the tackle over the prostrate blocker. If the ball carrier is a distance behind the blocker, the defender has time to gather himself and be ready to make the tackle.

Being aware of blocking progression is essential for intelligent and effective defensive line play. The defender must know which players are most likely to attack him. The normal concerns for a defender are listed as follows, but the scouting report should refine these because every team does not attack with all of the potential blockers. For this reason, each scouting report can refine the progression for that week.

Being aware of the blocking triangle enables the defensive lineman to read the most dangerous potential blockers.

The expected progressions are as follows:

A. Man on center (nose guard, nose tackle)

1. Man on
2. Strongside guard
3. Weakside guard
4. Near back
5. Strong tackle
6. Weak tackle

7. Tight end
8. Flanker in motion.

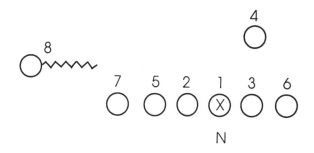

Blocking progression for man on center

The blocking triangle is the center and both guards.

Blocking triangle

B. Man on guard (defensive guard or tackle)

1. Man on
2. Lineman outside, near tackle
3. Lineman inside, the center
4. Far guard
5. Near back
6. Far tackle, flanker in motion.

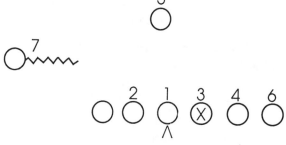

Blocking progression for man on guard

The blocking triangle is the man on and the two adjacent linemen.

Blocking triangle

C. Man on tackle (defensive tackle or end)

1. Man on
2. Man outside, tight end or wingback
3. Man inside, near guard
4. Near back
5. Far guard

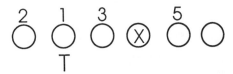

Blocking progression for man on tackle

The blocking triangle is the man on, the man inside, and either a lineman, wingback, or inside slotback to his outside; if no man is outside, it is the near back and flanker in motion.

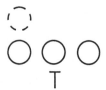

Blocking triangle

D. Man on end (defensive end or outside linebacker)

1. Man on, the end or inside slotback
2. Man inside, tackle
3. Near back, wingback or set back
4. Near guard
5. Far guard
6. Flanker in motion

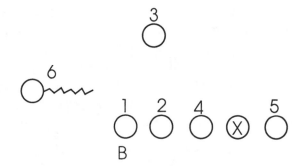

Blocking progression for man on end

The blocking triangle is man on, man outside, man inside; if no man is outside, it is the near back.

Blocking triangle

The blocks to expect from each person in the blocking progression are as follows:

Noseman:

- From center — drive, scramble, hook, post on double team
- From either guard — angle, scoop, drive man on double team, wedge
- From near back — delayed double team, lead block
- From either tackle — trap
- From end or wide receiver — trap or delayed double team

Man on guard:

- From near guard — drive, scramble, hook, post on double team
- From center or near tackle — drive, angle, scoop, drive man on double team, wedge
- From far guard — quick trap
- From near back — lead or delayed double team
- From far tackle — long trap
- From man in motion — trap or delayed double team

Man on tackle:

- From tackle — drive, scramble, hook, double team
- From end, or inside slotback — double team drive, angle block
- From near guard — angle, scoop, cross block
- From near back — kick out or log block
- From flanker in motion — trap inside or outside

Man on end:

- From end or inside slot — drive, hook
- From near tackle — angle, scoop, cross block
- From near back (wingback) angle, double team (set back) kick out, log, delayed double team
- From near guard — trap or log
- From far guard — trap or log
- From flanker in motion — trap, log, delayed double team

Coaches can set up their defensive reaction drills based on the types of blocks and the expected blocking progressions. For example, if no one in your league uses a scramble block or a scoop block, do not bother to practice against it. Defenders should practice against what they will see.

The pass rush begins with the recognition of a pass. It may be the drop step of the blocker. On play action passes, it takes longer to recognize. Once recognized, the defender should yell "pass" to alert his teammates. He should then start his rush by getting his hands on his blocker's jersey at chest to shoulder level. He must charge hard to defeat the blocker. There are several techniques that can be used, depending on how the blocker is blocking. Does he have too much weight forward or backward? Can his shoulders be turned? Are his feet quick enough to stay with the rusher? Does he have a weakness that can be defeated?

After the rusher has his hands on the blocker he can charge through the blocker, overpowering him, or he can attack one side. A big defensive end attacking a smaller offensive lineman or a back might decide to run right through his blocker. If the blocker is retreating fast and has too much weight on

his heels or has excessive momentum backward, he might also be susceptible to the head-on attack. If the matchup is even, it is better to attack one side of the blocker. Whatever the blocker's technique and size, there is a pass rush technique to beat him.

Basic Pass Rush Techniques

The bull rush is used against a fast retreating blocker whose weight is on his heels. It can also be used against an outmanned blocker. In this rush, the defender rushes hard at the blocker. He punches the heels of his hands into the outside of the chest or under the armpits of the blocker. He drives his legs hard as he pushes the blocker into the passer. Because the defender has momentum, he might be able to knock down the blocker. Linemen or big backers being blocked by smaller backs often use this type of rush to intimidate the blocker.

The jerk is used when the blocker has too much weight forward. The defender starts the charge forward and then, as the blocker lunges forward, grabs the blocker's jersey or pads and pulls him forward as he goes around him.

Most pass rushes will be to the side of the blocker. The defender should get the blocker's shoulders turned away from the line of scrimmage. As he does this, he can attack with power through that shoulder.

Following are techniques to attack through the shoulder that is turning backward:

The rip and run technique has the defender drive his far arm with a hard rip under the near arm of the blocker. If the defender is going to his right, which is the left side of the blocker, he hooks his left arm under the left shoulder of the blocker. He lifts up on the shoulder as he charges. This technique eliminates the hands of the blocker as weapons, turns the blocker's shoulders, and eliminates the blocker's ability to cut him as he moves past him.

Rip and run technique

Wrist club

The wrist club and swim is another technique that is used to the side of the defender's initial charge. The defender steps with the far foot and moves to the side of the blocker. When he is close to the blocker, he grabs the hand or forearm of the blocker or hits it with his forearm. (If going to the right, he hits the left hand or forearm of the blocker with his right hand.) This action knocks the blocker's arm off the rusher and creates a path for the rusher. Then he swings his far arm over the near shoulder of the blocker in a swim-like move.

Swim

The shoulder club and swim has the rusher hit into the shoulder of the blocker and then use his swim move. (If going to the right, he would hit the left shoulder of the blocker with his right hand.)

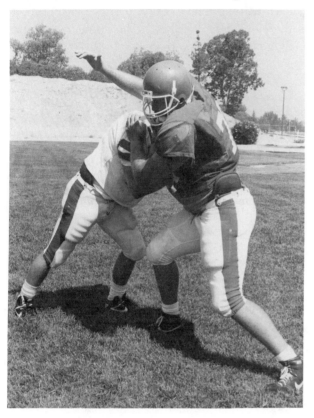

Shoulder club and swim

The shoulder club and slip has the rusher hit the blocker with a hard blow of his hand into the shoulder pad or upper arm of the blocker. The shoulder of the blocker should be lifted in either case. The rusher then drives his far shoulder under the armpit of the blocker. This is a good technique for shorter players working against taller blockers. In this case, the rusher can grab the area near the elbow of the blocker and lift as he charges under the arm.

Shoulder club and slip

The bull rush and slip is slightly different. The defender starts forward in the bull rush technique, but as the charge continues the defender lifts one shoulder of the blocker and then brings his far arm under the blocker's shoulder and drives past him.

Another method of pass rushing is to start the blocker's shoulders turning one way and then attack the other way. This should be done after the blocker has overcompensated for the outside rush and is somewhat off balance.

The pull and swim technique has the defender start in a hard rush to one side with his hands on the chest of the blocker. As the blocker turns his shoulders in one direction, the rusher either grabs the jersey or reaches behind the shoulder of the blocker and turns the close shoulder toward him as he swims over it with the other arm. For example, if the rusher is charging to his right and the blocker's shoulders turn in that direction, the defender grabs the blocker with his left hand pulling the right shoulder toward him as he swims his right arm over the blocker's right shoulder. This works well for taller defenders.

The reverse club and slip is used by shorter players. They start the rush to one side while turning the shoulders of the blocker in that direction. As the shoulders turn, the defender reaches up with his trailing hand and grabs the elbow or upper arm of the blocker pushing it upward and then ducking under it by driving his far arm under the blocker's upraised arm. If starting to the right, the defender lifts the right arm of the blocker with his left hand, then ducks under the blocker's right shoulder.

The club and spin is another technique to reverse the charge of the rusher. The rusher starts his normal rush, as above, but with the pressure to the outside the rusher hits hard into the midsection of the blocker with a hand or forearm and whips his other arm behind him, spinning to the inside. The spin must bring him closer to the quarterback, not back to the line of scrimmage.

The arm lift and charge is perhaps the most effective pass rush technique, but very few players have the strength and skill to use it. In this technique, the rusher grabs the wrist of the blocker with one hand and then raises it over the head of the blocker. He hits the blocker's chest with the other hand and raises him as he charges directly through the blocker.

The rushing lanes are important to understand as the defender moves past his blocker. The defender must realize where the passer is moving and his own responsibility for the rush. The outside rushers usually take responsibility for containing the passer. The inside rushers are then more flexible in the rush they take. However, they must be aware of the possibility of the draw play.

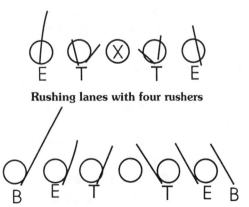

Rushing lanes with four rushers

Rushing lanes with six rushers

If the passer escapes the contain of the outside rusher, somebody must assume that responsibility to stop the passer and rush him again. If the passer is allowed to run unimpeded outside of the rush, he gains much more time for his pass or he can run. It is therefore essential that he be contained in the pocket by the outside rusher.

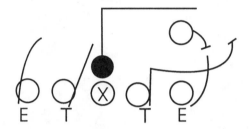

Inside rusher picking up contain

Stunts

Stunts are designed to confuse the blocking assignments of the offensive line. They are designed to make the big play, either a sack on the passer or a loss by a running back. The stunts may involve linemen, backers, and defensive backs. Two or more players may be involved in any stunt.

Because the stunts involve a guessing game, the defenders must be alert to plays that could have been called that would have defeated the stunt. For this reason, the man who is expected to break free into the backfield should check the play as he starts his stunt. If the play is coming at him, the stunt can be scrapped. Often a team that stunts when it expects a pass is fooled when the offense runs a play right at the spot vacated by the defender. Another important factor is that the stunts should take place on the offensive side of the line of scrimmage. They must be aggressive charges.

Twists involve two linemen. The first defender moves across the face of one or two blockers while the second goes behind and moves into the seam created by the blockers attacking the first man.

As the linemen move, they must be able to protect themselves with the block protection techniques described earlier. As they cross, they should be aware of the movement of the blockers. If the blockers move with them, it is a man-to-man blocking scheme. If the blockers stay, they are in a zone scheme. The stunts work better against the man schemes.

Tackles twist

End-tackle twist

Stunts against a zone scheme are usually more effective if the zone is overloaded with a three-on-two attack.

End-tackle-outside backer stunt

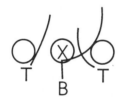

Two tackles and inside backer stunt

Pursuit

Pursuit to the ball is the next job of the defender. If the defender is not directly attacked, he must quickly discover where the ball is going and then take a path that enables him to intercept the ball. If it is a pass, the rusher must follow the ball and get to where he can make the tackle if the receiver is delayed or runs laterally.

In choosing a pursuit path, a cardinal rule is to "never follow your own color." Every defender must be taking a route that gets him to the ball carrier without having to run over his own man.

Trailing the play is the responsibility of one of the defensive linemen — usually the widest man away from the play. He should be alert to counters, reverses, bootlegs, play action passes, and cutbacks. His path should be as deep as the deepest man.

Drills

1. *Shiver drill.* This can be done into a bag, an arm shield, or a sled. The player explodes his body, makes the desired shiver (hand or forearm), then drives his legs. In beginning this skill it can be done with the defender on his knees popping his shiver into a blocking bag. The coach looks for proper technique — elbows and shoulders at a 90-degree angle for the forearm shiver; elbows in and down for the hand shiver.

2. *Pass rush contain drill.* This drill is done with four rushers against five blockers and a quarterback. The rushers start attacking in their lanes. The quarterback drops, then attempts to escape outside the contain rusher. If he escapes, the next rusher to the inside loops back and outside, then becomes the contain man and the rush continues.

3. *Pursuit drills* should be done in different parts of the fields and in different phases of the game (scrimmage play, punt coverage and so on).

4. *Ball stripping drills* can be done in one of several ways. One drill is to combine it with form tackling, with the first player making the tackle into the pit while a second player strips the ball by lifting the shoulder and punching the ball. A second drill is to have the ball carrier chased closely by the stripper, who rips downward at the ball carrying arm as he makes the tackle.

16
Linebacker Fundamentals

Linebackers are the backbone of the defensive team. They must be sure tacklers and premier run defenders, but they also must be prime pass defenders. Offensive strategies and tactics are often devised to fool the linebackers. Faking the run and then throwing the short pass, faking the drop back pass and then running the draw, starting the play one way and then countering opposite are all ways of fooling the linebackers.

In coaching the backers, it is important that they be disciplined in their responsibilities but they should not be robots. They should be able to play recklessly within the scope of their assignments.

Inside Linebackers

Stance for linebackers is a two-point stance. Inside backers can be more upright because they are farther from the blockers. The toes should be parallel to the line of scrimmage and the feet one-and-a-half to two feet apart. The knees are flexed. The torso flexes forward and the head is up. The hands are at about chest height if a blocker is an immediate threat. If the blocker is one-and-a-half yards away or more, the arms can be dropped comfortably in front of the body. The weight should be on the balls of the feet.

Movement of the linebackers is primarily lateral while remaining in the hitting position. The backer should shuffle sideways (not crossing his feet) while keeping his shoulders parallel to the line of scrim-

mage. It is only as a last resort that the backer should turn and run. Plays such as a quick pitch or a spot pass to a wide receiver would be such situations.

Keys for inside backers are essential so that they are not easily fooled. Linebackers can key a lineman or a back, or read through a lineman to a back. In some cases they can key the spin of the quarterback — if the basic plays (not the counters) always go to the side toward which the quarterback opens, the linebacker can start in that direction. Some teams always reverse pivot, so the backer can start to the side away from which the quarterback turned. Most teams open sometimes and reverse sometimes, so this key is not always valid. Check the scouting reports.

Keying the guards is standard in the Okie 5-2 or pro 3-4. The backer "mirrors" the action of the guard. If the guard attacks him he attacks the guard and then pursues. If the guard drops back in pass protection, the backer drops into pass coverage. If the guard pulls behind his linemen, the backer moves behind his linemen. If the guard blocks the next man in or out, the backer steps into the same area in which the guard moved.

Examples of keying the guard follow:

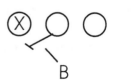 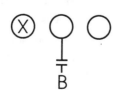

141

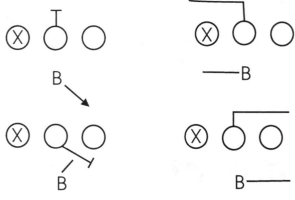

Keying the guard

Keying a near back is done similarly. If the back crosses the center, so does the linebacker. If the back attacks on his side of the center, the backer moves to that area. Generally the backer keys only the first step, but sometimes, in order to pick up counters, he keys two or three steps. A "near back key" is used when the offensive team does not cross its backs.

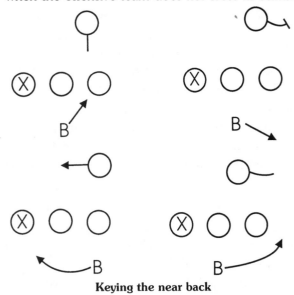

Keying the near back

Keying a far back (cross key) is often used when the offensive team crosses its backs such as in a cross buck or a belly series counter. The same principles apply as in keying a near back. If the far back comes at the backer he holds and protects his responsibility. If he moves the other direction, the backer pursues. Some teams start with a near back key and then switch to the far back, for a possible counter, if the flow goes away.

In playing against an "I" team, the backer may key the fullback or the tailback. Usually he keys the back who is most likely to run a counter.

Reading through a lineman to a back is a more complicated read, but is often much more effective because it can pick up counter plays in which a lineman leads. There is no reason to key linemen unless they lead in counters.

Reading through the near guard to the near back is the easier read. However, it should not be used if the offense crosses its backs. The backer should look through the guard to the near back. If he sees lateral movement from the guard, a pull, he honors that and starts laterally. If the guard moves forward, even at an angle, he disregards the guard and keys the back as explained above.

If a team crosses its backs and pulls one or both guards on counters, he should read through the near guard to the far back. He uses the same principles as above — lateral movement by the guard is primary; if no lateral movement he keys the back.

If a team is a heavy keying defense, this read through the lineman to the far back is the "universal" read. It works against any offense, but it is the most difficult to master. The only exception to its working is when a team employs key breakers, such as false pulling a guard or running the far side back away from the point of attack.

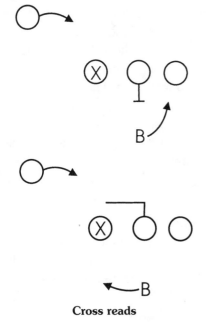

Cross reads

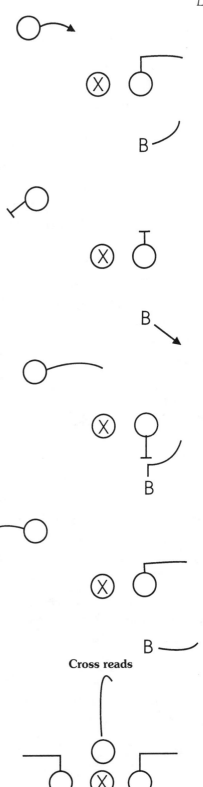

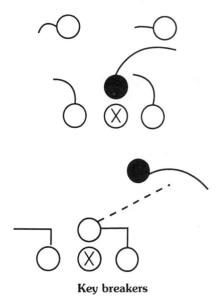

Key breakers

With practice, this can be done effectively, but it requires time to master. A heavy keying defense, if it is to be used, must be practiced all year.

Another type of key is reading a triangle. The triangle can be the guard, center, and near back or the guard, tackle, and near back. Some coaches prefer the guard, quarterback, near back. In this read, there is more emphasis on the blocking pattern of the linemen than the movement of the back.

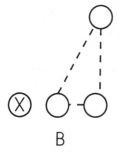

Triangle for inside backer

Another possible assignment of the backer can be to "get" a back. In this assignment, he is responsible for stopping one back, whether it is a run or a pass. This assignment might be used when the defense called is a man-to-man pass defense or it might be used when one offensive back is a controlling type of player. When this is the case, one or both inside backers may be told that their only responsibility is to stop that player.

Cross reads

Key breaker

Playing the Block

The blocking scheme gives the inside backer an even better idea as to where the play is heading. The blockers can attack the inside backers in one of several ways. The backer must focus on the potential blockers rather than looking at the back. He may read his key and then look at the blockers, but if he looks for the ball carrier he is likely to be blindsided by a blocker and knocked out of the play.

The drive block by a lineman head-up on the defender should be met with a shoulder charge and forearm rip by the inside shoulder and forearm. The inside leg is forward. The target is the inside number of the lineman. From the snap of the ball he should be checking the flow angle of the backs to tip off an inside or outside attack. Still, he must defeat the block before he moves right or left. If the backer is playing on the guard, as in an Okie or 3-4, he should squeeze the guard toward the center with his outside leverage (outside arm). Don't let the head of the guard get past the outside hip. If the ball goes outside, react and make the play from the inside out.

The cut block is a block aimed at the backer's knees or lower. If he is not looking at the blocker, this can be an effective block. However, if he sees the blocker coming low, he merely has to keep his feet back, put his hands on the back of the blocker and push him down while giving ground slightly.

The reach or hook block has the lineman stepping outside to get an outside position on the backer. The backer must step wide with his outside leg to meet the blocker head-up. He then plays the same technique as in the drive block.

The scoop or slip block has the lineman on the backer blocking the next defensive lineman toward the flow. The offensive man toward the flow is then free to slip his man and get a better angle on the backer. A key is that the offensive lineman on the backer moves directly down the line of scrimmage toward the backfield flow. The backer must step in the same direction and be ready to meet the next blocker with the near forearm and shoulder. Be ready for the cutback. If there is no cutback, take the best angle of pursuit, to either side of the blocker.

The cross block is expected when the lineman blocks down. The backer steps with his inside leg at a 45-degree angle toward the man who is attacking him. He makes the same type of hit, inside shoulder and forearm to inside number, squeezes the blocker into the hole with his outside leverage, then reacts to the ball carrier.

The down block should be met with the outside shoulder and forearm into the outside number of the down blocking lineman. Watch for cutback, then pursue.

The trap block is keyed when the lineman on him blocks down. The backer looks inside, expecting a pulling lineman to attempt to block him out. He meets it as with a cross block — inside shoulder and forearm to inside number of trapper. Squeeze the trapper into the hole. Don't let the trapper's head get past the outside hip. Make the play bounce outside.

The fold block requires the backer to take a lateral step to meet the blocker head on. Meet the blocker with the near shoulder and forearm. Pursue across the blocker's head.

The isolation block is keyed when the lineman blocks down or out and the near back or fullback is coming into the hole. He is played the same as a drive block — inside shoulder and forearm to inside number. Squeeze the back to the inside to make the play bounce out.

A pull and seal by a lineman is played by stepping laterally, hitting with the near shoulder and forearm, and checking for a blocking back or the ball carrier.

The inside backer must be aware of blocks coming from several areas. His concerns are, in the following order:

1. Man on
2. Man outside
3. Man inside
4. Near back
5. Far guard
6. Near end, tackle, or flanker

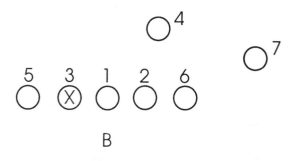

Blocking progression for inside backer

The blocks he might expect are as follows:

- From man on — drive, scramble, cut, double team
- Man inside or outside — angle block, scoop, fold, double team
- Near back — lead, delayed double team
- Far guard — trap
- Near end, tackle, flanker in motion — seal

The pursuit path of the linebacker can be based on the instinct of the player or can be planned. If he has no other assignment than to make the tackle, the onside backer should pursue keeping the runner on his outside shoulder. The offside backer should keep the runner about a yard ahead of him to prevent a cutback.

When his pursuit angle is planned as part of the defensive assignment, it can be into the line or behind the line. When the backer's responsibility calls for him to move into a hole in the line, it is called a "scrape" or "scrape off." When his responsibility calls for him to remain on his side of the line of scrimmage until he has a clear shot at the ball carrier, it is called a "shuffle."

Many defenses are designed to have the onside backer scrape into a hole created by the placement or the charge of the defensive linemen. This is really a controlled stunt. The backer doesn't know where he will penetrate until he has read his key. As he moves into the hole he must spot the ball carrier, stay slightly behind him to eliminate a cutback, then attack the ball.

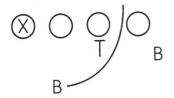

Scrape off hole created by alignment

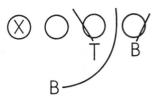

Scrape off hole created by charge of the linemen

The shuffling linebacker moves behind the line of scrimmage staying about a yard behind the ball carrier. When he sees an opening he can move across the line and make or assist on the tackle. In shuffling it is important to keep the shoulders square to the line of scrimmage and to move without crossing the legs for as long a distance as possible.

Playing off blockers is often essential to get to the ball but the backer should remember that his job is to make the tackle, not to play off blockers. Fighting the pressure is easier for linebackers because they are farther from their attackers and have more room to maneuver. Most defensive assignments expect the linebackers to have an outside responsibility. Because of this they generally use one of two techniques.

The backer may play the blocker with a forearm flipper, using the inside forearm and keeping the outside arm free to control the outside of the blocker. This is more often used if the blocker is upright. Against lower blockers or those coming at an angle, the backer may use his hands to ward off the blocker, always making certain to control the outside of the blocker. The hands should control the shoulder pads as the backer concentrates on the blocker while "seeing" the ball carrier.

As with defensive linemen, the backer should fight through the blocker's head. It is permissible for a backer to give a little ground as he plays through the head and continues his lateral movement. When the blocker is coming from directly in front of the backer and the ball carrier is directly behind the blocker, the backer must defeat the blocker while not taking a side. The forearm rip is generally the most effective technique to use. He should straighten up the blocker, push him away with the free (outside) hand, and make the tackle. He should never spin in this situation.

Outside Backers

Stance for an outside backer playing on a tight end or an inside slot back is usually low so that the potential block of his nearest opponent can be met.

Stance for outside backer (right)

Alignment is closer to the line of scrimmage, usually as close as possible if there is a blocker who is an immediate threat, such as a tight end or slot-back. If he is playing wider, such as in a walkaway position, he may drop off a few yards.

Keys for outside backers usually start with the nearest two lineman then the near back. If the backer is playing on a tight end, he would read the end and tackle and then the near back. If the end releases, it is likely to be a pass or a run away from the backer's side. The end is the major key.

Before the snap, the backer should recognize what types of plays that can be run at him from the backfield set. A wide halfback gives the offense the possibility of a quick pitch. With this possibility, he must be alert to the pull of the tackle leading the pitch. With backs in a veer set, he should be alert to the veer attacking his area and then play his re-

sponsibility — either the dive back, the quarterback option, or the pitch — whichever his coach has assigned on that defense.

In looking at his triangle, he must be alert for the end and tackle blocking down. This would probably indicate a trap, so he must prepare to meet it. If it is a veer set or a wishbone, he must be ready to play the option if the linemen block down.

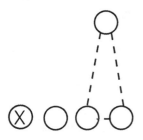

Triangle for outside backer

Most coaches assign the linebacker on the tight end to keep the end off of the middle backer, to be able to fight off a seal block, and to slow up the end on pass plays. The outside backer must be alert to several types of blocks and plays aimed at the off tackle area or wider. He must be alert to the drive block, the kick out block, and the reach block from linemen. He must be aware of a block from a back that can be designed to take him in (log) or out. He must also be alert to the sweep, quick pitch, and the option. Generally, the outside backer reacts to the step of the tight end on him. If he is a weak side backer with no one on him, he has more time to read his keys and to react.

Playing the drive block is done by stepping with the inside foot, striking under the shoulders with the hands or forearm, then bringing the hips closer to the blocker so that the blocker can be lifted. If using the hands he should lock out the arms, then react to the pressure or the keys. He should control the line of scrimmage and not be driven back. The blocker should be controlled with the outside hand and squeeze him inside, thus reducing the off tackle hole. By keeping outside leverage he can pursue the wide runs from the inside out.

Playing the reach block is done by stepping laterally as the tight end steps laterally to get an outside position. The backer hits with his hands into the shoulder pads of the end and keeps the end's shoulder pads from turning him inside. An effective outside backer will turn the blocker's outside shoulder away from the line, making it impossible to be hooked in. The end must not be allowed to get an angled position on the backer and wall him off from an outside play.

Playing the cutoff block is done by stepping inside as the end steps inside. He must hold the line of scrimmage while maintaining outside leverage with his hands or with a forearm rip with his inside arm and control with his outside hand.

Playing the pulling lineman is done by stepping into the end, who is blocking down, and controlling him with a hand shiver, knocking him off of the defensive end. The backer should check the flow of the backs and the depth of the pulling lineman to determine if they are attempting to run off tackle (to his inside) or wide. Guards pulling deeper or a back taking a looping path toward him (to log him in) indicate a wide play.

If the play is designed to run inside, he should control the end with his inside forearm and outside hand or both hands. He should close the hole down from the outside. If the play is going wide, he must avoid being logged in by a back or pulling lineman by using his hands and keeping his feet free as he strings the play out.

Playing the cross block of the end and tackle is done by controlling the end, keeping him off the inside defender, then closing the hole and meeting the tackle with the hands or an inside forearm. This block is recognized by seeing the tackle come directly at him from over the hip of the downblocking end.

Playing the tackle log or hook block is done by controlling the end as in the cross block. If he sees the tackle looping deeper, he can expect a log type of block pinching him inside. When he sees this coming he steps laterally to gain a head-up position with the tackle, hand shivering him, avoiding being hooked, and controlling the line of scrimmage.

Playing the inside out (kick out) block of a back is done after controlling the end who is probably blocking down. The backer should approach the back at a 45-degree angle. The back should be hit with the inside shoulder and forearm, but controlled from the outside with the outside arm. The hole should be reduced, forcing the ball carrier to bounce wide. If the guard is pulling shallow, it is a tip that the play will be inside. If the guard is pulling deep, it will be outside so the backer can be even more conscious of the outside play.

Playing the load block (arc block) of a back is recognized by seeing a wider, often arcing, pattern that enables the back to get outside. Hit the back with an inside forearm rip or with the hands, always making certain that he has outside leverage.

The blocking progression is as follows:

1. Man on
2. Man to either side (tackle, tight end, inside slotback)
3. Near guard
4. Near back
5. Far guard
6. Flanker

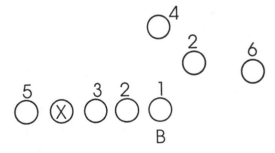

Blocking progression for outside backer

Blocks to expect are as follows:

- From man on — drive, cut, hook (reach)
- From man outside — double team, angle
- From man inside — angle
- From near guard — trap
- From near back — lead, log, delayed double team
- From far guard — trap, log

Playing the release of the tight end requires that the backer hit him to knock him off his path. If he releases inside, the backer should step down with him. The height of the end's head might tip off the type of play, run or pass. If the end's head is low he is probably blocking for a run. If his head is high he is probably releasing for a pass. The outside release might signal a pass, an option play, or a run to the other side. The backer hits the end, then looks to the inside to find the ball.

Playing the option depends on the theory of the defense being used. In some defenses the backer attacks the quarterback, making him pitch quickly. In other defenses he might be required to "slow play" the quarterback. In slow playing him, the backer remains at the line of scrimmage in a position where the quarterback will have trouble cutting back on him. The backer strings out the play as the defensive pursuit forms and the ball approaches the 12th man, the sideline.

Responsibilities of Backers

Stunts (or blitzes) give the linebackers the opportunities to make big plays. A stunting linebacker attacks the assigned area on the snap of the ball. He can either continue through the hole or make a read as he attacks and adjusts his charge based on the read.

For example, if the stunt is designed to work against a drop back pass but the offense runs a quick pitch, he would adjust and get into a proper pursuit path rather than continuing toward the quarterback.

The stunting backer should not tip off the offense that he is blitzing. He must start on the snap of the ball and charge toward his hole responsibility. As he approaches the hole he should adjust to the movement of the linemen or the backfield action. If the guards pull, he should follow. If they set in pass protection he should attack and use the techniques of pass rush described in the chapter on defensive line play. He should know whether he has an inside rushing lane or has outside contain on the pass.

Pass defense is a prime responsibility of the linebackers. They are usually called to drop into a specific zone, but are also often called upon to play man-to-man defense. Here are some concerns for the backers playing zone defense.

Zone Defense

Pass drops begin when the backer picks up his pass key. It might be the linemen setting in cup protection or, for an outside backer, it might be his tight end releasing. Most coaches teach to turn to the outside and run back to the assigned zone while watching the eyes of the quarterback.

Coaches generally also ask the backer to peek at the near receivers to get a tip on the pattern that will be run. If he sees a wideout starting to curl in, the backer might adjust to a wider and deeper spot than he had anticipated. If he sees the wideout running a quick slant, he might adjust to a shorter and wider position.

The most important concern should be the eyes of the quarterback. For this reason, some coaches don't let their players peek at the potential receivers. They merely get their keys from the eyes of the passer. Few passers at the high school or college levels do a good job of "looking off" the backers. This is especially true if there is a strong pass rush.

When reading the eyes, the backer starts to make his drop but adjusts his drop depending on where the passer looks. By watching the eyes, four short defenders at a 10-yard depth should be able to cover the entire width of the field. The problem, of course, is to be able to get to the proper depth.

Traditionally, the proper depth has been 10 yards. However, as 15- to 18-yard patterns have become more common, the drops have often been adjusted to compensate. Some coaches have their backers drop immediately to the 10-yard depth and then count 1001, 1002 and start drifting farther back. The thinking is that if the pattern was a 10-yard "hook" or "in" pattern, it would have been thrown by the time the backer gets to the 10-yard depth, so the backer can drift deeper to reduce the seam between himself and the defensive backs.

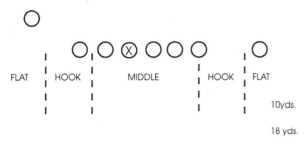

Five underneath zones

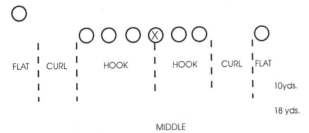

Six underneath zones

Reading the eyes of the quarterback can give the backer a big jump on the direction of the pass. As with so many other factors in football, the coach must choose between having him peek at the receivers or reacting only to the eyes of the quarterback. It is obvious that if he is peeking at receivers he has lost eye contact with the passer and might miss the early jump he could have had if he had not been looking for receivers.

Some coaches maintain that the backers cannot really see the eyes, so they must look at the face guard or the chin of the passer. Backers can get the jump on the ball if they move immediately as the passer looks at his target. Some coaches teach to start slowly and then run fast as the passer takes his long step. Most coaches teach the backers to run fast at the target when they see the passer look. They should keep their eyes on the quarterback while running. Some coaches teach to look at the target and run as fast as possible toward the target as soon as the key is recognized. This assures that the backer can cover the greatest distance toward the target. The coach must determine whether he wants to jump on the passer's eye key or to protect against a possible throwback. The coach must choose reckless pursuit or caution in determining which technique he will teach his backers.

Being conscious of the receivers is the other option for the backer. If he can see the potential receiver he should work to get about three yards in front of and no more than three yards inside the receiver. If no receiver is near him he can begin backpedalling and look for nearby receivers.

The backers should tell each other where the receivers are and who might be entering their zone. "Curl behind" or "deep cross" are examples of alerting an adjacent linebacker.

Man-to-Man Pass Defense

The backer must know whether he has deep help from the safeties or whether he has his man all over the field. If his assignment is to take away the underneath patterns, up to 18 yards, he can play more recklessly. In this assignment he can play under the man and knock down or intercept any short passes. If he has no deep help he must play more cautiously.

With deep help while playing a receiver wider than a tight end he can align himself inside and at a depth of six inches to four yards. He should not let the receiver inside of him. A tight end, wingback, or inside slot back should be played close and slightly inside.

The backer should concentrate on the receiver, chucking him, and keeping him outside. If he is playing tight to the line of scrimmage, as in a bump and run, he must slow up the receiver's pattern and knock him out of the pattern by making him run laterally rather than up field. He must then stay on the inside hip of the receiver.

If the defender is off the ball, he maintains his inside position. If the receiver tries to cross inside, he hits him. He should try to remain two to three yards deeper than the receiver and a yard to his inside. He should duplicate the receiver's cuts while maintaining his "air cushion" between himself and the receiver.

If the receiver gets behind him, he plays the same technique as the bump-and-run player and gets on the receiver's inside hip. The defender must be as close to the receiver as possible, continually looking at the receiver. He looks for the ball on one or all of the following keys: when the receiver looks for the ball, when the receiver's eyes are obviously concentrating on the ball (they usually widen), or when the receiver's hands move up to get into position to catch the ball.

If the backer's man is in a running back position, the backer checks for an immediate release by the back. If the back sets to block, the backer goes to him and plays him with his hands. This does two things: the back is occupied and cannot help to block a defensive lineman, and the backer is close to the back and behind the blockers in case the back releases for a screen pass.

Drills

- *Key, read, or "get" drills.* The type of drill depends on the key the coach wants the backer to learn. Examples: Key guard; read through the guard to the near back; read through the guard to the cross back; read center, guard, near back triangle.
- *Hand shiver or forearm flipper drill, maintaining outside leverage.* The coach signals one of the linemen to come at the backer. A ball carrier can be added to the drill. Use bags to limit the ball carrier's area to run.
- *"Reading the eyes" drill.* The coach simulates taking the snap, dropping and looking in each direction. The backer reacts to the eyes of the coach. The coach may throw the ball on his first, second, or third look.
- *Man-to-man pass defense drill.* The coach signals the receiver (tight end, wideout, or running back) to stay and block, then release inside or outside and run a pattern.
- *Pass rush drills.* See chapter on defensive line play.

17

Defensive Secondary Fundamentals

The players in the defensive secondary, the cornerbacks and safeties, must be intelligent, skilled players. They are the last line of defense to prevent touchdowns. Their techniques are predicated on the defensive theory of the coach — whether they play man-to-man or zone, loose or tight, deep or shallow. In any case, they must play mistake-free football.

Secondary rules should be very simple to reduce mistakes. Some coaches teach only one defense, with the defensive backs never varying in assignment. This greatly reduces errors, but it also reduces the ability to change coverages and attempt to fool the offense. At the high school level, simple rules are best. At the professional level, multiple coverages are a must. Still, broken assignments often occur at the pro level. This should make the high school and small college coach consider a simpler defensive scheme than they see on Monday Night Football.

Stance is a comfortable two-point stance. A "bump and run" cornerback would have his feet parallel or near parallel. If taking away one side of a receiver, he may play the near foot slightly closer to the receiver. Backs playing deeper play in a similar stance, but with the inside foot back.

The bump-and-run player has his hands up ready to hit or absorb the receiver. Backs playing deeper can keep their arms more relaxed. The closer to the receiver, the more important the stance.

Bump and run stance

The alignment of the backs depends on their responsibility. Some coaches prefer that they align the same on every play so as to reduce the pre-snap read of the quarterback and receivers. Other coaches align the defensive players so as to make their assignments easier to carry out.

The bump-and-run player should be very close to the line of scrimmage. The free safety should be 10 to 15 yards deep. The strong safety should be two to 10 yards deep and one to two yards outside of the tight end. The corners can be as deep as 10 yards, but usually start at a five- to eight-yard depth. The corners can play slightly outside or inside the receiver, depending on the width of the receiver and the responsibility of the defender.

Against a tight team, such as the tight-T or wing-T, the defensive halfbacks or corners might play three to four yards outside of the end or wing-back and four to eight yards deep. The safety or safeties might align only eight to 12 yards deep. If there is a single safety and he is required to play the deep outside zone, or if the defensive halfback has to rotate up, he might play as deep as needed to be able to beat the widest player into the deep outside zone. If there are twin safeties who rotate in an umbrella defense, they need only be deep enough to get to their zones ahead of any possible receiver.

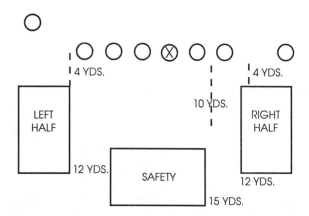

Possible alignment areas — three-deep secondary

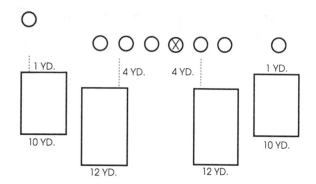

Possible alignment areas — four-deep secondary

Responsibilities of the defensive secondary depend on whether they are playing a zone defense, a man-to-man defense, or a combination of the two. In the zone defense, the defensive back should get to his area while watching the passer. The depth that he plays is determined by the zone he is assigned to cover. In the man-to-man defense, his major concern is to watch his man. The depth that he plays depends on whether the coach wants him to play

bump and run or play off him, giving him a cushion of air and not allowing him to complete the deep pass. If giving him a cushion, he generally plays five to seven yards deep.

Jamming the potential receiver is a technique that is used in a man-to-man, "bump-and-run" defense and in some zone defenses, if the corner has a shallow zone pass responsibility. The technique is similar to the hand shiver used by defensive linemen, but is generally made from the inside out or the outside in. The hit should be made with the palms open and the thumbs up. The blow should be struck from low in the numbers up and through the receiver. This throws the receiver off his path, and the timing of the pass might be hindered. The jam can also be done with the defender hitting the center of the receiver's chest with the hand nearest to the receiver.

Since generally the defensive back should be able to maintain his balance, he should not overextend into the hit. He must keep his balance. However, when he knows that he has *effective help* in the deep zone he can really unload on the potential receiver as long as he can keep his balance.

Some coaches, afraid that the bump-and-run player will overextend while hitting, have their players "absorb" the body of the receiver. In doing this, the defender stays in front of the receiver, puts his arms out and allows the receiver to make some forward progress. This softer approach to "bumping" allows the defender to stay more balanced and to keep his body in front of the receiver longer.

Coaches often teach that if the defender is inside of the receiver, he should bump him only on an inside release. Playing the inside is much simpler and more effective for most players playing man-to-man defense, because they can prevent the quick inside release and still maintain the preferred inside position on any outside release patterns. The major problem is against a team that is proficient in completing a fade pattern.

The defender should try to run the receiver out of his route and slow the timing of the pattern. Because the receiver is trying to get into his planned route, the longer he is delayed the more the overall pattern is disrupted and the greater the chance for a sack. If the receiver is forced to run along the line of scrimmage, he has been effectively delayed.

Some coaches teach to bump with one hand only. This stops the defender from overextending into the hit. The hand that hits should be the hand farthest from the direction that the receiver is moving. This enables the defender to open up in the same direction that the receiver is moving. The movement of the receiver actually helps the defender to turn toward his opponent and run with him. A combination of the absorbing bump and leaving the far hand on the receiver as he moves past the defender also works well.

Zone Defense

Zone responsibilities require that either two or three defensive backs cover deep. If three backs are used, they will generally play the three-deep zones if it is a drop back pass. They may rotate into a two deep on a long sprint out or roll out pass if the defensive halfback on the side of the flow is given the assignment of the flat zone. With two safeties and two corners, many combinations are possible to cover two- or three-deep zones.

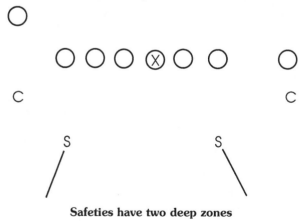

Safeties have two deep zones

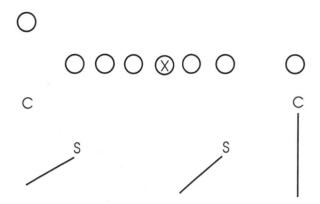

Safeties and one corner take three deep zones

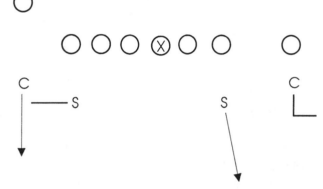

One safety and one corner take two deep zones

If flow goes away from the defensive halfback (three deep) or the corner (four deep), he should remain cautious of the bootleg, reverse, reverse pass, counter action, or play action pass. His rotation should not continue until he is certain that there is no possibility of a play coming back to his area.

Man-to-man responsibilities can be either bump and run, a press technique, or playing off the receiver with a cushion of air. In a bump-and-run technique, the defensive back takes away the underneath patterns by playing between the passer and the receiver. This is called "trailing." The long pass is taken away because of the speed of the defender. If the team is playing bump and run with the deep zones covered, the speed of the corner is not as critical.

In the "press" technique, the defender plays up to a yard-and-a-half off the receiver. He backpedals with the receiver, then as the receiver makes his cut the defender hits him with his "far" arm, the arm away from the direction of the cut. This hit should slow the receiver a bit and also helps to turn the defender so that he can run with the receiver.

When using the press technique, many coaches teach that the primary responsibility is inside. If a receiver has cut inside and then outside, the defender is told to honor the inside fake then, on a double-cut pattern, turn away from the receiver getting depth as he relocates the receiver on his outside. Double-cut patterns such as post square-out (a "dig" pattern) or a post curl-out leave the receiver open. However, the more dangerous post corner has a good chance of being well covered.

If the defensive theory is for the defensive back to play off the line he does not have as much responsibility for the very short passes, but is asked to take away the intermediate routes and still play the deep routes. However, he may also have a safety behind him for the deep routes so he can play the intermediate routes more aggressively.

Defenders playing off the line should "shade" to one side or the other — playing about a yard inside or outside of the receiver and taking away one possible cut. Most often they take away the outside cut, inviting the receiver to cut into the middle of the field where the linebackers can help.

Zone techniques start with getting whatever depth is necessary to get to the proper zone. This must be done prior to the snap of the ball. If a safety in a three-deep alignment is required to cover the deep outside zone in a rotation (against a sprint-out or roll-out) he might start 12 to 15 yards deep. On the other hand, a corner who is required to cover the deep zone behind him might be able to line up six to eight yards deep and still have plenty of time to get to his zone.

The first steps of the defensive back in most defenses are backward. Some teams have the defender turn and shuffle or start to run into his zone. This gets him there more quickly. Today more teams have him backpedal toward his zone. In either case he is reading his keys for run or pass as he takes his first steps. If a certain run key is read he can forget his zone and play his run responsibility. If he is in doubt, he plays the pass.

If running backward into the zone, the defender must have the agility to turn right or left whenever the quarterback looks in that direction.

Backpedaling is the more common technique used today. The backpedal is preferred for the following reasons:

- It enables the defender to keep his original alignment and leverage on the receiver.
- It keeps the defender's shoulders parallel to the line of scrimmage and enables him to move forward, right, or left quickly.
- It is more effective than the shuffle if playing a loose man-to-man coverage.

The technique of the backpedal requires that the defender keep his torso forward with his chin over his toes and his shoulders over his knees. Keep the head down, and the elbows bent at 90 degrees. The defender steps back quickly while driving his arms hard. By keeping his head and torso forward he remains balanced and able to stop and break forward for any short pass. His feet should be no wider than his hips. The player should concentrate on "stepping back" rather than "pushing off" because emphasizing pushing back may force him to lean back on his heels and make him stand up straighter, both of which will slow him down.

The defender should backpedal at three-quarter speed. At full speed he would not be able to change directions as fast to come up for a run or break for a short pass. The steps should be small to medium in length. The feet should stay close to the ground. The knees should be bent to enable the feet to reach back. The arms should pump forward and back, not across the body.

As he backpedals, he should remain in the proper leverage position, usually outside, in order to take away one of the receiver's options in cutting. After the receiver cuts the defender should whip his near arm toward the direction he will be running. This helps him to change directions more quickly.

The defender should be able to keep his leverage on the receiver for about 15 yards before he has to turn and run with him. This occurs after the receiver is about three yards from the defender. Receivers want to get to the defensive back as quickly as possible and force the back to turn and run. They also want to get head-up with the defender. Backs therefore must work on staying in the backpedal as long as possible while keeping the shade on the receiver.

Defensive backs should work on backpedaling straight back and on backpedaling both in a weave pattern and at 30- and 45-degree angles to their initial straight drop. They must continually work on keeping the cushion (at least three yards) and the shade (at least one yard) on the receiver.

The speed and depth of the drop depends on the coach's theory. Some coaches prefer that the defensive back be much deeper than the receivers. If using this theory, the back is much more likely to be able to intercept the long ball or to react more effectively laterally to any long ball. It should be noted that a long pass released when the receiver is 15 to 20 yards downfield will be caught after the receiver has run an additional 20 to 30 yards. So it is not important to be close to the receiver if he is running a long pattern. (On quick-in patterns, the receiver runs about six yards to the reception point after the ball is thrown. On quick-out patterns, he runs about 10 yards.)

The deeper the defender is before the release of the pass, the more he can come under control as the passer sets, and the greater lateral distance he can cover after the ball is released. Of course if he is very deep, the seam between him and the undercoverage is greater. The advantage to playing closer to the receiver is that the defender is closer to the target area if the pass is thrown into the intermediate zone of 15 to 22 yards. The coach must therefore decide whether he wants a more effective coverage of the long pass or a compromise in which there is more help by the deep backs in the intermediate coverage.

Whichever theory is utilized, the defender must watch the quarterback. While many coaches have the defender peek at the receivers in his area, doing so may take away the defender's ability to react quickly to the eyes or arm of the passer. It generally takes more than a second to change focus from peeking at a receiver to establishing contact with the passer's eyes.

Some coaches have the defensive backs turn their bodies and even move a bit toward the direction that the passer is looking. However, the main key to release the defender to go to the ball is the "long arm action" of the passer. Most passers fake a pass with a short arm action and a short step. When passing long, their arms come back farther and they take a longer step. By watching the "long arm" action of the passer, the defender can start to go in the direction of the pass before it is thrown.

After the ball is in the air, the defender should move to the area in which he can intercept it at the highest point. Because he will have a greater depth than the offensive receiver, at least five yards, he should have more room to maneuver for the ball than the receiver, who is running at top speed to the point of reception.

Playing through the receiver to get to the ball is essential. Once the ball is in the air it belongs to either team. Neither team can interfere with the other. Interference occurs only when one player plays the man rather than the ball.

Catching the ball should be done by squaring the shoulders to the ball, reaching or jumping high (catching the ball at its highest point), looking the ball into the hands, and catching the near end of the ball. If the defender concentrates on catching the end of the ball, it won't go through his hands. If it were to bounce out of his hands and forward, he would still have an opportunity to catch it after he had stopped it. After making the interception and tucking the ball under his arm, the defender should yell the code word, usually "oskie" or "fire," to alert his teammates that he has intercepted and that they should block for him.

Verbal communication on the pass is essential. The sequence is as follows:

1. "Pass" when it is recognized that a pass play is operating.

2. "Ball" when the ball is released.

3. "Got it" when the defender knows he can intercept it. This alerts the nearby teammates to get ready to block for him or to be ready for a tipped ball. Without this call, it occasionally happens that two defenders are in position to in-

tercept and they hit each other knocking each other off the interception.

4. "Oskie" or "fire" when he has made the interception and tucked the ball away. This alerts all of his teammates to block.

Also, the backs should call out the patterns in front of them as they unfold. By calling "slant," "hook," "out," "in," "comeback," or "curl," the linebackers have a better chance of adjusting their drops and making the interception or knocking the ball down.

Man-to-Man Defense

Responsibilities vary according to the theory of the defense. Bump and run requires a tight defense geared to take away the short and intermediate area passes. Deep man-to-man coverage is designed to take away the intermediate and long passes.

Bump and run coverage is designed to slow the pattern by hitting or absorbing the receiver on the line of scrimmage and making him take a lateral move before heading upfield. The defender should nearly always take away the inside of the receiver.

The defender lines up just outside or slightly inside the receiver. The stance should be parallel to the line of scrimmage so that the defender can step with the receiver, hit him, and block his release downfield. He should align as close as possible to the line of scrimmage.

On the movement of the receiver the defender should move his feet quickly, mirroring the feet of the receiver. This keeps him in front of the receiver. He then either absorbs the receiver or steps into him and hand shivers ("chucks" or "jams") him on the chest or shoulders. He should make the receiver run laterally as long as possible to throw off the timing of the play. When the receiver has released he should "get into his hip pocket" and run with him, duplicating the receiver's moves.

Watching the receiver's head and hands tells the defender when to look for the ball. Some coaches have the defender concentrate on the turn of the head and the receiver's eyes. The eyes may open

Man-to-man defense

wider as the ball approaches. Other coaches have the defender watch the hands and arms. As the arms come up in preparation for the catch, the defender turns and looks for the ball.

The defender should be aided by his teammates calling "ball" as the ball is released. After the ball is in the air, the defender plays the ball. His inside position gives him an effective advantage in intercepting or batting down the ball, if he has remained close to the receiver. If the defender does not turn to play the ball and the ball hits him, he may be called for pass interference because he was playing the man rather than the ball. This is particularly true if the defender sees the arms raise and he raises his arms to block the receiver's vision without looking for the ball.

When a defender turns to look for the ball, he often unconsciously moves closer to the ball and away from the receiver. Because of this, the man-to-man defender should be coached to lean in the receiver's direction as he turns. This reduces the chance of a completion over the head of the defender.

A newer technique used by many teams has the defender watch the arms of the receiver. As the arms come up, he sees "the flash of the ball" out of the corner of his eye. He then grabs the far shoulder with his near hand and rips through the near elbow with his far hand. (If the receiver is to the right and outside of the defender, he would hit the left elbow of the receiver with his left hand and grab the right shoulder of the receiver with his right hand.) Normally the ball hits the receiver's hands just before the defender hits him, so the receiver is playing the ball not the man.

The man-to-man defender must be particularly conscious of the types of patterns that should work most effectively against him — the out and up, the hook and go, the post corner, and the lean-in (on the defender) and break-out. The double fake is better countered by watching the eyes. The adept receiver might raise his hands on a fake (the hook, the out, or the post move of the double cut pattern) but his eyes probably will not bulge in anticipation of the catch.

Secondary responsibilities begin when the defender recognizes that the play is not a pass or when it is recognized that the pass is thrown out of his area.

After the ball is snapped, the defensive back, who is playing a zone defense, thinks pass as he reads his keys. If the key definitely shows run he adjusts his backward movement and begins his movement forward or laterally into his proper rotation or pursuit path.

The man-to-man defender must listen for verbal instructions from his teammates to alert him for "pass," which he is covering, or "run" which takes him out of his pass coverage responsibility and gets him into a pursuit path. If he is covering the pass and hears "ball," he can look for the ball and play it rather than play his man.

If the pass is thrown into another area, the defender must sprint to the area in the hope of accomplishing the following:

- Making the tackle if the pass is complete
- Catching the tipped ball if it is short and tipped by a linebacker, or long and tipped by the receiver or the covering back.
- Stripping the ball if it is caught by the receiver
- Recovering a fumble if one occurs
- Blocking for a teammate if he has intercepted the ball; the receiver should be the first target for a block

Stripping the ball from the receiver can be done as he is catching it or after it has hit his hands. When the receiver has his back to the defender, such as in a hook pattern, the defender can bump him hard with his chest while bringing his hands under the elbows of the receiver and ripping the arms outward and upward. This is called "playing through the receiver." The defender's contact should occur just as the ball contacts the receiver, not before.

Out and up strip

Another type of strip on a hook or comeback type of pattern comes from top to bottom, with the defender bringing his arms around the receiver and downward, attempting to make contact with the ball and forcing it downward.

Downward strip

When stripping from the side, the defender should grab at the receiver's far arm with his own near arm. If going to the right, he should grab the receiver's right arm with his right arm. The far arm is mostly used to stop the ball on the catch.

Far arm strip

If the far arm of the receiver cannot be reached, the defender can reach with his far arm for the near arm of the receiver while wrapping up the receiver with the near arm and making the tackle. If he is moving to his right and the receiver is moving and ahead of him, he can reach for the receiver's left arm with his left arm while wrapping up the receiver with his right arm. This is more effective if the ball is thrown ahead of the receiver and he reaches for it.

Near arm strip

Supporting the run responsibilities depend on the defensive theory. The cornerback may have the wide responsibility on a sweep or option. However, that responsibility might be given to a safety, who may be able to read the run more quickly because he is more likely playing a zone or, if in a man-to-man defense, watching the tight end on his side.

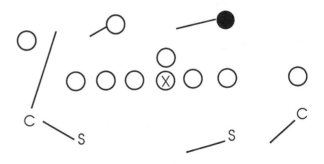

Corner supporting the wide run from wide position, with safety rotating

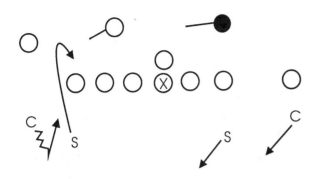

**Safety supporting the wide run, corner
in a secondary support responsibility**

A "hard corner" may take an "outside in" support movement, attempting to stop the flow and turn it in to the linebackers. More often, however, the defensive backs use the sideline as a 12th man and take an "inside angle out" on the support. The backs away from the point of attack should take the path necessary to make certain that they can make the tackle if necessary. This requires a deeper angle for the backs farthest from the point of attack.

Defensive backs must never be knocked down. They have plenty of room in which to maneuver, and should use their hands to play off the block.

Playing the blocker is another skill defensive backs must master. Often the defensive back has room to maneuver around the blocker who is moving fast. A simple fake one way and a move the other might be sufficient to get the blocker out of the way and be ready to make the tackle. This can be used if the ball carrier is some distance from the blocker.

If the ball carrier is close to the blocker, the defensive back must meet and defeat the blocker. When this is necessary, the defender must drop his weight over the leg with which he makes his lift, usually the inside leg. He anchors his back leg to absorb the hit of the blocker. He gets his pads under the blocker's. He rips with the arm over the forward leg. The other arm, usually the outside arm, punches up through the blocker's shoulder. The elbow must stay close to the body and under the shoulder. The palm and fingers should be up.

Tackling must be "sure" in the secondary. For this reason, the defensive backs may tackle high. They should be adept at working the high form tackle. They must be able to slow the ball carrier to enable the pursuit to catch up.

When tackling, the defensive back is not concerned with knocking the ball carrier backward, but with "wrapping him up" with his arms or forcing him out of bounds. The defensive back should never allow the ball carrier two ways to go. He must always take away one path and then make the tackle.

Be alert for the pass at all times. Teams are likely to pass in the following circumstances:

- After a timeout
- After penalties on the defensive team
- At the end of the half or game, if behind
- After a substitution
- After a sudden change of possession (fumble, interception, long kick return)
- On first and ten, especially in four-down territory
- On second and short
- On third and long
- After an injury to a defensive back or linebacker.

Goal Line

The closer the offensive team moves to the goal line, the closer the defenders must play the receivers. Most defenses call for a tight man-to-man, even a bump-and-run, type of defense in this area. Because of this, the defensive secondary must be aware of pick plays with a flanker and tight end or two tight ends crossing.

Drills

1. *Three steps and turn.* This drill, which is essential to zone defense, is also an excellent agility drill. The player starts his step with his left leg, moving at a 45-degree angle to his left rear. His next step is a crossover step with his right leg. The next step is with the left leg. As the left toe hits the ground he pivots 270 degrees on the ball of his foot and then steps to his right with

his right leg, then a left leg crossover, then a right step, then another 270-degree pivot. He should face the quarterback on each move. As he increases his ability, he increases his speed. He will also increase his angle of running so that eventually he can do this drill going straight back.

2. *Running backward and reacting to the ball.* This drill can be done backpedaling or running. The player gets to his zone and continues backward. As the passer looks, the defender turns his body in the direction that the passer is looking. When the passer makes the "long arm" action of the pass, the defender breaks for the ball in the direction that the passer is stepping.

3. A variation of this is the *three-passers drill.* The deep three defenders each have a passer to watch. The coach tells each of the three passers to do the same thing (three-step drop, throw right corner, roll right, throw back left, boot left, and so on). With this drill, all the rotations can be practiced and three defenders get work at the same time.

4. *Backpedaling.* After the technique of backpedaling has been learned, the player is taught to weave, running a serpentine or "S" pattern and backpedaling at 30- to 45-degree angles. Another backpedaling drill is to align the defensive back five yards from the receiver. On the signal, the receiver runs at the defensive back to tag him. The defender works on the speed of backpedaling.

5. *Backpedaling and reacting to the ball.* The defender starts in his backpedal, watching the eyes of the coach. The coach looks to an area and throws.

6. *Running into the ball* enables the defender to practice catching the ball when moving into it. The speed of the pass can be increased as the defenders become more adept at catching. They can improve their ability to catch by softening the catch. This is done by reaching for it and giving with it to cushion it.

7. *Line drill.* Start with one receiver on each hash mark and a defender in the middle of the field. The receivers start downfield while the defender retreats. The coach can throw to either receiver. It shows the defensive back that he can cover a wide lateral area if he has sufficient depth and reacts on the long arm action of the passer.

8. The drill also can be done across the field, with the receivers running on yard lines 20 yards apart and the defender on the yard line between them.

18

Kicking Fundamentals

Perfecting the fundamentals of the kicking game helps teams protect against the game-breaking mistakes that often occur on special teams.

The Long Snap

The punt long snap is one of the most important skills in football, and one of the most rare. Professional teams often draft a lesser player if he is an effective long snapper. A few years ago, a Washington Redskins long snapper missed three snaps on Sunday and was cut on Monday — even the pros don't always have the skill to make this pass.

Legendary coach Paul "Bear" Bryant estimated that 98 percent of blocked punts occur because of a poor center snap. This should convince coaches to make certain they have a couple of excellent snappers on their squad.

The long snapper does not have to be a center. Because so many teams use the spread punt, with the punter 12 to 15 yards back, the center does not need to block effectively, but it is essential that he get the ball back fast and accurately.

The long snap requires that the snapper pass the ball quickly to a punter standing 12 to 15 yards behind him in a spread punt formation. The snap should take about .7 second to get the ball back 10 yards, about .75 second if the punter is 13 yards back, and about .8 second if the punter is 15 yards back. This requires strong latissimus dorsi, lower chest, and triceps muscles. The pass can be made

directly from the ground or by picking up the ball then snapping it. The snap directly from the ground is the fastest and is definitely the preferred method.

The snapper's stance should be such that his feet are a good distance from the ball, so that he can reach out comfortably. By reaching for the ball the muscles are stretched — and a stretched muscle reacts more quickly. The feet should be even, with the toes equidistant from the line of scrimmage. If one foot is back it might cause the ball to drift to the other side. Most of the weight should be on the balls of the feet. Little weight should be on the football.

The strong arm, generally the right, grips the ball as if a forward pass will be thrown. The last two fingers usually grip the laces. The other hand can rest on top of the ball and aid in keeping the ball straight. The ball should be nearly flat on the ground. Lifting the nose of the ball can cause an error in the snap. With both arms moving between the legs, errors which would move the trajectory right or left are minimized. A one-handed snap is more likely to have errors to either side.

The target should be the inside thigh or knee of the kicking leg of the punter. The punter should give a target with his hands. This low target is important, because snappers tend to snap too high rather than too low — especially in the heat of a game. If the snapper aims at the knees and snaps two feet above the target, the ball will still come to the punter's waist. He would have to miss the target by six feet or more to snap it over the punter's head. (Many punters give a target at chest or shoulder level. When the snap is two or more feet above this high target, the punter must reach or jump and loses his rhythm.

The snap count should be up to the center. The punter can yell "set" when he and the team are ready. If a defensive team is trying to stunt through the center's area to block the kick, he should be alerted by a guard if he does not see it himself. The center can then look around for a possible stunt near him, get ready to snap, and then snap it.

The snap should be hard at the target. The pre-snap movement of the center's hips should be minimal. Most snappers raise their hips just before starting their backward snapping movement. This upward hip action signals punt blocking teams to start their charge and get a jump on the offense.

As the snap is made, the snapper must watch his target until the ball has left his hands. The snapper must follow through with both arms, with the palms facing upward, then as the ball is released snap them forward and lift his head quickly, looking for someone to block. The center blocks passively, as in a pass protection block, then releases downfield toward the punt receiver. The other men in the punt coverage wave set their lanes by where the center is moving.

The field goal and extra point snap must be both fast and accurate. Because the kick must be away in 1.2 to 1.4 seconds, the snap should be in the holder's hands in .4 to .5 second. Accuracy is more important than speed, however. A high fast snap must be controlled by the holder and then placed down. This takes a great deal of time.

The snap should be low, between one and two feet off the ground. One foot high is perfect. If possible, the laces should be pointed upward as they hit the holder's hands, so that he doesn't have to spend much time spinning the laces forward.

Because the distance from the snapper to the holder is always the same, the ball can be snapped so that the laces are on top most of the time. The snapper can take his normal grip and snap several times, noting where the laces land in the holder's hands. The snapper can then adjust the laces on his grip if necessary.

For example, if the laces are on the bottom when the holder catches it, the snapper can rotate the ball 180 degrees from where the snapper had it originally. If the laces are off by 90 degrees, the snapper should turn the ball 90 degrees one way or the other to make them land high in the holder's hands.

Punting

The punter should set up at 10 yards in the tight punt formation, at 12 or 14 for a high school spread punt, and at 15 yards for a college spread punt.

The stance of the punter should be leaning slightly forward with the feet parallel or the kicking foot slightly forward. The legs should be shoulder width, with the weight on the balls of the feet. The punter should be ready to move right or left, always anticipating a bad snap. The hands should give the snapper a low target, just inside the kicking leg knee.

Punters not instructed in giving the low target usually give a target at chest or shoulder height. A small error in the height of the snap can be disastrous, both in throwing off the punter's timing and in increasing the likelihood of a blocked punt.

Proper punter's stance

The equipment used should aid the punter. The hip pads should not restrict his hip movement, and he should wear low-cut shoes to enable maximum ankle extension. Many professionals remove the tongue of the shoe and kick without a sock, because they do not want shock absorbing materials between the football and the bones of the foot. They also often tie their shoes on the inside of the shoe so that the knot is not at the point where the ball makes contact with the foot. Punting barefoot reduces the shock absorbing material between the ball and the foot, and enables maximum ankle extension. However, it doesn't really make much difference in the kick. It is more of a psychological factor.

The mechanics of the punt start with the punter moving in front of the ball. If the ball is snapped to his right, he steps right with his right foot and then moves his left foot to the right and re-establishes his stance. He should never reach for the ball, but always move his whole body in front of it. If the ball is over his head, he should back up and reach up for it. If it is way over his head, he must turn and run back. The punter should then run away from the opponents and kick the ball. If it would be blocked, he should just run with it.

Ball at one o'clock position

The punter then looks the ball into his hands. He adjusts the laces to the right, to a "one o'clock" position if right-footed, as he starts his first step with his non-kicking leg. Both the laces and the valve are "dead spots" that should not hit the foot. The punter's foot drives halfway into the ball upon contact and the ball bounces faster off the foot the more it is compressed. Kicking a dead spot reduces the reaction of the ball off the foot.

The punter should hold the ball away from his body from the catch to the kick. It should not be brought into the body.

The first step is with the non-kicking leg. It is a short step made as the ball is being adjusted.

The second step is a normal length step. During this step, the punter makes the final adjustments to the ball and prepares it for the drop. Beginning punters usually adjust the ball and then start forward. This wastes tenths of a second. Most punters angle the ball slightly inward and downward so that it spirals better. The inward angle should have the front end of the ball over the big toe or slightly outside it.

Experience tells the punter the correct angle for him. Some coaches prefer that the ball be held so that it is pointed directly upfield with the longitudinal axis of the ball bisecting the laces of the shoe. This often gives an end-over-end kick that should bounce farther.

During this second step, the ball is brought up to chest height and held away from the body. The ball should not be lifted or lowered from this chest height position. The head should be down with the eyes on the ball.

The third step is a longer step. At the finish of this step, the kicking leg is starting forward. The ball is dropped during this forward whip of the kicking leg. The body must continue to lean forward.

The drop is the most important part of the punt. Without the correct drop, the ball does not hit the foot correctly. The punter should experiment with the several methods of holding the ball so that it drops consistently, but the distance the ball is dropped should be as short as possible. The longer the ball is in the air, the more mistakes in the drop are magnified. Also, when there is a wind, the mistakes are magnified even more.

Most coaches teach that the kicking-side hand be near the back of the ball with the other hand being forward. Some coaches prefer that the hands be under the ball, with the hands sliding out from under it on the drop. Other coaches prefer to have the rear hand on top of the ball so that less contact with the ball is possible after the initial release. Their thinking is that with a hand under the ball the releasing hand might pull the ball with it to the outside as it releases.

The ball should be dropped from a spot over where the kicking leg swings. It should not be dropped in the center of the body. This requires that the punter kick toward that spot rather than having a free swinging, straight leg action.

A punter with a "quick" leg can drop the ball from a lower point. A punter with a slow leg must drop it from a higher position in order to get the ball to the foot at the proper spot.

For a higher punt, hold the ball higher and closer to the body. For a lower punt, such as one into the wind, the ball should be held lower and farther from the body. If the ball is dropped correctly, the nose drops earlier than the rear of the ball. This should enable the ball to be angled downward as it hits the instep. It should be at the same angle downward as the angle of the instep. A correct drop and foot contact results in a spiraled kick.

If the nose of the ball is too far down or the toe is pointed upward upon contact, the ball might be kicked end-over-end with the front end going upward and backward. This results in a very ineffective punt that falls short and probably will bounce back toward the scrimmage line after it hits. If the ball is not angled downward sufficiently, the rear tip might be contacted first and another end over end kick, with the back end of the ball going up and forward may result.

The kicking action starts with the kicking leg back. It is whipped forward through the ball. The kicking foot is extended so that the top of the foot continues in a straight line from the lower leg.

Final step and drop

For most punts, the ball should be contacted just below knee level. This should give the punt good height. In cold weather, it should be contacted higher because the ball does not compress as much and leaves the foot quicker.

The height at which the ball is contacted determines the trajectory of the ball. If the ball is kicked high and short, it indicates that the ball is being met too far above the ground. Meeting it too high also generally reduces the time that the ball is on the foot. The kicking leg also might be nearly fully extended if the ball is met too high. Both of these factors affect the amount of force imparted to the ball.

The follow-through should be as high as possible. If the kicking leg is stopped quickly, it means that the leg was slowing down as the ball was contacted. This takes speed off the ball. The force of the kicking action tends to give the body a rotating motion, forcing the kicking leg to finish on the opposite side of the body. This must be eliminated or minimized for maximum efficiency.

Hang time of more than four seconds is essential if a team is covering the kick rather than kicking it out of bounds. Some punters get hang times of more than five seconds. An excellent hang time for high school is 3.8 seconds; for college kickers, 4.3; for pros, 4.5.

An acceptable hang time would be .1 second per yard from the line of scrimmage, so a 38-yard kick should have a hang time of 3.8 seconds. This would be acceptable for high school. An average college punt should be 43 yards, with a hang time of 4.3 seconds.

Individual differences account for some variation in technique. A punter with shorter arms probably needs to hold the ball closer to its end. The long-armed player may hold it more in the middle. The punter with less ankle flexibility might need a greater angle of the ball to the foot so that the toe does not contact the ball and create an end-over-end punt.

Angling the punt to the "coffin corner" is done by turning the body toward the target after catching the snap. The point of aim is determined by whether the punt drifts after it is kicked. A good punt goes straight. Some punters, however, get a drift. This drift is usually to the side of the punting leg, so a right-footed punter might get a drift to the right.

If this drift is common, the punter can aim at the goal line if he is right-footed. A lower punt generally goes straighter to the target and varies less in the wind. If you have a punting specialist, he might be able to practice both low and high kicks.

The punter should aim his body at the target point after the ball is snapped. Another method of aiming is to put one or two markers on the ground — pieces of white athletic training tape will do. He can then check them as he makes his steps. These markers should be placed on the spots where his feet land as they step into the punt.

The pooch punt is aimed down the middle. It might be fair caught at the 10-yard line or allowed to bounce by the receiver and downed by the punting team. The pooch punt is easier to teach, especially if the punter is not a specialist and has limited time to practice his kicking. The punt is kicked high to enable the coverage to get down under the punt and force the fair catch or down the ball before it goes into the end zone.

The ball should be held with the nose up and kicked with the toe up. This increases the chance that the ball will bounce straight up after it hits the ground, which in turn reduces the chance that the ball will bounce into the end zone.

Time of the punt depends on the distance the punter is from the snapper. At 12 yards, the punt should be away in 2.0 seconds, at 13 yards in 2.2, and at 15 yards in 2.3. If it takes .3 second longer than the above noted times, the punt is likely to be blocked if the opponents are rushing. Generally, punts take less time in a game than in practice because of adrenalin.

The Place Kick

The place kick and the drop kick can be used to score extra points, field goals, and to kick off. The once-popular drop kick isn't seen today because the shape of the ball has been changed from the rounder rugby ball shape to the more streamlined ball. The older style of place kicking was the straight-ahead kick. This is quite accurate, but lacks the distance of the more popular soccer style kick. The soccer style kick enables the player to get a longer leg whip prior to the kick, increased power from the hip rotation, and to get more of the foot into the ball. These three factors enable increased force to be imparted to the ball. Also, because more of the foot contacts the ball, there is more margin for error than in the straight-ahead kicking technique where a slight misplacement of the kicking toe may misdirect the ball.

Whichever style of kick is used, it must be away quickly. To avoid the block, the kick should be away in 1.3 seconds. The kick in the game generally gets away about 0.1 second faster than in practice because of the excitement of the players.

The hold is done from a point 7½ to 8 yards behind the snapper. Because the rushers are much taller than they used to be, the traditional seven-yard depth is generally not far enough back. This is particularly true when kicking off the grass and for soccer style kickers who don't get the quick lift of the ball as the straight-ahead kickers do.

The tee (high school) or hand target (college and pros) should be at the 7 ½- to 8-yard depth because if it is shorter the kick might be blocked from the middle. If it is deeper, the outside rushers have a better chance to block it.

The holder should be on one knee; the down knee is the one closest to the center. The other leg should be flexed and near the armpit closest to the kicker. The cleats under the toe should be on the ground so that the holder can stand up if necessary to handle a bad snap or to move out if a fake kick is called. The hand closest to the kicker may touch the target (tee or spot on the grass) to help the kicker, with the other hand providing a target for the snapper about a foot off the ground and slightly in front of the knee which is on the ground.

Hold and approach

Proper position for holder

As the ball is caught, the holder must turn the laces forward so that they do not affect the flight of the ball after it is kicked. Laces to the side might make the ball drift in that direction. Laces at the rear might affect the kick if the kicker's foot contacts them.

The hold is done with one finger of either hand. In holding for a soccer style kicker whose kicks drift, the holder and kicker can experiment with holding the ball at an angle. By holding the top of the ball in the direction opposite the drift of the ball, the drift might be straightened out. So, for a right-footed kicker whose ball drifts left, the top of the ball can be held to the right. A properly kicked ball will not drift. If wind is a factor, the holder can tilt the top of the ball into the wind about an inch. This will help to offset the effect of the wind.

The European soccer style or "sidewinder" kick has greater power and is generally recommended by the major kicking coaches for those players who want to be able to kick off long or to kick long field goals. Because the ball is contacted higher and with the thick part of the foot, more lineal power but less rotary power is imparted to the ball. This does not enable as much quick height on the ball.

The kicker must experiment with the exact starting point for his stance. Most kickers walk three normal steps straight back from the ball and then take two small steps (about two to two-and-a-half feet each) to the side, the side away from the kicking foot. This puts them at a 30-degree angle to the ball.

From this point, the kicker may step up or back another foot to get to the precise spot where he feels the most comfortable in his approach to the ball. If the kicker starts too far away from the ball, greater than a 30-degree angle, the ball usually slices to the right. If the kicker isn't far enough over laterally, less than a 30-degree angle to the ball, the kick usually hooks to the left.

Most kickers take a stance with the kicking foot back. This gives them two long steps into the kick. But whatever stance is comfortable should be used. The head should be kept down with the eyes on the target — the tee. As the ball is contacting the hands of the holder, the kicker starts forward with his non-kicking foot. This step can be as short as six inches. He then steps with the non-kicking foot with the foot landing even with the ball. The exact spot depends on the kicker. Most kickers land with the instep to the heel of the foot even with the ball. The non-kicking foot should be aligned with the desired flight of the ball. The toes should be pointing at the target (the middle of the goal posts or a wider target if a cross wind is expected to affect the flight of the ball.)

The foot plant of the non-kicking foot should be six to eight inches to the side of the ball. If kicking off the grass, the toe should be six to eight inches ahead of the ball. If kicking from a two-inch tee, the toe should be two to four inches forward of the tee. This placement varies a bit from kicker to kicker.

The correct placement of the non-kicking foot is essential to an accurate kick. Right-footed kickers can look for mistakes in foot placement by following these cues:

- If the kick hooks left (to the right for left-footers), the foot probably is too close to the ball.
- If the kick slices to the right (to the left for left-footers), the anchored foot is too far from the ball.
- If the kick is too low, the planted foot is too far back or the body is leaning backward.

The correct placement of the non-kicking foot is essential for an accurate kick, so it must be practiced continually. Adjust the starting point and the angle of approach until the kicking foot's plant is perfect every time. The kicking leg swings down through the ball, contacting it about one-and-a-half inches below the center. The toes must be pointed down (ankle extended) throughout the arc of the kicking leg's downward swing. The knee extends quickly, called a "fast knee" by the pros. To get greater distance, approach the ball the same as normal but make the leg whip quicker.

The body must remain forward to obtain maximum power. The eyes must be on the ball and the body must lean forward throughout the kicking action. Being straight up or leaning backward causes a hook or a low kick. To get more height when kicking off the grass, the kicker can bend the knee more forward and contact the ball with the outside part of the instep. This gives a "9-iron" effect and lifts the ball quicker than when the ball is contacted with the inside part of the instep.

The kicker's toes should extend past the ball. The follow-through should be straight toward the goal posts. The more the body turns, the greater the chance of error. The follow-through should be high. The shorter the follow-through, the greater the chance the leg is losing power and speed as it contacts the ball.

The kicker should hop on the non-kicking foot as his body moves through the ball and as his leg follows through.

Soccer-style kicker's follow-through

The kick should be away in 1.4 to 1.5 seconds in practice. In games, when adrenalin is flowing, it is generally about .1 second faster.

The American straight-ahead kick is seldom used at the higher levels of play, but because it doesn't drift, as the soccer style kicks often do, it can be more accurate. It also tends to get into the air more quickly, and is therefore more difficult to block.

The disadvantage is that it is less likely to get the distance of the soccer style kick because only the toe, rather than the instep, contacts the ball. However, the NFL-record field goal, a 63-yarder by Tom Dempsey, was kicked with the straight-ahead style.

The kicker should have the kicking foot forward, with the torso bent at the waist. The eyes must be on the target (tee). As the ball hits the holder's hands, the kicker should take a short step with the kicking foot. The step should be about one-foot long. (A longer step can generate more body speed and leg power, but it takes longer, so the kick is more likely to be blocked.)

The eyes must continue to focus on the target (the tee) as the steps are being made. This eye contact must continue until the ball is kicked, then the eyes should follow the ball. Many coaches teach to keep watching the ground or the tee during the follow-through. This is wrong because it reduces the ability of the leg to follow through and it reduces the ability of the kicker to kick through the ball with his whole body. It is absolutely essential to kick with the whole body in every type of kick.

The second step is a long step. During this step, the kicking leg is swung back. The farther back it moves, the greater the power that can be generated. The non-kicking foot lands about four inches outside and eight to 10 inches behind the ball. The exact distance depends on the height of the tee and the length of the kicker's leg.

If kicking from the ground, the planted foot should be six to eight inches behind the ball. If using a two-inch tee, it should be eight to 10 inches back. The eyes should concentrate on the spot on the ball that is the kicker's target. This target should be one to one-and-a-half inches below the center of the ball. One inch is better because more distance is possible. A lower target gets the ball up quicker, but it reduces the distance of the kick because much of the power is used to speed up the rotary, end-over-end action on the ball rather than the linear distance of the kick.

The thigh should come forward as the abdominal muscles and hip flexors contract. The knee extensors straighten the leg as the ball is being kicked. Depending on the speed of the leg, the toe of the kicker's foot may go as deep as three to four inches into the ball. The ball stays on the toe from the time it is contacted until it is 12 to 18 inches off the ground. The greater the speed of the leg, the greater distance the ball remains on the foot.

The foot must remain locked at a 90-degree angle from the time it starts forward until the follow-through is completed. It must not vary from this angle until the ball has left the foot. Some kickers tie a shoelace from the bottom lace to the ankle to keep the foot up. This requires an adjustment in the step and the hold, so is not recommended.

The foot also should remain parallel to the line of the arc of the kicking leg. Even one degree off of the parallel might create a twist of the leg or ankle when the ball is contacted. This reduces the power and accuracy of the kick. The muscles that control the twist (rotation) of the thigh and the rotation of the ankle must be strong enough to overcome the torque that could be created at the instant of the contact of the foot with the ball.

The leg should continue up and through the ball and finish as close as possible to the kicking-side shoulder. After the kick, the kicker lands on the non-kicking foot.

American-style kicker's follow-through

The Kickoff

The kickoff can be done with the soccer style or the straight-ahead style of kick. The soccer style usually gets more distance, and is generally preferred. The objective is to kick the ball consistently inside the 10-yard line with a hang time of four seconds.

To determine the proper number of steps, the soccer style kicker should start 10 yards back and five yards to the side. The straight-ahead kicker should start at the tee and then run back toward his goal line until he feels comfortable. Then he kicks an imaginary ball. The coach marks the spot. The kicker repeats this several times until the run at the ball seems comfortable.

This approach is used for either style of kick — straight ahead or soccer. Some kickers feel comfortable with a few steps, while others want several. After the steps seem comfortable, they should be marked off with the traditional stepping method.

The ball is generally teed up as straight as possible. However, individual preferences as to tilt can be considered.

As the kicker approaches the ball, he generates more speed than he would with the field goal. His strides are longer and the kicking leg flows through a greater arc, thus generating more speed.

The kicking action is the same as described for the field goal — a quick leg snap. However, power is more important than accuracy in the kickoff. For this reason, the kicker must "attack" the ball with a very quick leg action. The whole body is used to kick; it is not uncommon for a kickoff man to lift his body two feet off the ground.

After the follow-through, the kicker lands on his kicking foot. This is different from the landing on a field goal or extra point, in which he lands on the non-kicking foot. A hang time of four seconds is considered very good at any level of play.

For *soccer style kicks* from a two-inch tee, the kickers foot plant should be six to eight inches to the side of the tee and two to four inches behind it. From a one-inch tee, the toe should be two to four inches in front of the ball. This varies slightly from kicker to kicker.

The ball is kicked just below the center of the ball. As the ball is kicked, the hips and shoulders should be parallel to the goal line. If the ball hooks to the left (for right-footers), the planted foot is probably too close to the ball. If it slices to the right, the foot is probably too far from it.

For *straight-ahead kicks,* the planted foot should be about four inches to the side of the ball. If kicking off the grass, it should be eight to 10 inches behind it. Off a one-inch tee, 12 inches is about right; off a two-inch tee, 14 inches; from a three-inch tee, 18 inches. The higher the tee, the greater the height and hang time possible.

If the kicker is told to aim toward a particular spot on the field (such as kicking away from an outstanding returner), he should follow through toward that area. As the follow-through is completed, the kicker continues directly toward the ball and is the safetyman. Because of this additional duty, kickers must learn how to tackle.

The squib kick is used when a team wants to change the timing of a return or to reduce the possibility of a long return. It can also be used when a team does not have an effective kicker. The kick should no go long, probably between the 20- and 30-yard line, but it should be difficult to control and perhaps cause a fumble. For the squib kick, the ball is placed on its side with the long axis parallel to the goal line. The ball should be kicked to the side of the center so that it bounces unpredictably.

Onside Kickoffs

The kickoff specialist must also know how to perform the onside kickoff.

One method is simply to kick the ball softer straight downfield, about 12 to 15 yards deep, and then try to recover it.

A second method is to kick high on the ball — the "tip-off" kick. If properly done, this makes the ball take a short hop and then a high bounce that should enable the cover men to get to the ball and outnumber the receivers at the point where the ball will come down. This should be aimed at the sideline about 12 to 15 yards deep.

A third method, the most difficult to perform, has the kicker kick the side of the ball, imparting spin to it. If properly done, the ball spins past the 10-yard mark and then starts spinning back toward the kicking team. The ball moves like a top, with the spin creating a circular path of the ball.

Catching the Kicked Ball

The kick receiver must learn to adjust to the kicked ball, particularly the high kicked ball. The ball often goes farther than it appears it will go. Because of this, the inexperienced returner might misjudge the ball and let it go over his head.

When catching the ball, the returner must keep his elbows in close to his body so that if he misses the catch with his hands, his elbows can still secure the ball. If the elbows are wide, a missed ball goes right through his hands and arms.

The ball should be caught in the hands and then brought down to the ball carrying position in the crook of the elbow with the hand cupped over the end of the ball. Then he can look up and start to run.

If fair-catching the ball, the receiver must wave his hand overhead. He should be clear in his intention. Occasionally a returner puts his hand up to shield his eyes from the sun and inadvertently signals for a fair catch.

The returner's job is to make certain that he catches the ball. If he fumbles, the kicking team probably will recover it. This amounts to about a 35-yard gain for the kicking team. If he lets it go over his head, the kicking team may gain another 10 to 20 yards on the kick. Because yardage is very hard to get, it behooves the receiver to not give up any yards. After he has accomplished this, he can start his return and hope to gain additional yardage for his team. But the major concern is to catch the ball!

Drills

For the snapper:

1. Pass the ball overhand (overhead) with both arms.
2. Snap at a target (a manager or a fence).
3. Snap the ball and quickly assume blocking position.

For the punter:

1. Bad snap drills. Make the punter continuously aware of a high, low, right, or left snap. Even during full team punting, the coach should occasionally (once each day) signal the snapper to snap high or low, left or right.
2. Time the punt with a snapper (2.2 seconds or less if 13 yards back) and without a snapper (1.1 seconds or less).
3. Angle for side lines. A right-footed punter punting to his right should aim at the goal line. A right-footed punter punting to his left ("coffin corner" should aim at the 12-yard line.
4. "Pooch" punt to the 12-yard line.
5. Ball drop drill. The punter drops the ball without kicking it. When it hits the ground it should bounce back past the kicking foot to the outside. This ensures that the ball has been angled in and that the nose was slightly lower than the back end.

For all place kickers:

1. Practice from a very sharp angle to the goal posts. This makes the target very small and makes the kicker much more aware of the importance of alignment and follow-through.

Soccer style kickers:

1. From a point four to five feet from a wall, kick a soccer ball continually into the wall to get the proper feeling of the foot on the ball.

Returners:

1. Catch punts and kickoffs as often as possible.

2. Stand farther back than where you expect the kick to go and run toward it, catching it on the run.

3. Stand closer to the kicker than you expect the ball to land and run back to catch the kick. If a Jugs ball-throwing machine is available, use it as often as possible to catch as many kicks as possible.

4. When it is windy, practice catching punts in the cross wind, into the wind, and with the wind.

Weight Training Exercises

For the snapper:

1. Straight arm pulldowns on the lat machine

2. Straight or bent arm pullovers on the bench

3. Snapping a small medicine ball or a weighted football.

For the punter:

1. Leg extensions on a quadriceps machine for the leg snap

2. Hip flexions on a high bar. Bring the kicking leg up as high as possible. Do this with both a straight leg and with the knees bent

3. Abdominal curls

4. Flexibility work:

- Ankle extension. Work to make the ankle extend back as far as possible.
- Splits with the kicking leg forward. To stretch the connective tissue in the lower groin and the back of the thighs.
- Sitting toe touching. To stretch the connective tissue in the hamstrings and lower back.

For the place kicker:

1. Abdominal curls

2. Leg extensions

3. Hip flexion

4. Flexibility work:

- Splits with kicking leg forward
- Sitting toe touches
- Ankle extension

For the straight-ahead kicker:

1. Thigh rotation (inward and outward) with a partner giving resistance to the foot

For the soccer-style kicker:

1. Hip abduction, curling sit-ups and side sit-ups

19

The Scouting Report

Strategy is an absolute essential in preparing to play a football game, and strategy can only be planned by knowing as much as possible about your opponent. You must know what the opposing coach has done over the years and you must know what the team is doing this year, right up to last week. You find this out by talking with other coaches, exchanging films or videotapes, seeing the opponent play in person and reviewing last year's films.

Scouting by film or video is the simplest and most thorough method. You can exchange films with your opponent, ask to borrow films from other coaches (if it is legal according to your league rules), and watch last year's films (which should have been thoroughly analyzed in the off-season).

When you videotape your own game, you should have two videos made. One should be the traditional game film that is relatively close up and shows the offensive backs, both lines, the linebackers and perhaps some secondary coverage. The other video, which is not nearly as technical to take, is from a wide angle.

With the closeup you can see the backfield action and the blocking schemes as well as the play of the defensive line. With the wide angle you can see the pass patterns and the secondary coverage that does not show in the normal video.

If at all possible, shoot another video from the end zone. Shoot either from the end zone stands, a scaffold, a portable hydraulic lift, or a high ladder.

This gives you the line splits, blocking schemes and backfield action.

Analyzing film should include the entire staff, because each person might see something different or propose a plan that would not otherwise have been considered. At the highest levels of football, one or more coaches might be assigned to find out everything about an opponent by studying all of the films of the opponent's previous season. In doing this, the analysis may be as complete as watching the exact angle of foot movement of a lineman or back on each play, with the hope of finding a key to when a particular play or blocking scheme will be run.

For example, a halfback might take a step inward on a draw play but a step outward on a pass, or an offensive lineman might step with the inside leg first on a cross block or trap, but step with the outside leg on all drive blocks. Finding these keys can help your defenders carry out their assignments.

Scouting in person is best done with more than one person. You can talk into a tape recorder to note the down, distance, yard line, hash, formation, defense, play, and secondary coverage. However, because electronic toys often malfunction, it is best to write down the information also. Some coaching staffs designate one coach to write while the others observe. Sometimes the writing is done on a computer card that can be put directly into the computer. Most coaches must punch their data into their own computer, so they should design scouting forms that will assist them in doing this. If you have a laptop computer, you might be able to do this at the game. The Pocket Coach is one computer that can be taken to the game. (See the list of distributors of various programs at the end of this chapter.)

Many coaches find that it is best, after getting the basic information (such as down and distance), to watch the guards and the direction of the pivot of the quarterback as the ball is snapped. The quarterback's pivot is sometimes a major key in setting defensive strategy. If the quarterback always opens or always reverse pivots, except on counters, it might be a major key. The pull of the guards or other linemen can be effective keys, especially if they pull on counter plays and reverses. If you watch the guards, you will be able to see other linemen pulling at the same time.

After watching the first step of the guards, switch to the backfield pattern. If a pass shows, either because the guards set in a pass block or the quarterback drops into pocket protection, switch to the downfield action of the receivers. Using this system, even a beginning coach can see quite a bit of the action.

With an entire staff scouting one team at a game, one coach might be assigned to watch the offensive and defensive line play, another to watch the backfield on offense and the linebackers on defense, and a third to watch the receivers on offense and the defensive secondary on defense. If both teams are being scouted by two coaches, one might watch the line play of both teams while charting one team and the other watches the secondaries of both teams while charting the other team. Or each coach can watch and chart just one team while they exchange information on things that they have seen that the other might have missed.

After the information is obtained, whether from videos or from in- person scouting, it should be entered into the computer as quickly as possible. For teams without a computer available, the scouts should enter the information on several different types of charts. Following are some types of analysis for an opponent's offense that many coaches desire:

- *Down and distance.* List the plays according to these categories: First and more than 10 to go, first and 10, first and less than 10; 2nd and 10 or more, 2nd and 7 or more, 2nd and 4 or more, 2nd and less than four; 3rd and 10 or more, 3rd and 6 or more, 3rd and 3 or more, 3rd and less than 3; 4th and more than 3, 4th and more than 1, 4th and 1 or less.
- *Formations.* Diagram each formation and chart the path of the ball (noting the type of play) for every time that formation is used. If charting more than one game use a different color pen for each game, because each opposing team might have different defensive strengths (either personnel or alignment). Include the pass routes with the formation.
- *Hash mark.* List plays according to the left, middle, and right areas of the field.
- *Score.* Does being ahead or behind make a difference in play selection? List plays by quarter, such as first quarter ahead, tied, behind; second quarter ahead, tied, behind, and so on.
- *Field position.* You might want to chart every 20-yard section or you might use goal line to 15, 15 to 35, 35 to 35, 35 to 15, 15 to goal.

Defensive scouting can be similar using the same charts as above, substituting alignment and coverage charts for the offensive formation charts. Determine when the opponent slants, stunts, and blitzes. Remember that you are scouting the coach. That is why following a team's strategy from year to year is so important.

Analyzing the Scouting Reports

The "data base" function of computers is used to handle the scouting data. Most coaches use their own computers so they must enter the data by hand. Some coaches have access to programs done by professional card-reading machines. In this case, just enter the specially marked cards into the computer. Among the facts entered into the computer are the following:

- Down, distance to go for a first down, usually entered as short (one to three yards), medium (four to six yards) or long (more than seven yards) yardage
- Territory ("minus" territory is on your own side of the 50-yard line, "plus" territory is on the opponent's side of the 50)
- Hash mark (left, right, or middle of the field)
- The line set designated by the placement of the tight end
- The set of the backs (I, right, left, split, single back)
- The set of the receivers (flanker [tight end and wide flanker to one side], slot [flanker back inside the split end], double slots, double flankers, triple set to one side)
- Whether or not there was motion and, if so, by whom and in what direction
- The defensive front (3-4 eagle or Okie, 4-3 pro or college, 6-2, and so on)
- The secondary (two, three, four, or five deep backs)
- The stunts of the linemen or backers
- The secondary blitz
- Type of coverage (zone 4-3, 5-2, five-under man with two deep safeties)
- The hole run (1 to 8) or the passing zones (in letters — see the offensive scouting report form for the zones)
- The yardage gained or lost
- Any extra remark (sack, punt, interference, two-minute offense and so on)

Defensive Analysis — the Basis for Offensive Strategy

The chart at the top of the following page is a sample of a defensive play list for the first part of a game. It lists each play run, in sequence, and becomes the basis for several types of analysis.

Many reports enable the coach to put in his own terminology for the printout. To aid in reading this report form, here are some of the symbols used:

Column three (distance) — 123 means one to three yards to go, 456 means four to six yards to go, 10+ means 10 or more yards to go.

Column four (territory) — -0-19 means from the goal line you are protecting to your own 19. +40-21 means from your opponent's 40 to its 20.

Column five (hash mark) — R, M, L means right, middle, left.

Column six (line) shows tight end strength. TE-R means tight end right, 2-SE means two split ends, 2-TE means two tight ends.

Column seven (back set) — I means I-formation, Ace-M means one back set in middle (the fullback's spot), Ace-R means one back set in the right halfback's spot, SP-BK means split backs, left means backs set left (fullback and left half).

Column eight (receiver set) — Slt-L means slot left, Pro-R means a pro right formation.

Column 10 (front) gives the defensive front. 3-4 would be a 3-4 defense, Okie means a 5-2.

Column 11 (adjust) indicates an adjustment to alignment or to linebacker pass defense alignment. Reduc means a reduced front — an Eagle alignment on the side of the split end. Walk means that the outside backer is in a walkaway position, halfway out to the wide receiver. Eagle means that the 3-4 or 5-2 is in an Eagle alignment with the defensive tackles inside the offensive tackles and the backers on the offensive tackle or end. Okie means an Okie adjustment with the defensive tackles on or outside the offensive tackles and the backers on the guards.

Column 12 (secondary) — 40 means four deep. Nick means nickel (five defensive backs). Goal means goal line defense.

Column 13 (stunts) tells whether they did not stunt ("base"), whether they slanted ("angle") or whether they used a linebacker stunt.

Column 14 (blitz) shows the type of secondary stunt used.

Column 15 (cover) shows the type of pass coverage. 3-sky means that the secondary rotated to a three-deep cover, with the safety taking the strong side flat, MN-FR means that they were in a man-to-man defense with a free safety, 2-5UN means a two-deep, five-under cover.

PLAY	DOWN	DIST	TERR	HASH	LINE	BACKS	REC	MOTION	FRONT	ADJUST	SECOND	STUNTS	BLITZ	COVER	AREA	YARDS	REMARK
1	1ST	10+	-0-19	R	TE-R	I	SLT-L		3-4	REDUC	40	ANGLE	S-RAM	3-SKY	6	5	
2	2ND	456	-20-39	R	TE-R	LEFT	SLT-L		3-4	OKIE	40	BASE		3-SKY	2	2	
3	3RD	123	-20-39	M	TE-L	I	PRO-L		3-4	EAGLE	40	JET	D-RAM	3-MAN	Y	-7	SACK
4	4TH	10+	-0-19	M												21	PT-RT
5	1ST	10+	-40-49	L	TE-R	I	PRO-R		3-4	REDUC	40	ANGLE	W-RAM	3-WK	Z	0	
6	2ND	10+	-40-49	L	2-SE	ACE-M	2-SLT		3-4	WALK	NICK	JET	S-RAM	2-5UN	F	0	INT-R
7	1ST	10+	-20-39	M	TE-L	ACE-R	SLT-R		3-4	OVER	40	BASE		3-CL	7	7	
8	2ND	123	-20-39	L	TE-L	I	SLT-R		4-3	PRO	40	D-PIN	D-RAM	MN-FR	2	1	
9	3RD	123	-20-39	M	TE-R	I	PRO-R		4-3	PRO	40	D-PIN	BULL	MN-FR	X	72	TD
10	4TH	456	-20-39	R													

Partial defensive play list

Column 16 (area) shows the area which the play hit. Numbers indicate the holes, letters indicate the area into which the pass was thrown (see chart 20-9).

Column 17 (yards) shows the yards gained or lost.

Column 18 (remark) adds other information. PT-RT is a punt toward the right side, 2-min means a two-minute offense.

The next consideration would be the frequency of each defense according to the down, distance, and hash mark. From the first line, you can determine that on first down the defense ran this defense six times — a reduced 40 line that slanted, with the safety blitzing or filling, and the secondary rotating from a four-deep to a three-deep with the safety (sky) covering the flat.

```
1ST DOWN
--------------------------------------------------

  6)  3-4  /REDUC/40   /ANGLE/S-RAM/3-SKY
  8)  3-4  /REDUC/40   /ANGLE/W-RAM/3-WK
  2)  3-4  /OVER /40   /BASE /     /3-CL
  2)  6-2  /EAGLE/GOAL /JET  /D-RAM/3-MAN


2ND DOWN
--------------------------------------------------

  4)  3-4  /OKIE /40   /BASE /     /3-SKY
  8)  3-4  /WALK /NICK /JET  /S-RAM/2-5UN
  2)  4-3  /PRO  /40   /D-PIN/D-RAM/MN-FR
  2)  4-4  /EAGLE/GOAL /JET  /D-KNF/3-MAN


3RD DOWN
--------------------------------------------------

  6)  3-4  /EAGLE/40   /JET  /D-RAM/3-MAN
  4)  4-3  /PRO  /40   /D-PIN/BULL /MN-FR
  2)  6-2  /EAGLE/GOAL /OUT  /D-KNF/3-MAN
```

Frequency by down and distance

Next is the evaluation of hash mark tendencies. Some teams generally slant or stunt to the wide side of the field. When coaches find this happening, they might attack into the short side of the field. A sample of hash mark tendencies (right hash, middle of field, left hash) is on the following page.

The next area of concern is the type of defense they use on each down in each territory (from the opponent's goal line to its 19 [-0-19], -20-39, -40 to -49), then into the opponent's offensive territory (+49 to +40, +39 to +20, +19 into their goal line). It is also categorized by down and distance in the following summary. The example used here is only for first down:

```
1ST DOWN  10+ DIST   -0-19 TERR
--------------------------------------------------

  4)  3-4  /REDUC/40   /ANGLE/S-RAM/3-SKY

1ST DOWN  10+ DIST   -20-39 TERR
--------------------------------------------------

  2)  3-4  /OVER /40   /BASE /     /3-CL

1ST DOWN  10+ DIST   -40-49 TERR
--------------------------------------------------

  4)  3-4  /REDUC/40   /ANGLE/W-RAM/3-WK

1ST DOWN  10+ DIST   +50-41 TERR
--------------------------------------------------

  2)  3-4  /REDUC/40   /ANGLE/S-RAM/3-SKY

1ST DOWN  10+ DIST   +40-21 TERR
--------------------------------------------------

  2)  3-4  /REDUC/40   /ANGLE/W-RAM/3-WK

1ST DOWN  10+ DIST   +20-8 TERR
--------------------------------------------------

  2)  3-4  /REDUC/40   /ANGLE/W-RAM/3-WK

1ST DOWN  789 DIST   +7-0  TERR
--------------------------------------------------

  2)  6-2  /EAGLE/GOAL /JET  /D-RAM/3-MAN
```

Frequency by down, distance and territory

```
              RIGHT HASH          |          MIDDLE HASH           |          LEFT HASH
------------------------------------|--------------------------------|------------------------------------
-0-19

 1/10+ 3-4  /REDUC/40   /ANGLE/S-RAM/3-SKY I 4/10+    /    /    /    /    /    I
 1/10+ 3-4  /REDUC/40   /ANGLE/S-RAM/3-SKY I 4/10+    /    /    /    /    /    I
 1/10+ 3-4  /REDUC/40   /ANGLE/S-RAM/3-SKY I                                   I
 1/10+ 3-4  /REDUC/40   /ANGLE/S-RAM/3-SKY I                                   I
                                           I                                   I
------------------------------------|--------------------------------|------------------------------------
-20-39

 2/456 3-4 /OKIE /40  /BASE /    /3-SKY I 3/123 3-4 /EAGLE/40   /JET /D-RAM/3-MAN I 2/123 4-3 /PRO /40  /D-PIN/D-RAM/MN-FR
 4/456    /    /    /    /    /    I 1/10+ 3-4  /OVER /40   /BASE /    /3-CL I 2/123 4-3 /PRO /40  /D-PIN/D-RAM/MN-FR
 2/456 3-4 /OKIE /40  /BASE /    /3-SKY I 3/123 4-3 /PRO /40   /D-PIN/BULL /MN-FR I
 4/456    /    /    /    /    /    I 3/123 3-4 /EAGLE/40   /JET /D-RAM/3-MAN I
                                        I 3/123 3-4 /EAGLE/40   /JET /D-RAM/3-MAN I
                                        I 1/10+ 3-4  /OVER /40   /BASE /    /3-CL I
                                        I 3/123 4-3 /PRO /40   /D-PIN/BULL /MN-FR I
                                        I 3/123 3-4 /EAGLE/40   /JET /D-RAM/3-MAN I
                                        I                                         I
------------------------------------|--------------------------------|------------------------------------
-40-49

                              I 2/456 3-4 /OKIE /40   /BASE /    /3-SKY I 1/10+ 3-4  /REDUC/40   /ANGLE/W-RAM/3-WK
                              I 2/456 3-4 /WALK /NICK /JET /S-RAM/2-SUN I 2/10+ 3-4  /WALK /NICK /JET /S-RAM/2-SUN
                              I 3/123 4-3 /PRO /40   /D-PIN/BULL /MN-FR I 1/10+ 3-4  /REDUC/40   /ANGLE/W-RAM/3-WK
                              I 2/456 3-4 /OKIE /40   /BASE /    /3-SKY I 1/10+ 3-4  /REDUC/40   /ANGLE/W-RAM/3-WK
                              I 2/456 3-4 /WALK /NICK /JET /S-RAM/2-SUN I 2/10+ 3-4  /WALK /NICK /JET /S-RAM/2-SUN
                              I 3/123 4-3 /PRO /40   /D-PIN/BULL /MN-FR I 1/10+ 3-4  /REDUC/40   /ANGLE/W-RAM/3-WK
                              I                                         I
------------------------------------|--------------------------------|------------------------------------
+50-41

                              I 1/10+ 3-4  /REDUC/40   /ANGLE/S-RAM/3-SKY I
                              I 1/10+ 3-4  /REDUC/40   /ANGLE/S-RAM/3-SKY I
                              I                                           I
------------------------------------|--------------------------------|------------------------------------
+40-21

 1/10+ 3-4  /REDUC/40   /ANGLE/W-RAM/3-WK  I                              I
 2/10+ 3-4  /WALK /NICK /JET /S-RAM/2-SUN  I                              I
 3/456 3-4  /EAGLE/40   /JET /D-RAM/3-MAN  I                              I
 1/10+ 3-4  /REDUC/40   /ANGLE/W-RAM/3-WK  I                              I
 2/10+ 3-4  /WALK /NICK /JET /S-RAM/2-SUN  I                              I
 3/456 3-4  /EAGLE/40   /JET /D-RAM/3-MAN  I                              I
------------------------------------|--------------------------------|------------------------------------
+20-8

                              I                              I 1/10+ 3-4  /REDUC/40   /ANGLE/W-RAM/3-WK
                              I                              I 2/789 3-4  /WALK /NICK /JET /S-RAM/2-SUN
                              I                              I 1/10+ 3-4  /REDUC/40   /ANGLE/W-RAM/3-WK
                              I                              I 2/789 3-4  /WALK /NICK /JET /S-RAM/2-SUN
```

Field tendencies

Next the defenses are categorized by offensive formations, because it is possible that the defensive coordinator has selected his defenses according to the formation tendencies rather than to down, distance or hash.

```
TE-R /SP-BK/SLT-L/
-------------------------------------------

(2) 6-2  /EAGLE/GOAL /JET  /D-RAM/3-MAN
(2) 4-4  /EAGLE/GOAL /JET  /D-KNF/3-MAN


TE-R /I    /PRO-R/
-------------------------------------------

(8) 3-4  /REDUC/40   /ANGLE/W-RAM/3-WK
(2) 3-4  /WALK /NICK /JET  /S-RAM/2-5UN
(4) 4-3  /PRO  /40   /D-PIN/BULL /MN-FR


TE-R /I    /SLT-L/
-------------------------------------------

(6) 3-4  /REDUC/40   /ANGLE/S-RAM/3-SKY


TE-R /LEFT /SLT-L/
-------------------------------------------

(4) 3-4  /OKIE /40   /BASE /    /3-SKY


TE-L /I    /PRO-L/
-------------------------------------------

(6) 3-4  /EAGLE/40   /JET  /D-RAM/3-MAN


TE-L /I    /SLT-R/
-------------------------------------------

(2) 4-3  /PRO  /40   /D-PIN/D-RAM/MN-FR
```

Frequency by offensive formation

The defensive tendency chart by down and distance shows the stunts (slants and other defensive line movements), the blitzes, and the coverage. The distance is determined by 10 or more yards to go; seven, eight or nine yards to go; four, five or six yards to go; or one, two or three yards to go.

```
1ST DOWN  10+ DIST
---------------------------------------------
STUNTS****  (2) BASE    (14) ANGLE
BLITZES***  (2)          (6) S-RAM   (8) W-RAM
COVERAGE**  (6) 3-SKY    (2) 3-CL    (8) 3-WK


1ST DOWN  789 DIST
---------------------------------------------
STUNTS****  (2) JET
BLITZES***  (2) D-RAM
COVERAGE**  (2) 3-MAN
```

```
2ND DOWN  10+ DIST
---------------------------------------------
STUNTS****  (4) JET
BLITZES***  (4) S-RAM
COVERAGE**  (4) 2-5UN


2ND DOWN  789 DIST
---------------------------------------------
STUNTS****  (4) JET
BLITZES***  (2) S-RAM    (2) D-KNF
COVERAGE**  (2) 2-5UN    (2) 3-MAN


2ND DOWN  456 DIST
---------------------------------------------
STUNTS****  (4) BASE    (2) JET
BLITZES***  (4)          (2) S-RAM
COVERAGE**  (4) 3-SKY    (2) 2-5UN


2ND DOWN  123 DIST
---------------------------------------------
STUNTS****  (2) D-PIN
BLITZES***  (2) D-RAM
COVERAGE**  (2) MN-FR


3RD DOWN  456 DIST
---------------------------------------------
STUNTS****  (2) OUT     (2) JET
BLITZES***  (2) D-RAM    (2) D-KNF
COVERAGE**  (4) 3-MAN


3RD DOWN  123 DIST
---------------------------------------------
STUNTS****  (4) D-PIN   (4) JET
BLITZES***  (4) D-RAM    (4) BULL
COVERAGE**  (4) MN-FR    (4) 3-MAN
```

Stunt, blitz, coverage summary

Offensive Analysis — the Basis of Defensive Strategy

A chronological list of plays that the offense ran in one game follows. Just as with the defensive list, the offensive play list includes (according to column): down (2), distance (3), territory (4), hash mark (5), tight end placement (6), backs set (7), and the position of receivers (8). It also notes the back in motion (9), the type of run (10), ball carrier (11) and hole hit (12). If it is a pass it notes whether it was a drop back, play action, sprint, roll out, or boot leg (13). It notes the receiver (14), the result (15) the pattern run (16), the zone into which the pass was thrown (17), and the yardage gained (18). In the "remarks" category (19) it notes whether it was a turnover, penalty, touchdown and so on.

##	DOWN	DIST	TERR	HASH	LINE	BACKS	REC	MOTION	RUN	CARR	HOLE	PASS	REC	RES	PATT	ZONE	YDS	REM
1	1ST	10+	-20-39	M	2-TE	ACE-H	2-FLK		DRAW	QB	2			RUN			6	
2	2ND	456	-20-39	M	TE-R	I	SLT-L		BLAST	TB	1			RUN			1	
3	1ST	10+	-20-39	R	TE-L	I	PRO-L					PLA-L	TE-L	SCK	OUT	A	-7	
4	2ND	15+	-0-19	M	TE-R	ACE-H	DBL-R	SL-R	BUCK	TB	2			RUN			4	
5	3RD	10+	-20-39	R	2-TE	ACE-H	2-FLK					BTL-L	TE-L	CMP	OTH-1	F	21	
6	1ST	10+	-40-49	M	TE-R	I	PRO-R		POWER	TB	4			RUN			3	
7	2ND	789	-40-49	M	TE-L	ACE-H	DBL-L	SL-L				SPR-L	TE-L	INT	OUT	A	0	TURN
8	1ST	456	-20-39	L	TE-L	ACE-H	2-FLK		POWER	TB	3			RUN			4	
9	2ND	456	-40-49	L	2-TE	ACE-H	2-FLK		POWER	TB		BTL-R	TE-L	CMP	DRAG	E	7	
0	1ST	10+	-40-49	R	TE-L	LEFT	PRO-L		POWER	TB	3			RUN			2	
1	2ND	789	-40-49	M	TE-L	I	PRO-L				4	PLA-L		RUN			2	
2	3RD	456	+50-41	R	TE-L	RIGHT	PRO-R					DP-BK	FLK-R	INC	STK	E	0	
3	1ST	10+	-20-39	M	2-TE	ACE-H	2-FLK		POWER	TB	3			RUN			7	
4	2ND	123	-20-39	L	TE-R	I	PRO-R		BUCK	TB	2			RUN			2	
5	3RD	123	-20-39	M	2-TE	I	FLK-R		SWEEP	TB	7			RUN			9	
6	1ST	10+	-20-39	L	TE-R	I	PRO-R				8	PLA-R		RUN			14	
7	1ST	10+	+50-41	M	2-TE	ACE-H	2-FLK					BTL-L	TE-L	CMP	OTH-1	F	19	
8	1ST	10+	+40-21	L	TE-R	RIGHT	PRO-R					BTL-R	TE-R	CMP	CURL	C	9	

Offensive play list

The first nine columns and the last two columns for the offensive play list are the same as for the defensive list. The remaining columns are as follows:

Column 10 (run) tells the type of run.

Column 11 (carr) is the ball carrier (TB for tailback, and so on).

Column 12 (hole) tells where along the offensive line the ball carrier ran.

Column 13 (pass) — PLA-L means play action left, DP-BK means drop back, SPR-L means sprint out left.

Column 14 (rec) receiver — FLK-R means flanker right, and so on.

Column 15 (res) result — CMP means completed pass, SCK means sack, and so on.

Column 16 (PATT) tells the type of pass pattern.

Column 17 (ZONE) tells the area to which the pass was thrown.

Based on the information on the list of plays, the defensive coach would want to know the frequency of plays at each hole and the number of passes to each area. He would use a play frequency chart, with the holes and passing zones shown.

This summary tells which running holes (0 being over the center, 1, 3, 5, and 7 being left guard, left tackle, left end (off tackle), and a wide play to the left;

2, 4, 6, and 8 being the holes to the offensive right side) and which passing areas were targets. X, Y, and Z are the zones behind the offensive line; A through E are the five short zones up to about 15 yards deep; F, G, and H are the three deep zones.

Each of these run or pass possibilities is charted for each down and distance in each territory.

TOTAL RUN PASS

ALL PLAYS

PLAYS	92	52	40
YARDS	644	240	404
AVER.	7	5	10
PLAY %		57%	43%

RUNNING HOLES

7	5	3	1	0	2	4	6	8
12	8				8	16	8	
92	12				12	56	68	
8	2				2	4	9	
13%	9%				9%	17%	9%	

PASSING ZONES

A	B	C	D	E	F	G	H	X	Y	Z
8		4		4	8			4	8	4
40		32		36	20			288	-12	
5		8		9	3			72	-1	
9%		4%		4%	9%			4%	9%	4%

Detailed play frequency chart

	TOTAL	RUN	PASS	RUNNING HOLES									PASSING ZONES										
				7	5	3	1	0	2	4	6	8	A	B	C	D	E	F	G	H	X	Y	Z
L PLAYS				7	5	3	1	0	2	4	6	8	A	B	C	D	E	F	G	H	X	Y	Z
AYS	48	29	19	3		3	7		7	4		5	6	1	1		4	2		2			3
RDS	244	111	133	16		13	33		25	7		17	0	12	9		31	48		33			8
VER.	5	4	7	5		4	5		4	-2		3	0	12	9		0	20		17			3
AY %		60%	40%	6%		6%	15%		15%	8%		10%	13%	2%	2%		8%	4%		4%			6%
ST DOWN				7	5	3	1	0	2	4	6	8	A	B	C	D	E	F	G	H	X	Y	Z
LAYS	21	13	8			3	4		2	1		3	3		1		2	1					1
ARDS	118	70	48			13	24		10	3		20	-4		9		24	19					0
VER.	6	5	6			4	6		5	3		7	-1		9		12	19					0
LAY %		62%	38%			14%	19%		10%	5%		14%	14%		5%		10%	5%					5%
ND DOWN				7	5	3	1	0	2	4	6	8	A	B	C	D	E	F	G	H	X	Y	Z
LAYS	17	12	5	2			2		4	3		1	1	1			1			1			1
ARDS	52	33	19	7			6		14	4		2	0	12			7			0			0
VER.	3	3	4	4			3		4	1		2	0	12			7			0			0
LAY %		71%	29%	12%			12%		24%	18%		6%	6%	6%			6%			6%			6%
3RD DOWN				7	5	3	1	0	2	4	6	8	A	B	C	D	E	F	G	H	X	Y	Z
PLAYS	10	4	6	1			1		1			1	2				1	1		1			1
YARDS	74	8	66	9			3		1			-5	4				0	21		33			8
AVER.	7	2	11	9			3		1			-5	2				0	21		33			0
PLAY %		40%	60%	10%			10%		10%			10%	20%				10%	10%		10%			10%
4TH DOWN				7	5	3	1	0	2	4	6	8	A	B	C	D	E	F	G	H	X	Y	Z
PLAYS	0	0	0																				
YARDS	0	0	0																				
AVER.	0	0	0																				
PLAY %		0%	0%																				
R HASH				7	5	3	1	0	2	4	6	8	A	B	C	D	E	F	G	H	X	Y	Z
PLAYS	19	9	10	1		1	4		1	2			5				1	1					3
YARDS	71	42	29	7		2	27		4	2			0				0	21					8
AVER.	4	5	3	7		2	7		4	1			0				0	21					3
PLAY %		47%	53%	5%		5%	21%		5%	11%			26%				5%	5%					16%
M HASH				7	5	3	1	0	2	4	6	8	A	B	C	D	E	F	G	H	X	Y	Z
PLAYS	18	12	6	2		1	2		2	2		3	1	1			2	1		1			
YARDS	121	33	88	9		7	3		10	5		-1	0	12			24	19		33			
AVER.	7	3	15	5		7	2		5	3		0	0	12			12	19		33			
PLAY %		67%	33%	11%		6%	11%		11%	11%		17%	6%	6%			11%	6%		6%			
L HASH				7	5	3	1	0	2	4	6	8	A	B	C	D	E	F	G	H	X	Y	Z
PLAYS	11	8	3			1	1		4			2			1		1			1			
YARDS	52	36	16			4	3		11			10			9		7			0			
AVER.	5	5	5			4	3		3			9			9		7			0			
PLAY %		73%	27%			9%	9%		36%			18%			9%		9%			9%			

Plays according to down and hash mark

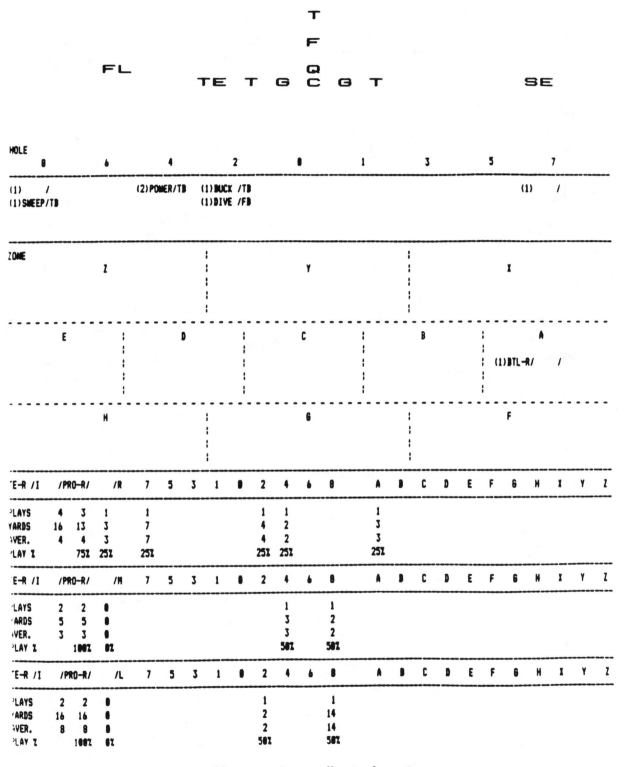

```
                                    T
                                    F
                 FL                 Q
                        TE  T  G  C  G  T                    SE


HOLE
        8          6          4          2      8      1      3      5      7
----------------------------------------------------------------------------------
(1)     /          (2)POWER/TB  (1)BUCK /TB                          (1)     /
(1)SWEEP/TB                     (1)DIVE /FB

==================================================================================

ZONE              :                 :                 :
         Z        :        Y        :        X        :
                  :                 :                 :
- - - - - - - - - : - - - - - - - - : - - - - - - - - : - - - - - - - - - - - - -
     E            :   D         C   :        B        :   A
                  :                 :                 :   (1)BTL-R/     /
                  :                 :                 :
- - - - - - - - - : - - - - - - - - : - - - - - - - - : - - - - - - - - - - - - -
     M            :                 6 :               :   F
                  :                 :                 :
                  :                 :                 :
```

E-R /I	/PRO-R/	/R	7	5	3	1	8	2	4	6	8	A	B	C	D	E	F	G	H	I	Y	Z
PLAYS	4 3	1	1					1	1			1										
YARDS	16 13	3	7					4	2			3										
AVER.	4 4	3	7					4	2			3										
PLAY %	75%	25%	25%					25%	25%			25%										

E-R /I	/PRO-R/	/M	7	5	3	1	8	2	4	6	8	A	B	C	D	E	F	G	H	I	Y	Z
PLAYS	2 2	8						1		1												
YARDS	5 5	8						3		2												
AVER.	3 3	8						3		2												
PLAY %	100%	0%						50%		50%												

E-R /I	/PRO-R/	/L	7	5	3	1	8	2	4	6	8	A	B	C	D	E	F	G	H	I	Y	Z
PLAYS	2 2	8						1		1												
YARDS	16 16	8						2		14												
AVER.	8 8	8						2		14												
PLAY %	100%	0%						50%		50%												

Plays according to offensive formation

The next summary, shown on Page 180, indicates all the plays run according to down and hash mark. It also lists them according to the running hole or passing zone. It then gives a percentage of plays for each hole or zone.

The next chart, shown on Page 181, shows what the team does from each formation. Illustrated is a pro-right I-formation. There will be a full sheet for each formation.

Coaching Aids

Depending on the size of your staff, the level of your competition, and the locations of your opponents, you might be limited in what can be done. Generally, a film exchange is possible. Sometimes you can talk to other coaches who have played your opponents. Perhaps a professional scout or an ex-coach can be hired to scout an opponent. Whatever information you can get, within the rules, should be learned so that your strategy can be based on the best information possible.

Scouting aids can be purchased from many companies, including the following:

Lafayette Instruments (800-428-7545). Everything needed for game video analysis (cameras, projection, multi-deck recorders).

Pocket Coach (Dave Fisher Productions) 3127 S.W. Huntoon, Topeka, Kansas 66604, 800-444-7215). Prints game analysis on roll of paper tape. Has programs for football, basketball, weight training, and other sports.

Quality Coaching (Box 11051, Burbank, CA 91510-1051, 818-842-6800). Software and books.

Quick Scout (Box 70, North East, PA 16428, 814-725-9279). Software scouting program.

Sports PC (800-752-7222, 813-398-6633 in Florida). A top-of-the line computer software producer that can sell you programs for whatever you want for your game analysis. It is used by many college and professional teams, but lower level teams might be interested in using just a few of its programs.

20

Planning Strategy

Because each football team uses basically the same offensive and defensive theories throughout the year, opponents have a pretty good idea what to expect in terms of formations, basic plays, and basic defensive alignments. One team that didn't fit this pattern was one of the teams from the California Institute of Technology during the late 1950s. The coach believed that since they couldn't "out-physical" anybody, they would have to try to "out-mental" their opponents. Every week, the coach gave his players an entirely new offense. While they could master the new offense, they still couldn't master their opponents. Their record was 0-9 that year.

Scouting an opponent by attending a game or watching game films is standard at all levels of football. The formations, hash mark tendencies, field position tendencies, and strongest and weakest players are all a part of the evaluation.

Some high schools may scout a team only once, but most major colleges and the pro teams scout many games. Generally the previous three games of the opponent and the games it has played against your team gives more than enough information. This should give some insight into the opponent's basic theories and strategies, and it gives a pretty good idea of which players will play against you.

Most high schools and colleges, and all professional teams, take their scouting data and enter it into a computer. The computer can quickly give a great deal of data on the upcoming opponent. Per-centages play a big part in developing the week-to-week strategy for an opponent. Do they have certain tendencies on third-and-one when the game is tied? Do those tendencies change if they are ahead or behind? Are they likely to pass from inside their own 20-yard line? Do they usually run to the wide side of the field or to the right side of their formation? When are they likely to blitz or stunt? The answers to these and hundreds of other questions help coaches develop their strategy for next week's opponent.

Developing the Offensive Strategy

After the tendencies of the defense have been charted, the coach can begin to plan his own strategy of attack. If the opponent has shown marked tendencies against every team they have played, it gives the coach a good hint as to what might work against that opponent.

Does the team nearly always stunt in a third-and-long situation? Do they tend to play man-to-man defense against a short passing offense or when they are in a goal line defense? Do they generally slant to the wide side of the field? Do they usually stay in the same pass coverage, or do they vary it? What are we likely to see when we are faced with third-and-long? What is their goal line defense? These are some of the questions that must be answered if an effective strategy is to be implemented for the next game.

If a team blitzes often, the quarterback should be taught to recognize the blitz before the snap. He might be able to "audible" a special play at the line of scrimmage to capitalize on the weakness of that defense. In addition, pass patterns might have to be adjusted in blitz situations. However, because a team might run only a certain blitz once or twice during a game, you must make certain that the quarterback and receivers can recognize special blitzes the instant they are evident.

It is not enough that all these decisions must be made, they must be made the day after your most recent game and formulated into a game plan within two days so that the practices can be geared to perfecting the game plan.

Beating the Defense

Offensively, you should first try to beat the opponent's basic defensive alignment, its theory of defense and its basic coverage. Does the team generally run a 4-3 or a 3-4? Do the linemen charge hard or do they play more of a "hit and react" technique? Are they primarily a man-to-man team or a zone team?

Next try to create a mismatch. In developing your passing strategy, perhaps you can put your best receiver on their poorest defender. Or if they run a lot of zone defense, you might try to get two men into one defender's zone. If they play a lot of man-to-man defense, try to get your fastest receiver on their slowest defender, such as a running back against a linebacker.

In developing your running strategy, you might try to create a mismatch by bringing your tight end to the side toward which you want to run so that he can double team a tough defensive end. Or you might motion a slot back to help block at a certain hole. Maybe he could trap a lineman from the outside or perhaps help out on a double team.

If a team plays a lot of zone defense and doesn't adjust well to strength when you might bring a man from one side of the field to the other, you might motion your flanker to the play side and thus gain an additional blocker.

At the higher levels of football, many teams like to have at least two ways to block every problem defender. The outstanding players just can't be handled on every play with a one-on-one basic block. They have to be hit by different people, both linemen and backs, and they may have to be double- or triple-teamed if you expect your quarterback to survive until halftime.

Coach Hank Stram was outstanding at scouting personnel and coming up with ways to beat certain individuals. He would look for the two or three best people, the ones that had to be controlled to win, then devise ways to beat them. He didn't want a person or a team to be able to effectively do what they had been able to do best.

If a nose guard can't be handled one-on-one, he might be double-teamed. If he reacts well to the pressure of a blocker, he might be blocked into the hole and then allowed to fight away from it with his excellent pursuing techniques. If a tackle is an aggressive rusher when he reads a "pass," you might run a draw trap. Against a quick reacting linebacker, you might run play action passes to keep him out of his zone, or a draw play might go if he reacts quickly to the quarterback's drop. Against a great defensive back, you might swing a back into his area or maybe the quarterback would "look him off" (look one way to get him moving one way, then quickly throwing the other way).

Coaches should not make major changes in offense or defense. Adjustments should be made depending on personnel, whether your team or the opponent has injured players who won't play, particular weaknesses or strengths of the opponent's offense, defense, or kicking games, or tendencies such as sideline, down and distance. Will a play or a defense work because of a technical weakness of the opponent or a weakness of one of their players?

You also have to think about what your opponent's expect you to do. Because effective coaches scout their own teams each game, they should know their own tendencies as well as the opponents do.

Self-scouting tells you what you have been likely to do on each situation. So if you come up with a third-and-three and have been running your tailback most of the time, you might decide to throw deep, or let the tailback throw the running pass.

Running Game Strategy

First the coach must determine whether the opponent's running defense is based on a "hit and pursue" or an "attacking and penetrating" type of defense. Against the strong pursuit type teams, the offense might well think first of quick plays and counter plays. Against the attacking defense, the offense might think of using wide plays, especially the quick pitch, and trapping plays.

Next, the coach has to look at the basic alignment used by the opponent's defense. How many "down linemen" does he use — three, four, five, or six? Do they stay in that set or do they overshift or undershift it often? (An overshift involves moving the linemen toward the strength of the offensive formation. An undershift involves shifting the linemen away from the strength of the formation.)

Does the opponent use multiple defensive sets? If so, which of our players must learn more than one assignment? Is the defense balanced? Draw a line through the center and then count the number of offensive players and defenders on each side of the ball. Does the offense have an advantage to either side? If so, does the defense cover the unbalance with a slant or backfield rotation? Does the team blitz or stunt? If so, when is it most likely to do so — on obvious passing downs, on long yardage, on short yardage, on first down? If the team stunts, who is most likely to stunt — a middle backer, an outside backer, a safety, a corner? Or do they prefer to "twist" the linemen when rushing a pass, while keeping their backers free to pursue the run or drop for the pass?

What are the keys of the linebackers? Do they seem to key the guards, the fullback, the halfback? If so, a false pull and a counter might work. Does the team pursue too quickly? Recently, a pro team, that didn't run many reverses was playing against a team that pursued very quickly. For that week, they worked on a reverse. It scored. The next week, knowing that the opponents knew about the reverse, the team faked the reverse and threw a pass for a touchdown.

Do the linemen try to fight through the head of the offensive blocker? (Defensive linemen who use a hit-and-react type of technique generally use the blocker's head as the key as to which way the play is going. So if a blocker puts his head on your right side you can assume that the play is going to your right.) If so, you might try to "false block" him. (That is have the blocker put his head away from the side to which you want to block him — then let him fight away from the play.)

Another way to work on a good defensive lineman who reacts well is to influence him. In an influence block, one man false blocks a defender and then releases on a linebacker or defensive back. A trapper then comes to take the defender in the same way he is reacting. In the following diagram the offensive tackle influences the defensive tackle by putting his head on the outside, then slipping the block. Meanwhile, the offside guard traps the tackle.

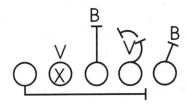

Using an influence block

What is the action of the defensive backs? If they are a four-deep team do they get their run support mainly from the safeties or from the corners? Do they play a lot of man-to-man? If so, perhaps a wide run at a cornerback who is watching his man run deep rather than watching for the run might work.

The offensive strategist also must look for weaknesses in the individual linemen and linebackers. Are there any injuries to the starters that must be filled by second stringers? Is one player adept at going to his right but not to his left, or is one player relatively slow? Does one linebacker react too slowly to a run, or does he commit so quickly that he might be vulnerable to a counter or to a special blocking technique?

Several years ago against Seattle, the Raiders decided to use the halfback pass. Marcus Allen was a quarterback in high school so he threw a pretty good pass. They waited for a short-yardage situation and then tossed to Marcus, who was running wide. He pulled up and threw a pass for a touchdown. A few weeks later against the Chargers, the play was used again, this time for 40 yards and a score. So, the coaches decided they needed this play in their offense. While it was put in originally as a "big play" for a specific game, it became an integral part of the offense and kept the defensive backs from coming up too soon to stop the run. The threat of the pass made the run more effective.

Sometimes you can predict, nearly without error, what a team will do in a highly specific situation. Several years ago in a playoff game, the Raiders were nearly certain that the Broncos would use a specific defense on third-and-one. They had a play that they were 98 percent certain would score. They never got into a third-and-one situation in the game, so were never able to use this piece of strategy.

Passing Game Strategy

Some teams, such as the Raiders, always want the threat of the deep pass. If it's there — great! If not, it opens up other things, like 20-yard curls or outs. Often those 20-yard patterns go all the way. While a "big play" team may actually call only six or eight long passes in which the deep man is the prime receiver, it will have potential receivers running deep patterns quite often — even if the quarterback isn't paying any attention to them.

When a coach expects a defensive line to hit and pursue on the run, he can expect a somewhat slower pass rush because the defender must first hit, then recognize the pass, then rush. This is slower than the defender who is aggressively attacking a gap. The 1985 Super Bowl champion Chicago Bears illustrated the hard charging type of defense that gets a good number of sacks. This makes it more difficult to get sufficient time for a complete passing attack.

To combat the hard charging linemen and the blitzing defenses, a coach might decide to just throw short. This is what Miami did in beating the Bears of 1985. Instead of having the quarterback drop seven steps, he might just use the patterns that have one-, three-, or five-step drops with quick releases. Or, if the coach has a mobile quarterback, he may have the passer sprint or roll away from the rush. Do the opponents always use a 4-3 or a 5-2 zone? Do they always use a tight man-to-man defense? If either of these is true, the types of pass patterns that will work against man-to-man or zone can be put into the game plan.

The offensive coach must also account for every possible rusher on or near the line of scrimmage. At the more advanced levels of football, the offense should have more than one way to block each of these defenders. If the defense is overloaded to one side, you should be able to slide your linemen over to pick up the possible rushers. Perhaps you might shift your tight end over to the defensive strong side. Or you may need to have a back ready to block to the side which the defense has overloaded.

Some teams blitz a lot when they are in the "nickel" defense. But from where will that extra blitzer come? The offensive team may be one player short at the point of the blitz. How will that be handled? On the goal line, are the opponents always in a man-to-man defense? If so, crossing patterns, hooks, or fade patterns can be put into the game plan.

In creating the mismatch, you might look for a weak defender against which you can put your best receiver? How can this best be accomplished? Perhaps he is a cornerback. If so, you can motion your best receiver toward him or flank your best receiver on his side.

Can you coax the defensive line to rush aggressively and then run screens and draws? Or can you get outside the rush with a quick pitch or a swing pass? Will the linebackers react to a run fake so that play action passes can be completed? Will defensive backs react up to a run fake so that a receiver can sneak deep on them for an easy touchdown?

When developing the passing strategy for the game, the coach should look at how he can match up his best receiver with the weakest defender. Every game plan should have the potential of hitting quick with big play potential for each receiver.

Developing Game Strategy

In preparing for a team, we have to think of the overall theories of the coach. What does he like to do? Is he conservative, or is he a gambler. If he has been in the league a long time, the other coaches know a lot about him.

But what about the new coach in the league? You can use a computer analysis that records a team's tendencies over several years to give an idea as to the coach's thinking on such concerns as the following:

- When does he like to block punts?
- Does he often use an onside kickoff?
- When is he likely to blitz?
- What types of plays does he like on third-and-long?
- What are his favorite goal line plays?

In football, you not only scout the players but also the coach. It is the coach who is directing the team? A team can't change its overall style every week and still be successful. The execution of the plays is of critical importance, so new plays, pass patterns, defensive reads, or pass coverages can't be changed on a weekly basis. However, you may change something just a bit. You might decide to run a pattern a few yards deeper than normal or throw the halfback pass to a different player or from a different formation. It may be just enough to throw off the opponent, but it isn't enough to take a lot of practice time to perfect it.

Another consideration is how an opponent has played a team similar to you. If your opponent was successful against teams similar to yours, they might use a similar strategy against you.

A major aspect of your strategy for every game might be the "big play." When is the opponent likely to play man-to-man or to blitz? What are they likely to do on third down and short yardage?

Most coaches call certain plays early in the game to see how the defense adjusts. The coach may look for defensive adjustments to such things as: stretch motion (running a back farther out to the same side on which he started); crossing motion (having the back go across the formation therefore changing formation strength); motion to a slot or flanker set; a formation with an unbalanced line; or, to the reaction of the linebackers on a play action pass. You will want to know what they do in short-yardage situations.

Years ago, Sid Gillman, one of the finest strategists the game has seen, used the first quarter to analyze the opponent's defense, and then attacked that defense for the next three quarters. Many coaches have followed his lead.

Often coaches attempt to beat the linebackers. By using draws and screens in passing situations and play action passes in running situations, they try to fool the backers who have both run and pass responsibilities.

Another factor that might change a team's strategy is the injury factor. If a team's best passer or receiver is out of the game, the running attack might become more important in the game plan. If the best runner or pulling guard is hurt, it might mean another type of change for the game plan.

The weather is another factor to consider. If the weather is expected to be very cold or wet, it might mean that the running game would become the dominant part of the game plan. Power plays, quick plays, or counters might have a better chance of working than long passes.

Or, perhaps the coach might decide to punt on early downs and wait for the opponents to make mistakes that result in turnovers. The opponent might be so strong that the only way possible to try to run on them would be with trick plays, such as reverses, counters, using an unbalanced line, or Statue of Liberty-type plays. It might be that their strengths can be used against them.

READY LIST

vs. _____

1st DOWN

FB
RUN
22/23 T
68/69 T
68/69 T
SPUN
68/65
68/69 Bom
60/61

DROP BACK PASSES

R: 89 W 10 CROSS
E: Y SLANT Z 2 OUT
E: Harp 95 Hort POSS
E: 95 IN 11 OUT
E: 94 Sheat 10 OUT
E: 91 CLOSE 920

I: 91 OUT 6 ARC
N: 99 213 CROSS
I: 91 HOOK 213 ARC
GRON: 95 CROSS 6 ARC
FAR: 86 T2 T13 POKE
N: 99 Y CROSS 6 ARC

SCREENS

Far Lt: Sh. Screen Lt HB
Ease Lt: Harp 95 OUT

3rd LONG

K PASS DEEP

East IR Max 2 K15
Far Lt Draw Tops Pass
Tites 2 99 K65 Wing
Green Tlt: 28 Arc XIN K14
K76

PLAY PASSES

East I Lt: 99 Post 2R K14
DIVR: 23 K69 SPOKE
IR: 23 K14
IB: 95 CROSS K14
IL: 99 YL K15
NL: 99 CR X UP K14
NR: K5OCMBK (XCOR)
RR: 50 SW. Z PIVOT

3rd MEDIUM

Pirate
NEAR: (Z sh) 89 Z CROSS 2/3 OPT out up
BRN NEAR: 99 CROSS 6 option
GREEN NR: 99 Z CROSS 2 OUT UP
N GAR: (Z sh) 94 Z CROSS 2 OPT.

THREE / TWO

I: 91 OUT Y CROSS 2/3 ARC
ENR: 91 IN U OUT 13 CROSS

ZONE OFFENSE

US
35 L
:GB
8/19 BOB.

REGULAR

Brown NEAR: 94 COR Z OUT 2/3 OPT.
Brown NEAR: 94 OUT Z CROSS 2/3 option
Brown NEAR: 94 OUT 6 UP ZONE 2/3 OPT.
GREEN N R: 99 IN Z CROSS 2 OUT UP
Full RT: 99 IN Y CROSS 2 SWING
GRAY N: 86 Y CROSS 2 POST

EAST

East FAR: 89 IN 10 option
East NEAR: 99 Z CROSS 2/3 OUT
East NEAR: 94 CORNER 2 CROSS
East Far: 99 Z PIVOT 10 CROSS

SPECIAL PLANS Charlie

DEEP

OUT UP
CORNER
E East Lt: Y 90 UP GP Z CROSS 2 OUT

MOVE POCKET
SPRINT Rt 26 ZCMBK
Turnol B (ZCMBK Go)

SHORT YARDAGE — GOAL LINE

1 SPEC UNBAL I LT 15 LM.
2 TBL FAR (Z) 64 SLM.
3 TBL I: FRONT SL 18/19 Y.Z.
4 TBL I (Z) CMR 14/15
1 TBL I: 68 OPT Z.
2 TBL FAR (Z) 68/69 YL

PASSES
1 TBL NR 2 app Roll 94 Sh. COR
2 TBL I R (Z) Sh. Yd. R.P. Ap 19

20 YARD LINE OFFENSE

15/20 YD LINE
Far Rt: Spec 26 10 IN UP
East Lt: 94 OUT UP 11 POST
N GREET: 86 Y CROSS 2 POT
East Trip Lt: 91 IN ZN 05 Flag
East: 41 CLOSE 20

15 YD LINE
East OUT (2 md) 85 POST
East FAR Lt (Z md) 89 OUT Z COR 11 CROSS
Tight Trips Rt: 28 SPEC 8 PIVOT

TWO MINUTE OFFENSE

EAST DOUBLE   3 MAC MAN

Moving Routes
94 OUT 6 IN
99 IN 6 CMBK (OUT)
89 IN 6 IN

HALF-TIME

3/4 d. LINE

1. TBL I RT: C+ Z TRAP 15
1A. SPEC UNBAL TLT 15 LM.
2. TBL FAR (Z) SLANT 18/19 U
6 LINEMEN TBT (Z) 14/15 BL
1. TDN: 16 68/69 YL.
3. 16 64/65 LM.

PASSES
1 TBL FAR (Z) 95 IN K16 FLAT
2 TBL R: East GL R.P. Ap 18 Y.Z.
4 LINEMEN
TBL Seal (Z) 18 CROR 14/4 G
TBL Seal (Half) 89 HE 85 Option

5-10 yd LINE
DOT: 28 85 POST

E RT (Z short) Run Pass Ap 18 G
2W Lt (Z East) Roll Rt PS Dolla

PIRATE
BRN NB: 95 IN Z CROSS 2 OUT UP
BAN R: 99 CROSS 2 option
NL (Z sh) 95 IN Z SWIRL 300 T

ORG
SPEC
Aide
Bandit

RUN PASS
E IR: F1 R.P. Flip1

Reverse
BRN IRT: Z ACK
REVER PASS
BRN Far Lt: Z K69 REV

The Offensive Game Plan

Most coaches develop a list of plays for each situation. Both the head coach on the field and the offensive coordinator in the press box have copies of this list. The list on the previous page was used in a recent Super Bowl appearance.

The list is intelligible to the team using it, but few other people could understand most of the numbering and code names.

The upper left-hand box lists the most probable plays which should work against the opponent's most probable first-down defenses. "FB" on the top left corner means "fullback." The 31 and 32 plays are fullback plays. 66/67T are trap plays at the 6 and 7 holes. Drop back passes are listed in the top right corner of the box and screen passes are listed in the bottom right corner.

Because second down is not as critical a down, it is not listed. Third down, however, is extremely important, so plays are listed for third-and-long, medium, and short (under two yards) to go. Notice that on third-and-two, both choices are pass plays.

The third box down in the right corner lists the plays from the plus 20 to the 15-yard line, then plays from the 15 to the 10, then plays from the 10 to the 5. Inside the 5-yard line look at the next box up for the goal line offense. The upper right corner of that box lists plays specifically from the 3 or 4 yard lines.

The bottom box in the right column is used for any new plays that will be added based on what the opponents have done the first half.

Developing Defensive Strategy

Your first consideration is to take away their bread and butter plays, whether it is the off-tackle, the isolation series, or the short passing game. You must stop what they do best and get them to try to beat you with their secondary attack.

Second, you want to know when you might get a big play. When are they likely to pass long or run a screen? If you can get a sack at this time, they lose a lot of yardage and their down. You should work a great deal on getting the big defensive play. Look for the big defensive play — the sack or the interception — when your opponents have been forced into an obvious passing situation. In these situations, you might want to gamble to get the "big play."

Look for the big play on both offense and defense. Remember that when you go for the big play you must gamble. But it's not like Las Vegas. Gamble when the odds are in your favor. If you are going to play the pass line, you want the dice loaded!

You also want to know how to get to the opponent's quarterback. Does he always drop back? Does he scramble a lot? When he does, is it usually to his right? Does he look for a hole in the middle to run through if his receivers are covered? You will certainly prepare differently for a pure drop back passer than one who runs often. Keep in mind the old coaches maxim to "rush the good passer and drop back defenders against the poor passer."

Against a team with one outstanding receiver, it might be determined to double cover him all the time, or perhaps only in certain passing situations. Or you might decide to just cover him with your best defender. Against a team with a good short passing attack, you might decide to go man-to-man often.

In looking at the scouting reports, one may find that a team has pet formations for favorite plays. Some teams nearly always pass from a split back set. Or, they may use their motion back extensively, using him to lead block or trap when he is near the offensive line, and using him as a prime receiver when he is wider. If so, he becomes a major key for the defense. Or, your opponent may ignore their back in motion, using him only to shift or spread the defense.

The scouting report might reveal that the team plays very conservatively inside its own 30. This means that the defense can become more aggressive and perhaps downplay the possibility of a pass. The report may show that the team favors running to its right or to the wide side of the field. This could signal the defensive coordinator to slant the line or stunt a linebacker into the expected flow of the play. An analysis of the scouting report may suggest that a team's basic keys might not be too effective. If your defensive line has been taught to follow a pulling lineman, but your upcoming opponent likes to pull one guard to influence the defender to follow him, then trap that defender — your defense might have to "unlearn" that key.

Perhaps the linebackers have been taught to key the guards, but the opponent never pulls the guards or double teams with them. In that case, a better key might be found for that game. Maybe your defensive backs have been taught to key the offside tackle and end to determine whether it is a run or pass play, but the tackle never releases immediately downfield; a new key might have to be found for your backs.

Some teams keep their keys the same throughout the season, others change somewhat from week to week to get the best possible defense for the upcoming opponents. It takes experienced teams to do this. Against a team that runs the I-formation, the key might be the fullback, or a read from the guard to the fullback, which would have a better chance at stopping the countering game. Against a team that doesn't cross its backs, the linebackers can key the near back, but if the backs cross, such as in a cross buck, it would be necessary to key the opposite back.

Sometimes the scouts pick up a "cheat" that can be exploited by the defense. A fullback might line up closer than normal on cross bucks or when he is expected to pass block. Or maybe a flanker lines up closer to the center if he is going to run a reverse. Or a tight end might cheat out a bit when he is going to release for a pass.

Sometimes a key signals the linebackers which way the play probably will go. A quarterback might always use an open pivot, opening up toward the flow of the quick or power plays. Or the fullback might always lead the tailback. If this is true, the defensive coordinator can start the linebackers toward the flow quickly, leaving only the necessary people on the offside to defend against a countering action or reverse.

Often a key of a back can be combined with another key that stops the counters. If one of the guards leads in counter actions, the backers might have to read through that guard to a back. If the guard moves laterally, the backer follows him. If the guard does not pull, the backer simply keys the back.

If the counters always come from a wingback, some defenders can key him and yell "reverse" when he starts opposite the flow.

Perhaps you can shake up the offense with a change of pace, or something the opponents have not seen before. In the 1985 Citrus Bowl, Ohio State started rushing Robbie Bosco of BYU with only two men while dropping back nine. This confused BYU. As BYU began to make adjustments, Ohio State began rushing three, four or more and blitzing others. The strategy was highly effective — Ohio State won, 10-7.

Teams should not be predictable on offense or defense! Smart coaches will pick up your tendencies and beat you with them.

Kicking Game Strategy

The kicking game is a highly scouted aspect of football. It is an area in which many "breaks" can be made, especially if they are planned.

Among the things to be considered when the other team is kicking off are the following:

- The average distance of their kicks
- The average hang time
- The type of kick coverage
- The speed of the kickoff team

If your opponent's kickoff is generally short, you may emphasize the return that week. If the kicking team coverage stays in lanes as they are supposed to do (about three to five yards apart) a middle return probably is best. If they converge quickly on the ball, a wide return is best. If most of them converge but those responsible for the wide plays stay wide, then a trap return probably is best. If the kicking team crosses their widest men to make it more difficult to trap, that has to be taken into consideration in setting up the blocking rules.

When you are kicking, you must consider the best return man for the opponent and kick away from him. You must know if the opponent is likely to wedge, cross block, or trap to prepare your coverage people for blocks from the side or from blocks from the front, such as occurs in a wedge return.

If the other team peels back quickly on the kickoff, you might consider an onside kick. In the 1966 Rose Bowl game, UCLA pulled off what might have been the biggest upset in this traditional game. Top-ranked and undefeated Michigan State was favored by two touchdowns. After a fumbled punt, UCLA scored. They kicked onside and recovered, then quickly marched 42 yards to score. The Bruins scored all of their 14 points without the Spartans touching the ball and held on to win, 14-12. Tommy Prothro, the UCLA coach, was a championship bridge player as well as a highly successful coach. His strategic and tactical decisions won a good many games for him — at the card table and on the field.

When the other team is punting, you must know how many seconds it takes for the center to snap the ball to the kicker and how long it takes the punter to get the ball off. (Taking more than 2.2 seconds is usually a signal that the punt can be blocked.) Does he take long steps? Is the center likely to snap high or onto the ground? If so, you can work on a block. Many teams put a man on the center to hit him as he snaps. If you can get him to start thinking about taking the hit instead of making the snap, you may be able to get a bad snap out of him. Or, he may snap extra hard so that he can quickly set himself to protect from the hit he knows he will receive. This hard snap is more likely to go high, thus increasing the time it takes to punt and increasing the likelihood of a blocked punt.

The coach must decide where the block should occur — usually the blockers aim five yards in front of the spot where the kicker lined up, but if the punter takes short steps the target for the block might be at four yards. Next, the coach has to determine where to attempt the block. Are their linemen tightly spaced? If so, you might be able to block from the outside. Or are their gaps wide so that an inside stunt might work?

As the punting team, you want to make certain that you get the punt off. But if a team never rushes your punter you might think of having him hold the ball for a second before he kicks it to give your coverage people a chance to get further downfield. If they hit and peal back to set up a return you might fake the punt and pass or run. If they always rush the punter, the fake punt might work. Should you decide to use a fake, maybe a pass into the area vacated by their rushers might work. For the punt return, coaches generally don't make any changes. However, if the other team has had a personnel change it might affect who and how you double team to slow the punt coverage.

While you normally wouldn't plan any changes in your field goal attempt, you might change your fake field goal play depending on the expected coverage by the defense. The field goal block might be changed if you find that one of the blockers generally creates a gap. If he always blocks a man on his outside, you might put a man on his outside and then stunt a man through the gap created. If the opponent's end always blocks down and the wingback always takes the outside responsibility, you might put a man on the end charging down and a man on the back charging outside and then stunt a man between them.

The Challenge of Making the Strategic Decisions

Some teams stay very basic with their offense and defense. Their idea is to minimize their own mistakes. Other teams look for technical advantages and change somewhat from week to week in their attack and defense.

Sometimes the strategy hinges on pre-game publicity. In 1904, Coach Fielding Yost at Michigan publicized the fact that his 265-pound lineman, Babe Carter, (the original "Ice Box") would carry the ball near the goal line. During the game he inserted Carter as a back when his team got near the goal line. Carter faked, and another back scored. Years later, Mike Ditka effectively used William "the Refrigerator" Perry, a defensive lineman weighing more than 300 pounds, in his goal line attack, both as a ball carrier and a decoy.

The hype of the 1986 Super Bowl between the Bears and New England Patriots had many people wondering. Would Tony Eason be able to play even though he had the flu, or would Steve Grogan start? Would Jim McMahon be able to play with his sore buttock, or would his acupuncturist have to start the game instead? A defense might prepare somewhat differently depending on which quarterback might start, so the supposed pre-game indecision by one coach might result in a lot of headaches for his opponent.

Before their playoff game meeting in 1986, John Robinson of the Rams said that Dallas often adds plays if there is a strategic reason for it, but that the Rams are not inclined to do anything different from week to week. Then in the game it was the Rams who had all the new plays — obviously Robinson was setting up his opponent.

When Mike Ditka unleashed the "Refrigerator," opposing coaches had to give some thought to defending him. Each week Ditka put in a new "wrinkle" for his new ball carrier. One week he led the ball carrier to the goal line. The next week he carried the ball. The next week, in an unplanned tactic, he carried the ball carrier over the goal. The next week he caught a pass. The "Fridge" was not really a major part of the offense, but he did have to be considered in the plans of the defense.

Prior to the "Fridge" with the Bears, San Francisco's Bill Walsh had used a lineman in the backfield on certain plays. You could always count on Walsh to come up with a new formation, an unbalanced line or some other gimmick. It caused opponents problems in preparation and adjustments.

But gimmicks don't necessarily bring success. Many successful offensive teams seldom use major changeups. The coaching staff generally sees many things that can be done, but do not have time to practice. The major question is whether the time spent in teaching the changes is more beneficial than focusing on fundamentals.

Most coaching staffs do not go "out of character" for a big play. They won't change a basic run or pass play just to gain a small advantage, because the practice time it takes to perfect the changes are not worth the expected result. When they do make changes it is more likely to be in the passing game than in the running attack, because passing changes are easier to install. Passes usually involve only two or three people, while a running change requires that the whole offensive unit be involved in the learning process.

Defensively, you not only have to be prepared for what an opponent has done, but what it might do. The "what if" part of the preparation can drive you crazy. What if they have their reverse man throw a pass? What if they run a hook and lateral? What if they try a reverse on the kickoff?

In 1985, San Diego Charger coach Don Coryell installed the power-I as part of his offense. It was a formation he had used as a college coach at Whittier. The Chargers already were hard enough to prepare for with their helter-skelter offense; this addition made them even more difficult. The Raiders made adjustments during the week, but Coryell added some motion and other formation changes that weren't expected. The Raiders' "what if" preparation wasn't quite complete, and they lost in overtime, 40-34.

For many coaches, the week-to-week strategic adjustments are the most interesting and challenging aspects of the season. This is, perhaps, the major factor in the "violent chess match" of football.

21

Strategy Checklists

This chapter presents checklists for planning strategies for an upcoming game. These checklists are based on the information found in chapters 4-11 and 19-20. The left-hand column poses questions that a scout should consider, and the right-hand column offers suggestions.

Offensive Strategy

OPPONENT

1. What is the basic front?

2. What is the basic line play? Hit and react or penetrate?

3. When do they stunt or blitz?

4. What is basic pass cover?

5. Which zones are usually covered on a pass?

6. What is their hashmark adjustment?

7. Do they pursue well?

8. Who contains on wide plays?

OFFENSIVE APPROACH
Attack weaknesses

a. Against a reacting defense, double team, influence block, quick plays, false block
b. Against a penetrating defense, trap, go wide
c. If they follow a pulling lineman, influence trap

a. Look for hot receiver if a pass play
b. Get wide quick on a run
See passing strategy checklist

See passing strategy checklist

a. Pass away from rotation
b. Run away from slant
c. If no adjustment, go wide

a. If good pursuit, counter
b. If poor pursuit, go wide

a. If waiting end, fake inside, go outside
b. If crashing end, go outside
c. If boxing end, go inside
d. If backer or back, force rotation and flood vacated area

9. Who trails the play?

    a. If no trailer, run wide counter

    b. Counter into the area vacated by the trailer

10. How can backers be fooled?

    a. Play action pass

    b. Counter or draw

11. Alignment of backers

    a. If deep, run quicks

    b. If shallow, run wide or play action pass

12. Is their defense balanced (as many men on one side of the ball as the other)?

Run or pass to the side on which they are out-manned

13. Do their defensive players have strong or weak responsibilities?

Shift tight end to make defense make multiple changes (strong backers, strong safety, etc.)

14. When do they use short yardage situations?

Anticipate their change on your short list. Look for big play potential

15. What is their short yardage defense?

    a. What are three weaknesses in their short yardage defense (responsibilities and personnel)?

    b. What six plays will work best?

16. When do they begin using goal line defense?

Anticipate their change on short list

17. What is their goal line defense?

    a. What are their weaknesses (responsibilities and personnel)?

    b. What four plays will work best (two runs, two passes)?

Offensive Personnel

1. Which starters are injured?

Is it worth attacking that area? If so, how?

2. Who are their strongest offensive linemen?

How can they be beaten or neutralized?

3. What are the strengths of their quarterback?

    a. How can the strengths be neutralized?

    b. If he is a good passer, rush rather than cover

4. What are the strengths of their receivers?

    a. How can these strengths be reduced?

    b. Who needs to be double covered in pass situations?

    c. Which are their favorite patterns?

    d. Should wide receivers be bumped?

5. What are the strengths of the running backs?

Take away their greatest strengths.

6. Who are the weakest players?

How can they be exploited?

7. What are the weaknesses of the offensive line-men?

a. Does he charge slowly? If so, hit and react.
b. Is he very aggressive and off balance in his charge? If so,slant, loop, or draw his block and stunt past him

8. What are the weaknesses of the quarterback?

a. Does he like to run? If not, apply a heavy rush
b. If he's a poor thrower, rush less and play for interceptions
c. If he rolls or sprints, which direction is most likely? Stop him quickly.
d. Is he an effective runner? How do you intimidate him?

9. What are the weaknesses of the receivers?

Who can be single covered in pass situations?

10. What are the weaknesses of the running backs?

Take away the stronger back's best plays

Defensive Personnel

1. Who is the best pass rusher?

How can he be handled? Draw, double team, traps?

2. Who is the best run defender?

How can his pursuit be reduced?

3. Who is the best linebacker?

a. How can his strengths be used against him?
b. Who is he keying?
c. If he pursues quickly, counter
d. If he plays the run quickly, use play-action passes

4. Who is the best outside backer?

a. How can he be handled?

5. Who is the best cornerback?

a. How can he be neutralized?
b. Will he cover our best receiver?
c. How can we get our best receiver away from him? Motion?
d. Will he play man-to-man defense? If so, when?

6. Who is the best safety?

How can he be neutralized?

7. Who is the weakest run defending lineman?

a. What plays will work against him?
b. How can he best be blocked?

8. Who is the weakest pass rusher?

a. Can he be single blocked?
b. Will the draw work against him?

9. Who is the weakest inside backer?

How can his weakness be exploited? By runs—quick hitters, draws, sweeps, counters? By passes—play action, sprint out, middle screen?

10. Who is the weakest outside backer?

a. What are his weakest points? Speed? Toughness? Inability to play the run or pass?
b. How can his weaknesses be exploited? Double team him?

11. Who is the weakest cornerback?

a. How can we get our best receiver on him?
b. What are his weakest points? Speed? Agility?

Passing Strategy

OPPONENT'S DEFENSE	OFFENSIVE APPROACH
1. Secondary playing loose	Automatics, hitch, out
2. Loose zone	Use quick game
3. Normal zone	a. Throw under backs (18-yard curls) b. Throw under backers (floods, drags)
4. Secondary blitz or dog	Inside out release
5. Heavy rush	Draw or screen on early down
6. Backer dropping quickly	Draw or delay passes
7. Secondary rotation	a. Throwback from sprint or wide rollout b. Play-action passes
8. Sky-cloud cover	Post read pattern
9. Man-to-man	a. Play-action with one receiver out b. Pick patterns c. Get physical mismatch d. Fade, hook, double fake
10. Two deep safeties (5 under-2 deep)	Send three receivers deep, two on the sidelines, one more shallow in the middle
11. Four short zones (4 under-3 deep)	Work high and low on a player underneath, such as an orbit pattern

12. How can each defender be beaten?

    a. Determine best matchups.

    b. Determine best patterns to use

    c. Determine best way for each potential receiver to make one or more big plays

Defensive Checklist

OFFENSIVE TENDENCIES	POSSIBLE ADJUSTMENTS
1. Is there a hash mark tendency for their running game?	a. Slant line to strength b. Rotate backs or set rover to strength c. Stunt into strength
2. Field position	a. Look for big defensive play in specific situation b. From which areas are they most likely to pass?
3. Down and distance	Look for predictable down and distance situation for a big play
4. Score	At what point in the game does the score change their tactics?
5. What function does motion play in their offense?	If motion man is an integral part of their offense, honor it
6. What is the action of the ball carrier on a draw or pass?	If the back steps wide, probable pass, if he steps to the side, probable draw
7. Personnel	a. Who is injured? b. How can you defeat their strongest players? c. How can you defeat their weakest players?

Kicking Checklist

OUR PUNTING TEAM

Do they rush or cover?

    a. If they rush, who is their best punt blocker?

    b. If they cover, who are the rushers?

    c. What is their favorite return play?

    d. Who is their best returner?

    e. If they prefer wide side returns, kick to short side of the field

    f. Do they hit the snapper?

OUR PUNT BLOCK—RETURN TEAM

1. Where is best area of line from which to block their punt?

Rush from wide angle against tight line and from the inside against split line

2. What is the timing of their snap-punt?   If more than 2.2 seconds, consider a block attempt

3. What is their hang time?   If short, consider returning the punt

4. Does the punter kick low?   Consider returning the punt

5. Are you trying to block the punt?   Where is the target area? 4 to 5 yards

6. Are you returning the punt?   Who must be held up?

7. Which direction does the ball travel from the punter?   Usually right of a right-footed punter

8. Do they stay in the proper lanes?   If not, where can we exploit their weakness?

OUR KICKOFF TEAM

a. What type of return should we expect?
b. Where should we kick the ball?
c. If they retreat fast should we use an onside kick rather than a deep kick?

OUR KICKOFF RETURN TEAM

a. How deep do they kick?
b. What is their average hang time?
c. Who are the first men downfield?
d. Do they stay in their lanes? Can we exploit this?
e. Who is/are their safeties?
f. Do they cross any cover men?

OUR FIELD GOAL/EXTRA POINT BLOCK TEAM

a. Do they block upward or inward? If upward, can they be split? If inward, where will the seam open? (outside tackle or end)
b. What is the time of their kick
c. Can they be pushed back for a middle block?
d. Does their kicker kick low?
e. How far must blockers penetrate to block the kick?
f. Who needs to be covered for their fake or muffed kick plays?

OUR FIELD GOAL/EXTRA POINT TEAM

a. How do they attempt to block?
b. What adjustments do they make to our fake or muff adjustments?

22

Making Game Adjustments

Perhaps the toughest part of coaching is making necessary tactical adjustments during a game. Adjusting to an unexpected defense, a substitute starting in place of a regular, new plays, different formations, or new types of motion can be very challenging. Also, reacting to the adjustments of your opponent can force some quick thinking. The major point is not to panic.

The information on the new "wrinkles" of the opponent usually come first from the coaches in the press box. Each one is responsible for charting and diagnosing some aspect of the opponent's offense or defense. They are usually quick to make suggestions for adjustments. If these adjustments are part of your overall theory of offense and defense, you can react quickly. Perhaps you hadn't practiced these adjustments since the early part of the preseason, but they are still in your playbook. Sometimes you have to make an adjustment that hasn't been practiced. This, of course, has much more chance of error.

Intelligent tactical decisions play the percentages. Going for a first down on fourth-and-two on your opponent's 45-yard line is generally not as good a percentage play as a punt. But if it is late in the game and you are behind, your chances of winning are much better if you try for the first down.

Another tactical concern is the emotional factor. This is a reason that coaches often go for the "sure" field goal on fourth-and-one on the one-yard line. If the defense holds you scoreless, your players expe-

rience an emotional letdown and give momentum to the defense. Even a field goal makes the offense feel good and the defense feel that it has failed.

Then there is the control-of-time factor. When you want the game to speed up, you call running plays and keep the ball in bounds. When you want to extend the game, such as in a two-minute offense at the end of a half, you throw the ball and get out of bounds.

Before it became legal to throw the ball away to stop the clock, coaches often had players feign injuries. Once in a Bear game, Coach George Halas told Ed Ecker to fake an injury late in the game. He did, but downfield there was a penalty against the opponent that stopped the clock. Ed just laid there. Nobody paid any attention, so he limped off the field. When he got to the sidelines Halas cussed him out for leaving the field and then ordered him back into the game. The crafty coach had changed tactics in mid-play.

Offensive Tactical Adjustments

At the professional level, some of the tactics relate to making substitutions based on the other team's subs. Most teams do this. While in the huddle the linemen peek at the incoming subs and alert the quarterback to a possible audible call.

When Dallas played the Bears a few years ago, every time Dallas sent in seven defensive backs on third-and-long, Mike Ditka called for a draw play.

When the Cowboys made their adjustment and started going for running back, the quarterback faked the draw and threw long to set up a key touchdown.

One of the first things a coach wants to find out is if the opponent's defense is playing similarly to what they have in the past. Are the linemen in different spots than usual, or do they have different responsibilities? Are they playing tighter than they were when you saw them in the films? The offensive line coach usually gets this information from your linemen when they come off the field.

Some years ago Kansas City planned to stop the Raiders' running attack with five defensive linemen rather than their normal four- man front. It took the Raiders by surprise, but they soon realized that by playing a 5-2 alignment up front the Chiefs had to play man-to-man in the secondary. The Raiders split Cliff Branch as an end and put one back outside the tackles in a double wing. This forced the Chiefs safeties to "lock up" on the wing backs and left no free safety to help on Branch. He faked outside and went to the post which, of course, was wide open. The 50-yard touchdown forced the Chiefs out of their five-man line and enabled the Raiders to revert to their game plan, which was primarily a running attack.

Are the defensive linemen and backers penetrating or stunting more often? What are they doing in each down and distance situation? You usually get this kind of information from your press box coaches. Are the backs playing man-to-man or zone? Are they up challenging you in a "bump and run," or are they playing loose? Are they doing what you expected? Do they change coverages with changes in the down and distance situations?

A prime concern of yours should be the depth that their corners are playing. This can change the patterns you might call. What are they doing on passing downs? Are they running five defensive backs (a nickel defense) or six (a dime defense)? Do they change from situation to situation?

One successful professional team often tries for a sack on second- and-long yardage by playing a nickel defense and rushing the linemen hard. How-ever, on a third-and-long they often play seven defensive backs and try for the interception by double covering all of the prime receivers.

You might want to go deep early to see how they are covering you. If they are too deep, maybe you can break off your pattern at 20 yards, catch the ball, and still score. A few years ago in the first game against New England, the Raiders threw deep seven times and completed one for 50 yards and another for a touchdown. In a playoff game between the two teams the Patriots wouldn't let the Raider receivers deep. It changed the offensive strategy, and probably cost the Raiders the game.

When something you think will work doesn't, you need to know why. How did they react differently than you expected, and how can you attack their new reaction? Do you have to keep in an extra blocker? Do you have to run the patterns a few yards deeper or shorter in order to make them work?

You must quickly find the strengths and weaknesses of the opponents and then attack them where they are weak. Darrell Royal, the former Texas coach, might have put it best when he said "No use fartin' against thunder" and "Don't get in a pissin' contest with a skunk." Both ideas emphasize the obvious — that you don't want to go at your opponent's strengths.

When it was revealed that Bill Walsh had a list of 20 or 30 plays he was going to call at the beginning of the game, it made people think that he was a genius. He was going to have his coaches quickly analyze the opponent's strategy in terms of formation, down and distance tendencies, then he was going to attack them where they were weak. The problem was that as other coaches heard what he was doing they just sent in defenses without any strategic reasons — then after 20 or 30 plays they began to use what they had worked on all week.

At the end of the game, when behind, a team is usually prepared to throw the "out" patterns and to run draws. These are expected tactics. Then there is the "Hail Mary" pass, thrown long downfield with the hope of a completion or a pass interference penalty.

Sometimes tactical adjustments involve nothing more than going at a substitute or an injured player. Throwing to your best receiver when he is covered by a weak defensive back or running at a weak defensive lineman are obvious tactics that are often overlooked by coaches.

One of the first adjustments that power teams look for is the play of the defensive tackle. When a power-I or single-wing team double-teams the defensive tackle again and again, he probably will start to fight to the outside. After this is observed, the play that hits the next hole in is called and the tackle who is now fighting to get outside is trapped out.

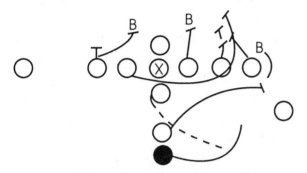

Defensive tackle is double-teamed

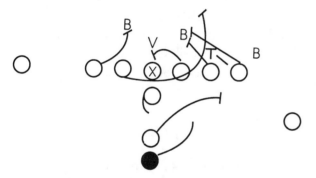

Play is run inside, tackle is trapped

One of the simplest checks for defensive coverage is to run a man in motion across the formation. If he is followed by a defender, they probably are playing a man-to-man defense. If the defense merely shifts a bit to compensate for the change in strength of the offense, they most likely are in a zone. Only the most sophisticated teams can totally disguise their coverage until the ball is snapped.

Another quick check can be done by shifting the backs. Does the defense adjust to the new strength, and if so how do they do it? Do they shift linemen, linebackers, or do they rotate their backs? Do they

slant into the shift? After the adjustment is found, the weakness can be attacked. For example, if they slant their linemen toward the shift, you might shift and then run a quick motion back to a balanced set and run the other direction — the direction toward which you looked weak.

If the defense is stunting linebackers a lot, you might alert your quarterback and ends to the "hot receiver" technique, in which the quarterback and the receivers both watch the backers. When a backer rushes, the receiver yells "hot" and goes to the zone vacated by the backer. The quarterback throws quickly, before the backer can make the sack.

Defensive Tactical Adjustments

Some teams have several defensive groups ready, depending on the tactical situation. There might be a regular defense, a nickel (five defensive backs), a dime (six defensive backs), a short yardage (elephant defense), and a goal line defense.

The offensive coordinator or the quarterback might wait until the defense is on the field before calling a play. If there is a 70 percent chance of a run you might substitute the short yardage "elephant" defense. If there is a 70 percent chance of a pass you would probably put in the nickel or dime defense and rush the passer hard.

Some coaches just count the number of wide receivers in the game to determine their defensive adjustment. Because a team can have from zero to five wide receivers in on any given play, it is often a good key as to the type of play which they have in mind — the more wide receivers, the better the chance that the play will be a pass. A weak or inexperienced player might be just the one to stunt against. He is less likely to pick up the stunt and more likely to give you the big defensive play.

When ahead, near halftime or at the end of the game, many coaches use a "prevent" or "victory" defense designed to prevent the long completion. But if the team goes into its "prevent" defense too early, there will be adequate time to run draws, "outs," and even some safe passes down the middle. This can set up a field goal, if not a touchdown.

Early in the regular season you have to be ready for anything. Some teams that pass a great deal might not show much of their passing attack because they don't want the scouts to see what they will do during the league season. Other teams might show a lot during the pre-season to drive the scouts crazy, then in the regular season might be quite basic in most of their attack.

It certainly helps a play to be successful if your quarterback has faith in it. A few years ago the Patriots had a rookie safety. He was a prime candidate for a mismatch against Cliff Branch. The Raiders planned on setting him up with some out patterns and then eventually going long on him. But Ken Stabler, the quarterback, was impatient. On the second play of the game he motioned Fred Biletnikoff from a slot position. This left Branch one-on-one with the rookie. Result — quick touchdown. The Patriot coach said he knew it was coming, but not that early in the game.

Tactics in the Kicking Game

In the 1986 Rose Bowl game, Iowa won the toss and elected to kick off. In the second half UCLA also elected to kick off. Both teams felt that their defenses could overpower the other's offense. Sometimes a team gives up its option of receiving the kickoff to take the wind at its back. Or it might choose to go on defense because it has a strong defensive unit or because the field is wet or the stadium is windy.

In the 1985 Rams-Bears NFC championship game, John Robinson second-guessed himself after the game when he said that he should have taken the wind rather than kick off when he had the chance. Former Rams coach George Allen said after the game that when you play in Chicago, you always take the wind if it is blowing more than 20 miles an hour.

In the previously mentioned 1965 Rose Bowl game, it was a tactical decision when UCLA coach Tommy Prothro chose to kick onside after his first touchdown. It worked. UCLA got the ball back and scored again. Its two touchdowns were all that it scored in the game, but it was enough to win.

Many people are not aware that in high school and college, after a fair catch the receiving team has the option of taking a regular "scrimmage down" or a "free kick down." A "scrimmage down" occurs automatically when a team takes a first and 10 option. This happens after all kickoffs, turnovers and punts in which there is no fair catch. A kickoff is an example of a free kick down — the opponent is not allowed to rush a kick. While it is not allowed to score points for a field goal on a kickoff, it is allowed on other free kick downs. So if a team fair catches a ball on its opponent's 30- or 40-yard line, it has the option of sending in its kickoff team, and if the kicker kicks it through the uprights three points are scored. While this option is seldom used, it does win some games — for coaches who know the rules.

A few years ago, San Francisco State coach Vic Rowen, a past president of the American Football Coaches Association, was two points behind Cal Lutheran near the end of the game. Cal Lutheran punted short from its end zone. The San Francisco State safety man fair-caught the punt. Vic sent in his kickoff team. It lined up in kickoff formation and his placekicker split the uprights with his kick. Cal Lutheran was helpless to stop it because during a "free kick" down the defense must remain at least 10 yards from the ball. Vic's knowledge of the rule enabled him to make a tactical decision that won the game by one point.

Making the Adjustments

Some people think that the quarterbacks ought to call all the plays — and a few do. But generally it is the coaches who call the plays, with the quarterback having the option of changing it by calling an "automatic" or "audible" at the line of scrimmage.

Some coaches allow the the quarterback to call the play, but have him signal the play back to the bench. The coaches must know the play so that they can concentrate on the defensive adjustments. Generally, the coaches in the press box are responsible for varying aspects of the opponent's offense and defense. It would be typical for a pro team on offense to have three coaches watching the defense — one looking at the defensive linemen, another at the linebackers, and another at the secondary.

If the coach responsible for the defensive backs knows that a play is to be run wide to the right from a set with two tight ends, and that the offensive left end is to release downfield but the right end is to block, he might be able to pick up the way the defensive backs are keying the ends.

If the safety on your right end starts playing for the pass, he is probably keying the release of the opposite end. If he comes up quick he is probably keying the end near him. If he is keying the end near him you might release that end, rather than have him block on the next running play to that side. Perhaps you find that the linebackers are well-drilled in keying the guards. If a guard fires out at the linebacker, the backer comes up hard to hit him. But if the guard sets up to pass block, the backer drops quickly. You might then call a lot of draw plays, with the guards setting to pass. If the backers come up fast, you might call play action passes and throw just behind the backers.

Maybe the linebacker on your tight end drops as the end releases. If so, you might run a delayed play at the spot that he vacated. Perhaps your coach looking at the defensive linemen finds that they are hitting and fighting the pressure (trying to get around our blocker's head). You might decide to influence block them and perhaps trap them. You would have your linemen put their heads on the opposite side of the defender from the way you want him to go. Then you would let him fight to get to where you wanted him to go anyway.

Generally, the major tactical adjustments are made at halftime, but some are made on the sidelines. Once in a while the television cameras zero in on a coach on the side line with his unit of players huddled around him as he hurriedly scribbles some X's and O's on the board and makes a quick adjustment to some of the opponent's unexpected strategy.

When Ray Perkins was the coach at Alabama he was asked what adjustment he made at the halftime of the Aloha Bowl against USC. He said, "We told them to stop making mistakes. Second, we told them not to lose their concentration and composure over the officials' bad calls. Third, we told them to get physical with USC." Hardly a gigantic change in strategy, but it worked. Tactical adjustments might need to be more psychological than technical. It is the coach's job to determine what is needed to win, and then do it.

23

Much more than X's and O's

While a coach must be concerned with his theory of the game and teaching fundamentals, other concerns are of primary importance too. The complete football program is much more than X's and O's. The coach must relate well with his staff, his players, the parents, and the community. He must set goals, organize, and evaluate his team's progress. And, he must keep up with the game.

The real crux of coaching is how the coach develops and handles the goals, organization, and evaluation of the total program.

Goals and objectives must be set for the year, the playing season, the upcoming week, the current day, and for each drill. Without goals, the coaching staff and the players do not know where they are heading. Some goals must be set by the staff, some can be set by the players.

Coaches also can help their players to set both short term and long term goals concerning such things as studying, attending college and preparing for a job. The effective coach up to the high school level should be concerned with the total development of his players. The boy with goals and accomplishments outside of football is more likely to be the kind of boy who will be a real credit to the program. Real pride comes from the whole player, not just that aspect of him that plays football.

Organization is required to make certain that the goals are achieved. As with the goals, the organizational plans include the long range goals of the year, the week-to-week goals for the upcoming opponent,

and the day-to-day objectives. Effective coaches can get more done in less time, so their teams are farther ahead. While some coaches practice four or more hours daily, others can accomplish as much in two to two-and-a-half hours.

Evaluation is necessary to determine whether the goals are being achieved and whether the organization is effective in achieving the stated goals.

Goals

Because of the nature of football, with the opportunity to regroup after every play, the game can be controlled by the coach more than can any other game. In the games that have a continuous flow, such as soccer and basketball, major adjustments can be made only during timeouts. In football, a major adjustment can be made on the next play.

Football, more than any other sport, is a game that is generally decided on the mistakes and errors of the teams. The number of the mistakes must be reduced to increase the chances of not losing. The emphasis on "not losing" rather than "winning" has long been the major concern of coaches. Coaches have long admonished themselves to "not beat themselves" in the game.

This requires that their mistakes be minimized. Close games are usually "lost" by one team rather than "won" by the other. A muffed punt, a blocked kick, a clipping penalty, a bad snap — are all errors that can be reduced or eliminated through practice.

One of the great advantages that an experienced coach possesses is that he has seen so many mistakes and made so many himself that he can plan his practices to minimize or eliminate the most costly errors. The offside penalty, the blocked punt, the unsportsmanlike conduct penalties, and the fumble are the types of mistakes that can be reduced. There is never enough time to eliminate all mistakes, but a coach can go a long way toward reducing them.

The coach must select goals to accomplish the most desirable outcomes for each important learning period, whether that be beating the next week's opponent or preparing for the year ahead. Consequently, both long term and short term goals are essential to developing the most effective program.

The football season is not long enough to practice sufficiently to eliminate all errors. It is therefore essential that the coach sets goals that can be accomplished. One coach may decide that the passing offense is the most important aspect of the game. Another coach may believe that defense or kicking is most important. These are decisions based on their theories of how best to win the game.

Setting Goals

After the coach has decided what he wants to emphasize during the season, he can set his goals. Does he want to beat his opponents with the run and shoot passing offense or play good defense and have a strong kicking game and hope that the opponents are forced into mistakes that beat themselves? Both theories have brought winning seasons for many teams.

Because the coaches should know more about how they want to win, they should set the major goals that relate to football. The goals set by the coaches should include both performance objectives of the team in the game and the conduct of the team members both on and off the field.

Players can be involved in setting some goals. Many coaches believe that players should set the goals relating to "off the field" conduct. Usually they set stricter goals than the coaches. Also, the fact that they make the rules makes it more likely that they will be enforced because they come from the intrinsic motivations of the team, rather than being handed down by the coaches. The areas of concern include smoking, alcohol and other drugs, academics, curfews, and absence from practice or meetings.

Setting performance goals can be done with the individual team members, making them aware of how they can be more effective players and team members. It also should be done on a team basis, setting goals for such things as the number of first downs per game the team should make; the number of interceptions the team is expected to make; the amount of return yardage on each type of kick, and so on.

The goals should be realistic and attainable. Goals such as holding an opponent to minus yardage on offense or blocking three punts per game probably are unrealistic.

Offensive goals include the following:

- Make 20 first downs a game
- Average 350 yards per game
- Have a 60-40 run-to-pass ratio in yards gained
- Have a 75 percent third-down conversion percentage

Defensive goals include the following:

- Hold opponents to 200 yards per game
- Intercept one of every seven passes
- Force four turnovers per game
- No eight-play drives

Kicking game goals include the following:

- Limit opponents' punt returns to a four-yard average
- Average 35 yards per punt
- Block one in 10 punts.

The performance goals should be specific for each coach and team. One coach might want a 90-10 ratio of run-to-pass, while another might want a 50-50 ratio.

Goals for Coaches

To increase the input of the coaching staff and to more fully develop the potential of each coach, coaches also should have performance goals. The coaches who have a primary interest in football should be encouraged to determine more goals. The coaches who are filling in parttime just because it needs more coaches should be allowed to pursue fewer goals.

Often the primary job of the head coach, especially at the high school level, is to coach the assistant coaches. They are the primary teachers of the game, so they should understand their duties and be very proficient at carrying them out.

Team goals can be set by the coaching staff. These goals include a desired win-loss record, the desired offensive output and defensive standards for the team and other objective measures, such as intercepting one of every seven passes or averaging 4.5 yards per offensive play.

Individual goals should be set with each player. How strong should he be in each lift? How fast should he run 40 yards? What kind of leadership should he exhibit?

Motivation

After the goals are set, the progress toward those goals is be determined by the motivation of the team members and the coaching staff. Motivation can be seen as intrinsic or extrinsic.

The goal of the coaching staff should be to keep the team intrinsically motivated. Intrinsic motivation comes from within — the desire to excel and the desire to win. Extrinsic motivation comes from the outside in the form of rewards and punishments — rewards such as athletic letters, newspaper articles on the player, and the praise of the coach. Negative reinforcement includes running extra laps for being late to practice, being kept out of a game or part of a game, or being "chewed out" by a coach.

Intrinsic motivation is far and away the best method of motivation. Positive extrinsic motivation is second best. Negative extrinsic motivation is third.

The worst way to motivate is to ignore the player. The intrinsic motivation is best accomplished by good genes and a positive first few years of living. Usually the coach can't do anything about those factors — unless the player is his own son! After you get a boy on your team, private talks with him in terms of goal setting and positive progress are more likely to be able to make the player intrinsically motivated.

Coaches have the reputation of "building character" in their players. But as former coach Pepper Rogers once said, "We don't build character, we just weed out those that don't have it." There is more than a little truth to that view. Still, we have all seen boys who have been honestly turned around because of their participation in football and their association with a loving coach who is deeply concerned about their development.

Organization

It has often been said that "coaching is a race against time," and that "you can never regain a lost minute." Because of this, it is essential that the whole year be planned. Spring football practice, summer passing leagues and the pre-season two-a-days are the times to accomplish the things that are important. While some coaches prefer to put in just about everything they expect to use early in the practice season (the gestalt method), others prefer to build slowly and perfect as they go, adding a few plays or stunts each week.

Staff meetings are the primary source for the organizational development of the season. The head coach should set the tone by having an idea in mind. He must then make certain that he does not have "yes men" on his staff. Don't try to reinvent the wheel every year — just try to perfect it.

Staff organization should include the duties of each coach: position assignments, scouting assignments, responsibilities for field equipment, player equipment, audio-visual machines, duplication of scouting reports, development of written tests and so on.

Yearly organization should include efforts to accomplish the following:

- The physical goals of the players and team (strength and flexibility program, perfecting kicking skills, perfecting non-contact skills such as passing and catching, snapping, backpedaling)
- The intellectual goals of the players and team (study halls for academic assistance, learning more about the total football program, especially for the offensive and defensive signal callers)
- The social goals of the players and team (social occasions that bring the team members, and perhaps parents, together during the offseason to keep the feeling of "team" as a year-round happening.

Organization of the Program

While beginning coaches might spend a great deal of time with the X's and O's, the mature coach spends more time on the overall program. How will the academic progress of the players be monitored and improved? How can each coach contribute most to the program? How can each player be utilized to make the most of his ability and desire? How can the practices be organized to best eliminate errors and to perfect the game skills necessary to be successful on game day?

One season is not enough time to practice and perfect *every* aspect of football. The coach must decide which aspects of the game are most important and then devote the proper amount of time to each one. For example, trick plays are fun to practice, but should you use 15 minutes each day practicing them? No. Look at what should happen on game day, then allot your practice time to make that happen. Focus your attention on winning.

The game is still won with fundamentals, primarily blocking and tackling. In teaching fundamentals you need to determine just what fundamentals are necessary to make your theory of football work on the field. Different coaches have different theories of offense, defense, or kicking, so the "fundamentals" taught vary somewhat from coach to coach. As a coach it is essential that you make your fundamentals fit your theory.

Coaches continually borrow from others. They attend clinics, read books and magazines concerning coaching, and watch other coaches practice. Just make certain that what you are borrowing fits what you want to do. Just because the Super Bowl champs use a certain blocking style or pass pattern doesn't mean that it will work for every other football team in the country — even other pro teams.

In organizing practice time for any fundamental (offensive, defensive, or kicking) the coach must determine the following four factors:

1. How many times during a game will the player be using a particular skill?

2. How difficult is the skill to learn?

3. How important is that skill to making your theory work on the game field?

4. What are the strengths and weaknesses of the individual player being coached?

5. *Early season organization* can start early in the summer or with the late summer official practice, depending on the rules of the league. The concentration should be on fundamentals and on the basic non-contact elements of team play. After the official practice season has started, the coach should have a master list of everything he wishes to accomplish and how much practice time is allotted for each skill and play. This can be adjusted depending on how fast or how slowly the team is progressing in each skill.

6. *The playing season* should have week-to-week objectives, depending on the strategy planned for the upcoming opponent. Perhaps more time is needed on man-to-man pass defense or on wedge blocking. If so, what will be given up?

7. While it is usually quicker to have an overall organization for practice with a certain amount of time devoted to offensive fundamentals, team offense, kicking, defensive fundamentals, and team defense, situations might require a change. Perhaps an upcoming opponent can be better prepared for by emphasizing one of the phases of the game at the expense of another. Or perhaps the team needs a psychological lift and a change from the daily ritual.

8. One method that has been used effectively is to change the practice organization completely. One such method is to break the practice into five- or 10-minute segments with a segment of five minutes for a particular fundamental and then a team segment of five to 10 minutes utilizing that fundamental. The short periods and the change in organization can often give a mental lift to the players and more learning can be accomplished. Give the assistants a chance to coach. Some effective head coaches give the assistants little to do, especially during the full team parts of the practice.

9. *Practice organization* is critical. Many coaches recommend that more time be spent planning the practice than actually practicing. While most staffs don't have that much time, they must make certain that they take the time to practice the individual skills and the team aspects of the game that are essential to winning.

10. When planning the practice, the coach must provide for skills, conditioning, mistake reduction, and agility work. Often they can be combined. Players running sprints, for example, also can practice getting off on the proper snap count (offense) or on the ball (defense). On the odd-numbered sprints the team can go on a snap count, varying the count, and on the even-numbered sprints the team can run on the movement of the ball, using snap counts to try to get them to jump "offside." Whenever a player jumps, either on a snap count (offensive sprint) or before the ball has moved (defensive sprint), the team is penalized five yards.

11. *Practicing the fundamentals* of catching may not have the glamour of practicing seven-on-seven. However, if a receiver drops a pass during a game one might wonder if more practice time should have been spent on concentrating on the ball and catching the near end of the ball, rather than reading three defenders and finding an opening. Perhaps a few simple pass patterns perfected with well-drilled fundamentals would be more effective than a complicated passing scheme that relies on the inherent skills of the players.

12. *Scripting* the full team aspects of the practice takes a great deal of guesswork out of the workout. Many teams use offensive scrimmages that include only third-down situations. After all, the third down is the critical down. So third-and-one, third-and-three, third-and-five and third-and-long situations should be addressed.

13. What is your opponent likely to do on a third-and-one on its own 30? On your 20? Analyze the films to determine the most likely defenses and then put them into your script. So if third-and-one at midfield is likely to find the opponent slanting to the wide side and blitzing its corners, set your offensive script to take advantage of this.

14. Scripting from the 10-yard line toward the goal line is also essential. At what point is the defense most likely to change from its normal defense to the goal line defense? What plays should you be ready to call? When is the defense likely to change from a zone to man-to-man? What pass play should you be ready to call?

Discipline

Developing a "we" feeling is essential for team unity. Football, more than any sport, requires that a team be unified to be effective. This attitude must be instilled in the players, especially early in the program. Once effectively instilled, it becomes infectious and passes on from year to year. But the initial development of team unity must come from the coaching staff, and it should be planned for. It must be emphasized that the whole team wins or the whole team loses, and that *every* player on the squad is important in either outcome.

Discipline is required by the players and the coaches if their goals are to be achieved. Discipline can be divided into two types: extrinsic discipline comes from outside of the individual, and intrinsic discipline comes from within the individual. This is the more effective type of discipline. A football player who loves the game, wants to be successful, and has the desire to work all year to win in the fall is intrinsically motivated. Count your blessings if you have a player of this type. He will not need any more reward than the improvement he recognizes in his skills and the positive results we hope he sees on the scoreboard. The coach can certainly be positive in recognizing that player's progress. Tell the player! This affirms his own feelings of success.

Extrinsic motivation is commonly used by coaches. The positive type can be such things as helmet decals for big plays, mention in the news articles, and compliments on the field. Negative extrinsic motivation is less effective, but is sometimes effective. "Chewing out" a player can make him play harder because of anger or embarrassment. But often the coach who spends much time chastising a player doesn't have the knowledge of the game to teach the player. If a player who is not intrinsically motivated is out for the team, you might be better off without him. He is playing for the wrong reasons.

Bear Bryant, once said that if you are going to criticize a player, make certain that it is one of your stars. Criticizing a fifth-stringer doesn't accomplish much. He already knows he isn't very good. Coaches must understand the psychological motivations of their players. Most players are motivated by the drive for power. Success in football is a very manly thing; hitting people is a physical aspect of the drive for power. Winning is essential to the psychological fulfillment of the power drive.

With this in mind, the way you motivate should be geared toward making the player more effective, whether it means moving from third string to second string or from first string to all-league. Because coaches are also power driven, as are most people in our society, the coach's feelings of inferiority are often taken out on the players. Sarcasm and other "put downs" are examples of the coach's personal insecurities being put ahead of the effective motivation of his players. There are relatively few times when a "put down" actually inspires a player, and when it does it must be selectively used. The coach must be in control, knowing that a certain remark will elicit an intensified effort in the player. Too often it makes the player embarrassed and results in the player sulking and reducing his effort.

Planning the progress of the season should be done before fall practice begins. A thorough review of all films of the opponents is a starting point. An analysis of how the game was won or lost is next. Was the game plan defective? Was the information from the scouting booth incomplete or erroneous? How can the problems be remedied? Remember that in football you are scouting the opposing coach as much as the players. The coach's tendencies in attack, defense, and kicking probably will not vary much from year to year. If you know as much as possible about the opposing coach, you can make part of your game plan before the season starts — when there is plenty of time. The more detailed aspects of the game plan, such as finding effective mismatches, should wait until the week of the game.

A coach should work to control the things that can be controlled. The all-time great basketball coach, John Wooden, spent little time preparing for his opponents, because he couldn't control them. He worked to control what he could — his own team. The fact he won 10 national championships in 12 years indicates his philosophy works.

Evaluation

Week-to-week evaluations. The team members and coaches should be apprised of the accomplishment of each goal each week. Most of these can be done by looking at the statistics. Individual goals can be evaluated by looking at the grades of the players after the film analysis.

While coaches generally know why they lost a game, they might not be as concerned about analyzing why they won a game. It is imperative to know what you are doing well and continue to work on these strong points.

Season-ending evaluations. Evaluation of all players about their progress as football players, students, and human beings is essential if the student is to improve. The coach must realize that in all probability he is one of the most important people in the lives of his players — often the *most* important person. His loving and concerned advice might make major improvements in the lives of his players.

Public relations. Head coaches are involved in relations with many "publics." Most important are his relations with his players and staff. But other publics include the school administration, the student body, the parents, the community, college recruiters (for the high school coach) or pro teams and agents (for college coaches), and the media. Coaches should learn to deal with all of these groups in a dignified manner.

Relating to the players. Because the football coach is the most important person in the school for a great number of students, he must accept that responsibility as an educator. Every player, from the All-American to the lowest scout team member, is a unique person with special needs. And while there is not enough time in a year to be the father-confessor-teacher of every player, there is time to do a great deal of counseling and to show interest in every player. The coach must understand how important he is in directing the life of his charges, whether that be getting off drugs or going to college.

Relating to the Staff

The head coach is responsible for the total program. He normally gets to hire his own assistants, but sometimes he must work with teachers who are already at the school or school employees who have been with the program. These people should be utilized in ways that aid the program the most.

Interview your assistants to determine their commitment to education, their knowledge of the game, their preferences as to which level of coaching they prefer and which responsibilities they would like to handle, and their personal characteristics. The interview should focus on several things, such as the following:

- Personal habits, such as chewing tobacco, drinking, or smoking, might not fit in with the overall philosophy of what you are trying to teach. In the ideal program it should be "do as I do, not do as I say."
- Will they be loyal to you? Some assistants are so intent on becoming the head coach that they undermine the program, "backbiting" the head coach with players, administrators,

parents, and others. This must not be allowed to happen. Laying out your expectations in the interview can reduce the possibility of this happening.
- What is their knowledge of the game? This might be the least important factor in selecting an assistant. While you should have assistants who are knowledgeable, it is easy to teach a person how to teach fundamentals, especially at the lower levels of your program. Learning to scout and to plan strategy or to make tactical adjustments takes much longer.

You should make it clear that you are open to private criticism. No head coach knows everything. In order to make the program the most effective possible, the head coach must be open to suggestions. Still he has to make the final decision.

As an assistant coach, you owe your boss loyalty. You should be able to talk to the head coach in private, but that is up to him.

Relating to the Parents

Most parents are highly supportive of effective coaches. These parents can be used as the nucleus of the booster club. They can host pre-game meals. They can put up players who live a long way from campus during "two-a-days" and host visiting players from out of town teams when overnight accommodations are required. They can videotape games and practices. And they can become great friends.

Relating to the Community

The high school football team is often the social focal point of a community, especially in the fall. The coach is therefore a highly visible person. Because of his position he is often looked up to by both students and adults. He must consider this lofty status in the way he portrays himself to the community. The community usually stands ready to help the football program in many ways, from building a new stadium to providing for needy players.

Keeping Up with the Game

Because football is continually evolving, the coach must keep up with the changing theories. Associations, clinics, books, and periodicals can help the coach keep up-to-date on the game.

The American Football Coaches Association is the best way to keep current in the field. Coaches from every major university as well as high school coaches and former coaches make up this association. Other members include foreign coaches and some of the professional team coaches.

The dues of the AFCA are inexpensive. This entitles the member entry to the annual four-day meeting each January, the clinic notes from the meeting, a special summer manual, and the directory of members. (American Football Coaches Association, 7758 Wallace Road, Suite 1, Orlando, Florida 32819 — 407-351-6113)

Local and state associations often have clinics. They also work to advance the profession in their area. They can be influential in developing laws or rules that are essential in the conduct of higher level physical education and athletics.

The American Association for Health, Physical Education, Recreation, and Dance (AAHPERD) is the primary physical education organization in the country. Athletics is becoming a more important aspect of this national association. State associations connected with AAHPERD are also important areas for the physical educator/coach. (1900 Association Drive, Reston, Virginia 22091 — 703-476-3430)

Football Coaches Professional Growth Association (13868 Olive Mill Way, Poway, CA 92064, 619-748-7566). Clinics, camps, and hundreds of videos and films that can be borrowed.

Scholastic Coach is a major magazine for coaches. *Scholastic Coach* not only presents timely articles on football and other sports, it also covers other areas such as weight lifting, administration, facilities and new equipment. (Scholastic Coach, Box 54490, Boulder, CO, 80322-4490).

24
Preventing Injuries

The risk of injury is always present in football. Growing children and teenagers in particular are prone to certain types of injuries. The responsible coach must be aware of these concerns so that temporary or permanent problems do not develop.

Injuries to the Bones

The bones in an adult skeleton are hard, making the risk of broken bones greater for college and professional players. Children's bones are soft, however, so that they can grow. They do not totally harden until the child is finished growing, anywhere from the early teens to the early twenties.

The most common bone problem for boys is a condition known as Osgood-Schlatter's. Estimates are that as many as 90 percent of boys have some evidence of this problem. In Osgood-Schlatter's, the tendon that attaches the muscle of the front of the thigh (the quadriceps) into the leg, just below the knee, pulls out on the upper leg bone. This is not only painful, but also causes a permanent bump just below the knee cap.

The normal activities of children and teenagers, such as running and jumping, are the major cause of this condition. Doing heavy leg exercises at too early an age also can cause or aggravate the condition.

Injuries to the Ligaments

The bones are held together by pieces of tough material called ligaments. When these ligaments are stretched, we call it a sprain. Stretched ligaments take years to shrink back to their original size — and some never do.

Many times a sprained ankle keeps getting re-sprained. Because the ligament does not immediately return to its original length, the outside of the foot isn't held up as high as it was before the injury. Therefore, the ankle is vulnerable to be sprained again and again. Sprains can be greater problems than breaks over the long run because they often do not heal completely.

Preventing Sprained Ankles

Sprained ankles can be prevented by having your players wear ankle braces or by taping the ankles correctly. Recent evidence indicates that some of the available braces work better than tape and are cheaper in the long run. High top shoes may also have some effect on reducing the ability of the ankle to be sprained.

Strengthening the muscles that hold the foot up might slightly reduce the chance of spraining the ankle. To exercise these muscles, push down with your hand on the outside of the foot (near the little toe), then bring the foot upward against the pressure of the hand.

Preventing Sprained Wrists

It is more difficult to prevent wrist sprains. Two arm bones attach to the eight wrist bones, which attach to five hand bones. This accumulation of bones requires a large number of ligaments to hold the bones together, and, as the wrist can move in so many directions, it is continuously in a position in which it can be sprained. With the increased use of the hands in offensive blocking, the wrists become even more likely to be injured. The best prevention is to wrap a few layers of athletic training tape around the wrist to help support the ligaments.

Preventing Knee Injuries

Knee injuries can be prevented by doing exercises that strengthen the muscles that move the knee joint and by wearing shoes that do not have cleats that anchor the foot to the ground. Exercises for the knee will be discussed in the weight training chapter.

One of the major causes of knee injuries is that the cleats of the shoe anchor the foot to the ground. If a player is hit from the side, the knee must take the brunt of the hit. If the foot were able to slide or twist on the ground, the force of the blow to the knee would be reduced.

Tennis shoes without cleats, or shoes with cleats in a circle, enable the foot to turn. They are the safest types of shoes.

Another way to protect the knee is to reduce the stress on it by reducing the amount of full speed running, jumping, and heavy weightlifting. Whenever there is a great deal of stress on the muscles of the front of the thigh (the quadriceps), the stress is transferred throughout the knee tendon (the patellar tendon) and into the top of the lower leg bone where the tendon is attached.

Preventing Shoulder Injuries

Strengthening the muscles around the shoulder is the best way to prevent shoulder injuries. Proper technique in performing the fundamentals and learning how to fall correctly are also very important.

You should be sure to teach your players to never fall with straight arms. Teaching them to bend their elbows ensures that they will absorb part of the force of the fall with their arms.

Preventing Elbow Injuries

The same preventive measures for preventing shoulder injuries apply to the elbows. Make sure your players practice falling so that bending their arms when they catch themselves becomes second nature. However, developing the biceps muscle is also important as it reduces the chance of dislocating the elbow.

Injuries to the Muscles

Muscle injuries can be reduced by beginning each practice with a proper warm-up and stretching routine and by encouraging your players to develop muscular strength.

Nobody, particularly younger children, should play when injured, but at the higher levels of competition bumps and bruises are part of the game. Playing with pain is part of the development of the "toughness" that is essential to the game. Certainly chapped lips and the like aren't enough to stop anyone from practicing!

The Warm-up

While teenagers are less prone to muscle injuries than adults, they still should learn to use proper warm-ups. The more intense the practice, the greater the need for a proper warm-up.

Start the warm-up by having your players jog while swinging or circling their arms. This will warm up the muscles of the legs. Jumping jacks will warm up the muscles that pull apart and bring together the legs (technically called abduction and adduction).

After the heart rate has increased and the blood flow to the muscles is improved, stretching can begin. Certain muscles should be stretched before an extensive practice session, as follows:

- The thigh muscles, for running
- The chest muscles, for blocking, tackling, or throwing the ball
- The lower back muscles, for blocking, tackling, or running with power
- The upper back muscles, for tackling
- The triceps (the back of the upper arms), for throwing and blocking
- The calf muscles, for running and jumping
- The fingers, for passing and catching

Flexibility

Flexibility is generally defined as the range of motion of a joint. All athletes need a certain amount of flexibility. Stretching exercises should be done slowly — holding the stretch for as long as 30 seconds.

A few simple flexibility exercises should be done before every workout or game. They will stretch your players' connective tissues and muscles, which improves reaction time and reduces the risk of injury. The ideal order for stretching exercises is as follows:

1. *Shoulder Rotation.* The players stand erect with their arms extended. They then rotate the arms forward in circles with their hands making circles of 12 to 15 inches in diameter. After 15 seconds, they rotate backward for 15 seconds.

2. *Chest Stretch.* The players bring their arms up to shoulder level and bend them at the elbow. They then pull the elbows backward until they feel a strong stretch in the upper part of the chest. Hold for 30 seconds.

3. *Groin.* While sitting on the floor or ground, the players put the soles of their feet together and pull them toward their hips with their hands. With straight backs, have them try to press their knees to the floor. Do this for 30 seconds.

4. *Lower Back and Hamstrings.* While sitting on the floor, the players spread their legs outward as far as possible. While keeping their back and legs straight, and with their toes pointed up, have the players reach as far as possible toward their right ankle. After 30 seconds, have them reach for their left ankle for 30 seconds.

5. *Trunk Twist.* The players sit on the ground with their legs straight and bend their right leg and cross it over their left leg. Their right foot should be flat on the ground. They then reach their left arm around their bent leg as if they were trying to touch their hip. Their right arm should be placed behind them as they slowly twist their head and neck until they are looking over their right shoulder. Hold for 30 seconds and then repeat the exercise to the other side.

6. *Thigh and Groin Stretch.* From a standing position, have your players step forward with their left leg. Then they should lean forward over their left legs while keeping their left feet flat on the ground. They will then push down with the right leg until they feel a good stretch in the thigh and groin area. (Hands are allowed on the floor for balance.) Continue this stretch for 30 seconds and then repeat to the other side.

7. *Triceps Stretch.* While standing, the players will pull their right elbows behind their heads until they feel the stretch. Have them hold this for 30 seconds and then repeat with the other arm.

Glossary

ANGLE BLOCK Blocking a player inside or outside who is not "on" or "shading" the blocker.

ARC BLOCK A block on the defensive end or corner by a running back with the back attempting to block the defender in. The blocker starts wide for a few steps then attacks the defender.

AUDIBLE Calling the offensive play at the line of scrimmage.

BACKPEDAL Running directly backward, a technique used by defensive backs and linebackers.

BLITZ A defensive play in which a linebacker or defensive back attacks past the line of scrimmage.

BOMB A long pass.

BOOT OR BOOTLEG The quarterback fakes a handoff to backs going one way while he goes the opposite way to run or pass.

BUMP AND RUN A technique in which a defensive back hits a potential receiver on the line of scrimmage (to slow him) and then runs with the receiver.

CHUCKING Hitting a receiver before the pass is thrown.

CLIP A block in which the defender is hit from behind. It is illegal.

CLOUD A commonly used term which indicates that the cornerback will cover the outside flat zone on a pass.

COMBINATION BLOCK A block in which linemen exchange responsibilities.

CORNERS OR CORNERBACKS The widest secondary players in an umbrella (four-deep) defense.

COUNTER A play in which the ends go in a different direction than the initial flow of the backs would indicate.

CRACKBACK BLOCK   A block by an offensive player who has lined up more than two yards outside of the tackle against a man inside him. It is illegal.

CROSSOVER STEP   A step by a lineman or back in which, when moving laterally, the player steps first with the foot away from the direction toward which he is traveling.

CURL   A pass pattern in which the receiver runs 15 to 20 yards downfield and then comes back toward the passer in an open area of the defensive coverage.

CUT BACK   The movement of a ball carrier away from the direction he was originally running so that he can run behind the tacklers.

CUT BLOCK   A block aimed at the ankles or knees of the defender. It is illegal at some levels of play.

CUTOFF   A block in which an offensive player blocks a player who is closer to the hole than the offensive player.

DASH   A planned action in which the passer drops back and then moves to his right or left. The blockers move with him.

DEFENSE   The team that is not in control of the ball.

DIME DEFENSE   A defense in which six defensive backs are in the game to stop a likely pass.

DIVE   A quick straight-ahead play with the halfback carrying the ball.

DOG OR RED DOG   A linebacker attacking past the line of scrimmage upon the snap.

DOUBLE COVER   Two defenders covering one offensive receiver.

DOUBLE TEAM   A block in which two offensive players block one defender.

DOWN   A play which begins after the ball is stopped. There are two types of downs, a scrimmage down and a free kick down.

DOWN BLOCK   Linemen block down toward the center.

DOWN LINEMAN   A defensive lineman.

DRAG   A delayed pattern in which a tight end or a wideout runs a shallow pattern across the center.

DRAW   A fake pass which ends with one of the backs carrying the ball after the defensive linemen are "drawn" in on the pass rush.

DRIVE BLOCK   A straight-ahead block.

DROP   The action of the passer as he moves away from the line of scrimmage. Three-, five-, seven- and nine-step drops are common.

EAGLE   A 5-2 defensive alignment with the tackles outside of the offensive guards and the linebackers on the ends.

ENCROACHMENT   Entering the neutral zone (the line of scrimmage bounded by both ends of the ball) before the ball is snapped. It is a penalty in high school football. At the college and pro level, it is a penalty only if contact is made with the other team.

END AROUND   A reverse play in which a tight end or a wideout carries the ball.

END ZONE   The 10-yard area between the goal line and the end line.

EVEN DEFENSE   A defensive alignment with no defensive lineman over the center.

EXTRA POINT   See "point after touchdown."

FADE   A pass pattern used generally against a man-to-man coverage in which the receiver runs deep and fades away from the defender.

FAIR CATCH   The opportunity for a receiving player to catch a kicked ball and not be tackled. It is signaled by waving one arm overhead. The ball cannot be advanced after making a fair catch. The team has an opportunity to put the ball in play by a scrimmage down or a free kick down.

FALSE BLOCK   Hitting an opposing lineman on the same side as you want him to move; used against a good reacting defensive lineman.

FAR   A player who is aligned away from where the ball will be run or passed. The "far" guard may trap block or the "far" back may be the ball carrier.

FIELD GOAL   A ball place kicked or drop kicked over the crossbar. It scores three points.

FLANKER   A back split wider than a wingback.

FLIPPER   A forearm shiver.

FLOOD   A pass pattern in which the offense sends more receivers into an area than there are defenders.

FLOW   The apparent direction of the ball during a scrimmage play. Most plays attack in the direction of the flow. Counters, reverses, and throwback passes go against the flow.

FOLD   A block in which an offensive lineman blocks the next defender on the line while the offensive lineman nearest that defender moves behind the blocker and blocks the near backer.

FOREARM SHIVER   A block protection technique in which the defender wards off the blocker by hitting and lifting him with his forearm.

FORMATION   The alignment of the offensive team. At least seven players must be within a foot of the line of scrimmage.

FORWARD PASS   A pass thrown forward from behind the line of scrimmage. College and pro teams are allowed one forward pass per play. High schools are allowed multiple forward passes on one play.

FREE KICK DOWN   A down in which the kicking team can tee up the ball to kick (as in a kickoff) or can place kick or punt the ball after a safety. The defensive team must stay at least 10 yards from the ball. Free kick downs occur after a touchdown or field goal. They can also occur after a safety (when the team scored against can have one scrimmage down or a free kick down in which it can kick the ball in any manner) or after a fair catch (in which the receiving team has the choice of a set of scrimmage downs or one free kick down in which it can score a field goal).

FREE SAFETY   The safety man opposite the power side of the offensive line (the tight end). He is usually free to cover deep zones.

FREEZE OPTION   A play in which an inside fake to one back running up the middle should freeze the linebackers. The play then ends as an option play between the quarterback and another runner.

FRONT   The alignment of the defensive linemen.

GAME PLAN   The offensive, defensive, and kicking strategy for an opponent.

GAP   The space between offensive or defensive linemen.

GAP DEFENSE   A defensive front with the defensive linemen in the offensive gaps.

GOAL LINE

The area over the inside edge of the chalk mark that marks the end of the playing field. The 10-yard end zone is beyond the goal line.

GUARDS

The offensive linemen on either side of the center.

HAND SHIVER

A defensive block protection in which the defender hits the blocker with his hands and extends his arms to keep the blocker away from his body.

HANG TIME

The amount of time a kick stays in the air.

HASH MARKS

Short lines parallel with the side lines that intersect each five-yard mark on the field. They are one-third of the way in from the side line (18⅔ yards) for high school and college and even with the goal posts for the pro game. Every play starts from a point on or between the hash marks.

HITCH

A quick pattern to a wide receiver in which he drives off the line and then stops.

HITTING POSITION

A balanced "ready position" in which the weight is on the balls of the feet, the knees are flexed, the torso is flexed forward, and the head is up.

HOOK BLOCK

A block in which the offensive player must get outside of a defender who is outside of him, then block that defender in.

HOOK PATTERN

A pass pattern in which the receiver runs downfield, stops, then comes back toward the passer.

HORIZONTAL STRETCH

Forcing the pass defenders to cover the entire width of the field on a pass.

HOT RECEIVER

A receiver who becomes open because the defender who would have covered him has stunted into the offensive backfield. The receiver yells "hot" when he sees he will be open and the passer passes quickly to him.

I-FORMATION

A formation in which the quarterback, fullback, and tailback are in a line.

INFLUENCE

Getting an opponent to move in the direction desired through finesse.

INSIDE SLOT

A slotback aligned close to the tight lineman.

INVERT

A four-deep defensive alignment in which the safeties are closer to the line of scrimmage than the corners. They are expected to quickly assist in run support.

JAM

Hitting a potential receiver before the ball is released by the passer.

KEY

Watching an opponent to determine what he/they will be doing.

LATERAL PASS

A pass thrown parallel with the line of scrimmage or backward. It can be thrown overhand or underhand.

LEAD

An offensive player goes through the hole and leads the ball carrier, usually looking to the inside to pick up a backer.

LEAD STEP

A step with the foot closest to the direction toward which the player is moving.

LINE OF SCRIMMAGE

An area approximately a foot wide (the width of the ball) which stretches from side line to side line.

LOAD

A block in which an offensive player coming from the inside blocks a wide defender on a wide play. The blocker will have his head and shoulders on the offensive side of the defender and the play is designed to go around him.

LOOP

A defensive lineman's move from a gap to a man, a man to a gap, or sometimes from a man to another man.

MISDIRECTION

A play which goes against the flow of the play, such as a bootleg, reverse, or throwback.

MUFF

A mistake in catching the ball on a kicking play.

NEAR

The player aligned close to the point of attack. So the "near" guard may trap, or the near back may be the ball carrier.

NEUTRAL ZONE

The area bounded by each end of the ball which extends from side line to side line and from the ground to the sky. Only the snapper can be in that zone before the ball is snapped.

NICKEL DEFENSE

A defense with five defensive backs.

NOSE GUARD/NOSE TACKLE

A defensive lineman playing on the offensive center.

ODD DEFENSE

A defense which has a man on the offensive snapper. This will result in a defensive line with an odd number of players on it.

OFFSIDE   Side of the line away from where the play will attack.

OFF TACKLE PLAY   A play which hits in the area of the offensive tackle and end.

OFFENSE   The team controlling the ball.

OKIE   The Oklahoma 5-2 defense (linebackers over the offensive guards).

ONSIDE   The side of the line to which the play will attack.

ONSIDE KICK   A short kickoff that travels at least 10 yards and can then be recovered by either team.

OPTION PLAY   A play in which the quarterback runs at a wide defender, forcing the defender to either tackle him or stop the pitch to a trailing back. The quarterback can keep or pitch.

OVERSHIFT   The alignment of the defensive linemen one man closer to the strength of the formation.

PASS PATTERN   The path or route that a receiver runs in attempting to get open.

PASSING TREE   The potential routes that a receiver can run. When drawn together they resemble a tree.

PENETRATION   The movement across the line of scrimmage by the defenders.

PICK   A pass pattern in which one of the potential receivers hits or screens off a defender allowing his teammate to be free. It is used primarily against a man to man defense. It is illegal to hit a defensive back before the ball is caught but it is legal to create a screen by stopping (as in a hook pattern) or having the receivers cross close to each other.

PLACE KICK   A kick in which the ball is either held by a player or held by a tee. It is used for kickoffs, field goals, and points after touchdowns.

PLAY ACTION   A pass off of a run fake.

POCKET   The area around a passer that is being protected by his blockers.

POINT AFTER TOUCHDOWN (P.A.T.)   An extra play allowed after a touchdown in which the team has an opportunity to score one point by kicking the ball over the crossbar and through the goal posts or two points by running or passing the ball over the goal line (high school and college game only). The ball is spotted at the three-yard line for this play.

PRE-SNAP READ   A cue read by the quarterback or receivers based on the alignment of the pass defenders.

PREVENT DEFENSE   A defense sometimes used by a team that is ahead late in a half. It uses extra defensive backs playing deeper than usual and fewer pass rushers than normal.

PRIMARY RECEIVER   The first choice of the passer in a pass pattern.

PULL   The movement of an offensive lineman behind the line as he leads the play.

PUNT   A kick made on a scrimmage down which is designed to make the most yardage when possession is changed.

PURSUIT   The movement of the defensive players to get them to a spot where they can make the tackle.

QUICK COUNT   A snap count which gets the ball in play quicker than normal, hoping to catch the defensive team unprepared.

QUICK SIDE   The side of the offensive line away from the strong side.

REACH BLOCK   An offensive lineman blocking a defender who is closer to the point of attack than himself or a tight end getting outside position on a backer who is slightly outside of him.

READ   Getting an idea of what the opponents are doing by looking at one or more of them as the play develops. It can be done by defenders watching offensive linemen or backs or by passers and receivers watching pass coverage defenders.

REDUCED FRONT   A defensive lineman playing closer to the center than normal. An example would be a tackle playing on the guard rather than on the offensive tackle.

RELEASE   The movement of a receiver in leaving the line of scrimmage.

REVERSE   A play in which a wide player on one side runs the ball against the flow of the other backs.

ROLLOUT   A deep, generally wide path of the passer behind the other backs.

ROTATION   The movement of the defensive backs to either a predetermined spot or to areas dictated by the movement of the ball.

ROVE
See dash.

ROVER
A defensive back who can be given various assignments. He is usually playing in a defense which has a 5-2 front and three defensive backs.

RUN FORCE
The responsibility of a defender to make the runner commit to an inside or outside path after he has passed the offensive end.

SACK
The tackling of the passer before he has a chance to pass.

SAFETY
A two-point play that occurs when an offensive player is tackled behind his own end zone.

SAFETYMAN
The defensive back or backs with the deepest responsibility.

SCOOP
A block in which a lineman blocks the next defensive man to the play side. This releases the next lineman out to block a backer.

SCRAMBLE
The running of the quarterback after he has been forced out of the pocket on a pass play.

SCRAPE
The path of a linebacker who is moving into the offensive line--usually on a key.

SCREEN
A pass, usually behind the line of scrimmage, after a deep drop by the quarterback. Some linemen pull to lead the receiver.

SCRIMMAGE DOWN
One of four attempts of the offense to advance the ball 10 yards and make another first down.

SEAMS
The areas between the defensive zones that are more likely to be open to complete passes.

SECONDARY
The safetymen and cornerbacks.

SET
The offensive or defensive alignment.

SETUP
The last step of a quarterback's drop — the spot from which he would like to pass.

SHADING
When the defender is not head-up on the blocker but part of his body overlaps the body of the offensive player.

SHIFT
A change of alignment from one set to another before the snap of the ball. It can be used by the offensive or the defensive team.

SHIVER	A defensive technique used to protect the defender from the block. It can be done with the hands or the forearms contacting the blocker.
SHORT LIST	The list of plays most likely to be used in a game with plays listed according to each situation.
SHOTGUN	A formation in which the quarterback sets several yards behind the center to be able to see the field better on a pass play. More wide receivers are also used. Some runs will be made from this formation to keep the defense honest.
SHUFFLE	The path of a linebacker who is moving nearly parallel with the line of scrimmage as he diagnoses the play and determines how he will attack the ball carrier.
SIGNALS	Offensive or defensive code words that tell the team which alignment and which play to use. Also the cadence called by the quarterback to get the play started.
SKY	A term used in pass coverage to indicate that a safety will cover a short flat zone.
SLANT	As a defensive term, a lineman making a hard move against an offensive lineman into a gap. As an offensive term it is a pass pattern, usually by a wide receiver, angling in toward the center of the field.
SLIP BLOCK	Same as scoop.
SLOT	A back lined up in the area between a split end and the tackle.
SNAP	The act of putting the ball in play. It can be handed to the quarterback or thrown (between the legs or to the side) to a back.
SNAPPER	The offensive lineman who puts the ball in play, usually the center.
SPEARING	An illegal action in which a player drives his head into a player, usually a player on the ground.
SPEED OPTION	An option play in which there is no inside fake. All backs run wide immediately.
SPRINT DRAW	A draw play off of a sprint out move by the quarterback.

SPRINT OUT A fast and shallow path of the quarterback.

SPY Keeping a defender near the line of scrimmage on pass plays to stop a draw play or a run by the quarterback.

SQUIB KICK A low flat kickoff that is difficult to handle. It is often used when the receiving team has an effective kick returner or when the kicking team does not have a long ball kicker.

STACK Playing a linebacker directly behind a defensive lineman.

STREAK A pass pattern in which the receiver runs long and fast.

STRETCH To widen the defense by placing offensive men in wide positions.

STRONG SAFETY The safety on the strong side (tight end) of the offense.

STRONG SIDE The side of the offensive line that blocks for the power plays. Usually the side of the tight end is designated the strong side.

STUNT A defensive maneuver in which linemen create a hole for a backer to move through the line, or a movement between defensive linemen that enables at least one to penetrate the line of scrimmage.

SWEEP A wide offensive power running play.

TIGHT END A receiver playing close to the offensive tackle.

TOUCHBACK A play that ends behind the receiver's goal line but in which the impetus of the ball was generated by the other team. There is no score. The ball is moved to the 20-yard line for the first down.

TRAP Blocking a defensive lineman by an offensive player who did not line up close to him originally. In a trap block the blocker will have his head on the defensive (downfield) side of the opponent and the play is designed to go inside the block.

TRIANGLE Triple key for a defensive player. A blocking triangle involves the three most dangerous blockers who could attack him. For a linebacker, it would involve one or two linemen and one or two backs.

TWIST A movement between defensive linemen, especially in a pass situation, in which the linemen cross hoping that at least one will get clear into the backfield.

TWO-MINUTE OFFENSE   The attack used by a team late in a half when they are behind and attempting to score while conserving time.

UMBRELLA   A secondary four-deep alignment, usually with the corners closer to the line of scrimmage than the safeties.

UNBALANCED LINE   An offensive alignment in which four or more linemen are set on one side of the line of scrimmage.

UNDERSHIFT   A defensive alignment in which the defensive linemen have moved a man away from their normal position away from the strength of the offensive formation.

UPRIGHTS   The vertical poles that hold up the crossbar of the goal posts.

VERTICAL STRETCH   Forcing the pass defenders to cover deep even if the pass is in the short or intermediate zones.

WAGGLE   A pass action off a running play in which the quarterback moves wide and deep after faking to a back. Some coaches call it a waggle if the quarterback move in the direction of the flow behind the backs to whom he has faked. Others call it a waggle if he moves opposite the flow and is protected by a pulling lineman.

WALKAWAY   A position taken by a linebacker or defensive back between a wide receiver and the offensive linemen. It enables the defender to be in position to stop the quick slant pass and still be able to play a wide run.

WEAK SIDE   The side of the offense away from the tight end.

WEDGE   A block in which three or more players block an area.

WIDEOUT   A split end or flanker.

WIDE RECEIVER   See wideout.

WING   A back lined up outside a tight end (usually a yard outside and a yard back).

ZONE BLOCKING   Pass protection blockers protect an area rather than blocking a specific man. It is used against stunting defenses.

ZONE DEFENSE   A pass coverage in which the linebackers and defensive backs protect areas and play the ball rather than watch specific men.

Get into the game!

Masters Press has a complete line of books on
football and other sports to help coaches
and participants alike "master their game".

All of our books are available at better bookstores
or by calling Masters Press at 1-800-722-2677, or
317-298-5706. Catalogs available upon request.

Our football books include the following:

Conditioning for Football

By Tom Zupancic

Designed to help coaches and players at all levels develop a
conditioning program that improves performance and safety. Includes strength training principles, aerobic and anaerobic conditioning, program design and motivation. A unique guide by the
strength coach of the Indianapolis Colts.

$12.95 • paper • 160 pages • b/w photos
ISBN: 0-940279-77-0

Football Crosswords

By Dale Ratermann

A collection of crosswords on each of the 28 National Football
League teams. Each chapter is devoted to a specific team and
features a history of the franchise, relevant statistics, and a cross-
word puzzle. Fun for all ages!

$12.95 • paper • 192 pages • photos, puzzles and graphs
ISBN 0-940279-74-6

Football Drill Book

By Doug Mallory

A collection of drills designed to improve the effectiveness of practice time and develop game-winning skills and teamwork. This book includes both offensive and defensive skills as well as drills for overall conditioning. Foreword by Bo Schembechler.

$12.95 • paper • 192 pages • b/w photos & diagrams
ISBN 0-940279-72-X

Youth League Football

By Tom Flores & Bob O'Connor

Includes drills and coaching suggestions for all positions on the field, along with equipment information and hints for keeping the emphasis on "play" rather than "work." A complete primer!

$12.95 • paper • 192 pages • b/w photos
ISBN 0-940279-69-X

Super Bowl Chronicles

By Jerry Green

The compelling story of that unique American phenomenon, the Super Bowl. Jerry Green, one of only 13 journalists to have covered the first 25 Super Bowls, tells of the unique characters and little-known facts he discovered along the way.

$19.95 • cloth • 192 pages • photo insert
ISBN 0-940279-32-0